John E. Taugren Alexander

WITTGENSTEIN
AND THE PROBLEM OF OTHER MINDS

WITTGENSTEIN AND THE PROBLEM OF OTHER MINDS

Edited by Harold Morick

State University of New York
at Albany

McGraw-Hill Book Company
New York   Toronto   London   Sydney

Library of Congress Catalog Card Number: 67-17201

ACKNOWLEDGMENTS

Grateful acknowledgment is hereby made to the authors and publishers
for permission to reprint the selections in this book.

"Critical Notice of Wittgenstein's *Philosophical Investigations*" is reprinted
from *Mind* (LXIII, No. 249, 1954) by permission of the editor and P. F.
Strawson.

"Wittgenstein's *Philosophical Investigations*" is reprinted from *Knowledge
and Certainty: Essays and Lectures* by Norman Malcolm, © 1963, with
the permission of Prentice-Hall, Inc., Englewood Cliffs, N. J., and the
author.

"Can There Be a Private Language?" is reprinted from *The Concept of a
Person and Other Essays* by A. J. Ayer (1963), by permission of Macmillan and Co., Ltd., The Macmillan Company of Canada, Ltd., St. Mar-
tin's Press, Inc., and the author.

"Two Arguments Against a Private Language" is reprinted from *The
Journal of Philosophy* (LXII, No. 17, 1965) by permission of the editor
and Moreland Perkins.

The excerpt ("Section D") from "Wittgenstein's Lectures in 1930–1933" by
G. E. Moore is reprinted from *Mind* (LXIII, 1954) by permission of the
editor.

"Persons" is reprinted from *Minnesota Studies in the Philosophy of Sci-
ence*, Vol. II, edited by Herbert Feigl, Michael Scriven, and Grover
Maxwell, © 1958, University of Minnesota, with the permission of the
University of Minnesota Press and P. F. Strawson.

"Wittgenstein's Conception of a Criterion" is reprinted from *The Philosophical Review* (Vol. LXXI, No. 4, 1962) by permission of the editor
and Carl Wellman.

"Operationalism and Ordinary Language: A Critique of Wittgenstein" is
reprinted from the *American Philosophical Quarterly* (Vol. 2, No. 4,

1965) by permission of the editor and of the authors, C. S. Chihara and J. A. Fodor.

"Could Sensuous Experiences Occur Apart From an Organism?" and "The Fallacy of Cogito Ergo Sum" are reprinted from *Mental Acts* by Peter T. Geach (1957), by permission of Routledge & Kegan Paul Ltd., Humanities Press, Inc., and the author.

"The Concept of Dreaming" is reprinted from *Dreaming* by Norman Malcolm (1959), by permission of Routledge & Kegan Paul Ltd., Humanities Press, and the author.

To my Mother and Father

PREFACE

THE ESSAYS in this book include not only several contemporary classics, but also some of the best recent writings which deal with the title topic. These have been selected and arranged with the intention of providing a general introduction to Wittgenstein's later philosophy, of assisting the reader in following what Wittgenstein says about other minds in his notoriously difficult *Philosophical Investigations,* of presenting leading analytic philosophers' evaluations of his work on this subject, and of giving a sense of the broader implications of the Wittgensteinian approach to the other-minds problem. Of course, one need not read the selections either in the order given nor from the perspective of the other-minds problem alone. However, this sequence and point of view are felicitous for someone who is just starting to study the *Investigations,* since so much of Wittgenstein's philosophical psychology revolves about this problem.

The book is divided into three parts. The first contains the only concise critical exposition in existence treating all the major aspects of Wittgenstein's later philosophy—Strawson's

critical review of the *Investigations*. In charting the main lines
of thought in Wittgenstein's major work, this essay provides the
necessary background for understanding his treatment of the
problem of other minds.

The second and largest section is meant to give a representa-
tive characterization of Wittgenstein's many-sided attack on
philosophical skepticism about other minds. First Malcolm gives
a panoramic but detailed picture of Wittgenstein's arguments
against the skeptical view of other minds. (The final section of
the essay is a discussion of part of Strawson's "Critical Notice.")
He devotes special attention to the celebrated private language
issue, with which Ayer is exclusively concerned in Selection III.
On this subject, Malcolm is perhaps the staunchest defender of
Wittgenstein, while Ayer is without question his most famous
critic. These first three selections appeared in 1954, within a
year of the publication of the *Investigations*. Writing more than
a decade later, Perkins makes fundamental contributions in
Selection IV toward resolving the issue.

In the next two essays we are concerned with Wittgenstein's
thoughts in the early 1930s, which greatly aid in understanding
his more mature but more elusive remarks in the *Investigations*.
In Selection V, Moore provides an invaluable supplement to
Wittgenstein's published writings, for his aim here is to give an
accurate transcription of Wittgenstein's views during the early
years of his later period. In Selection VI, Strawson begins by
attacking those of Wittgenstein's ideas concerning persons and
the ownership of experiences which Moore reports. Of course,
this essay is famous for Strawson's development of a highly
original solution to the other-minds problem and related ones
in the philosophy of mind. Yet Strawson's own view does develop the Wittgensteinian idea of behavior being a criterion for
inner states—the idea of a logical or conceptual connection between states of consciousness and their behavioral manifestations. Wittgenstein's conception of this connection is the difficult
but rewarding subject of the section's final two essays. Both
Wellman and Chihara-Fodor give detailed explications of Wittgenstein's conception of a criterion and also criticize it. (One

part of Chihara and Fodor's article is a criticism of Malcolm's "The Concept of Dreaming" insofar as Malcolm is applying Wittgenstein's remarks on criteria to dreaming.)

The Wittgensteinian treatment of the problem of other minds has implications for an array of related problems in the philosophy of mind. As Strawson says, "The topic of the mind does not divide into unconnected subjects." [1] In the last section, three of these issues are considered by Geach and Malcolm—two of Wittgenstein's most famous pupils who are also highly original philosophers in their own right.

Harold Morick

[1] P. 150 below.

CONTENTS

INTRODUCTION

IN PLATO'S *THEATETUS* the question is asked, "Are you quite certain that the several colors appear to a dog or to any animal whatever as they appear to you?. . . or that anything appears the same to you as to another man?" This is one expression of what Chihara and Fodor aptly call "the hoary problem of other minds." [1]

As Wittgenstein sees it, this problem arises from considering questions of knowledge from a self-centered perspective. Those who take this perspective find it problematic that one can have knowledge about the world and other people, while they take it for granted that clearly a person can have knowledge of his own psychological states. They suppose that in order to justify claims of knowledge about the public world one has to reconstruct the world from one's own private experiences or sense data. Wittgenstein questions this whole approach to knowledge, and in particular the skeptical conclusion to which it seems to

---

[1] P. 171 below.

lead: "I can never know what the contents of another person's mind are because I can't (directly) experience them." To make our explication more concrete, let us speak in terms of a large subclass of mental contents—thoughts and feelings. This skeptical inference of course tacitly depends upon a subsidiary premiss, something like: a necessary condition for knowing what another person is thinking or feeling is experiencing his thoughts or feelings. Wittgenstein never formally lays out the position he is attacking, and thus never says in so many words what the premiss or premisses of the skeptical inference might be because he believes that the temptation to say that one can never know what another person is thinking or feeling does not result from considering a cogent argument consisting of ordered and scrupulously expressed premisses. Indeed, apparently he finds that even the conclusion itself is not clear. For example, sometimes he puts it that only I can know what I'm really thinking or feeling, others can only surmise (believe) it; and sometimes that although others can (legitimately be said to) know what I am thinking or feeling, only I can know it with *certainty*. Nevertheless, from Wittgenstein's various formulations of the skeptical position we can extract a working model:

Premiss One (P_1): I can't experience another person's thoughts or feelings (nor, conversely, can he experience mine).

Premiss Two (P_2): A necessary condition for knowing what another person is thinking or feeling is experiencing his thoughts or feelings.

Conclusion (C): I can never know what another person is really thinking or feeling (nor, conversely, can he ever know what I am really thinking or feeling).

Wittgenstein believes that this view is a result of misunderstandings about language. His aim in his attack is not to provide a philosophical theory to replace this view, but rather to dissolve the view through linguistic analysis. He thought it important to do so because the view engenders tormenting and seemingly irremediable doubts which, queerly, are not consonant with the way we actually act when we are not thinking philosophically, in everyday dealings with other people. And furthermore, to the professional philosopher the success of Wittgenstein's dissolution would have an added dividend: it would vitiate any program which tried to reconstruct the external world and other minds from private experiences or sense data.

Since Wittgenstein's attack on this view is complex and manifold, I shall outline here only his main arguments. They deal with the idea of a private language, the ownership of experiences, the use of "know" as it appears in the skeptical argument, and the concept of a criterion. Let us look first at his attack on a private language.

One thing that the skeptical view presupposes is that I know what, for instance, pains and mental images are only from my own case since I can't experience other people's thoughts and feelings. But, Wittgenstein says, if I know only from my own case what "pain" or "mental image" means, "I know only what *I* call that, not what anyone else does".[2] Nor could I teach anyone else what these words mean to me, since in order for me to know that my teaching was successful, I would have to know that my pupil applied the word to the right private object. But by the hypothesis of the skeptical argument I can never know that. I.e., for all I know, what you call "pain" I should call "itch"; or perhaps you use "pain" to stand for some sensation I've never even had; perhaps you don't even use it to refer to anything that I should call a sensation. . . . Now in my own case the way I give meaning to such words as "pain" and "mental image" is by correlating them with certain recurrent experiences; I use them to name the experiences. "I simply *associate* names with sensations and use these names in descriptions."[3] Thus we may add the implication of a private language to the skeptic's argument: I can't understand another person's talk

---

[2] Ludwig Wittgenstein, *Philosophical Investigations*, trans. G. E. M. Anscombe, Second Edition (London: Basil Blackwell, 1963), sec. 347.
[3] *Ibid.*, sec. 256.

about his thoughts and feelings (nor can he understand mine).

If what the implication says is so, then only I can be in a position to know that I use a word for a certain thought or feeling to refer to the object which, in my usage, the word designates. Wittgenstein points out that a necessary condition for a word—referential or any other—to have meaning is that there be rules governing its use, and that the concept of a rule includes the possibility of checking whether the rule is followed. Now, Wittgenstein asks, can the skeptic's picture of people's talk about their thoughts and feelings meet this condition? This picture requires that the connection between the word and the thought or feeling it designates be brought about by a kind of ostensive definition. One can't, of course, point with one's finger to a thought or feeling; but one points to it, as it were, by concentrating one's attention on it while at the same time writing down the sign which is going to stand for it. The putative rule that I adopt then is that I will call, say, "S" any future sensation that is the same as this one I have today, Monday. But isn't this talk of adopting a rule here idle, Wittgenstein asks; for how on Friday would I ever know whether or not I lived up to this rule? Well, the check would be my remembering how S felt on Monday. But, Wittgenstein reminds us, we sometimes make memory errors. How could I distinguish really remembering the sensation from merely believing I was remembering it correctly? That is, how can I distinguish true from false memory impressions, in this case, of a private sensation, only by another memory impression—for instance, of what I called "S" on Tuesday.

But surely, one may reply, there is nothing wrong with my doing that; for we do sometimes check one memory impression by another. If I'm not sure that I remember rightly when the train leaves, I call to mind an image of the time table. It assures me that I did remember the train's departure time correctly. But, Wittgenstein points out, one memory impression can corroborate another only if it is itself actually correct; and obviously there must be some means which are not themselves memory impressions of determining whether a particular impression is correct. For instance, in the case of the train's departure, I can take the time table out of my brief case and look at it, or I can telephone the train station. But since by hypothesis in the case of "S" there are no other means available, I am in the position of a man who buys extra copies of the morning paper to check the correctness of what he reads in the first copy he buys!

Wittgenstein's point is stronger than simply claiming that no one could ever know whether or not "S" was used correctly (here, i.e., consistently). In such circumstances, "correct" or "incorrect" are inapplicable: "Here we can't talk about 'right' [4]." Since it makes no sense to speak here of applying or misapplying a rule, neither does it make sense to speak of rules of word usage at all; i.e., the putative private language is not a language. And this means that any philosophical view which implies a private language must be inherently confused.

One of Wittgenstein's attacks on the skeptic's conception (or perhaps better, lack of conception) of the ownership of experiences turns on reminding us that when I say "Another person can't have my pains," I must have a principle of identity for distinguishing my pains from his: "Which are *my* pains? What counts as a criterion of identity here?" [5] And his second argument is based on pointing out that "I" doesn't refer to anything in the skeptic's argument. Let us look first at the argument concerning the criterion of identity.

The skeptic might reply to Wittgenstein that the principle of identity seems obvious: what makes it *my* pain is that I feel it in *my* body. Through an unusual situation Wittgenstein shows that this is incorrect and therefore can not be the justification for saying "You can't have my pain." A bee stings the connecting part of a pair of Siamese twins. They both cry and grimace, describe the quality and course of the pain with the same words; and when asked where it hurts, they point to the identical place.[6]

[4] *Ibid.*, sec. 258.
[5] *Ibid.*, sec. 253.
[6] I have here drawn on two sources in Wittgenstein to produce this example: *Ibid.*, sec. 253, and *The Blue and Brown Books* (Oxford: Basil Blackwell, 1960), p. 54.

Wittgenstein notes that not only is there only one cause involved here, but insofar as pain can be capable of being located, what they refer to has the same location. And, contrary to the skeptical view, in one ordinary sense they *would* be having the same pain, just as we would say that they had two coats of the same color if the colors of their coats fit the same description (hue, saturation, and so forth). But the person who is tempted to skepticism will say that this is not the point. There is a difference between "same" and "identical." For instance, the criticism about conformity used to be that men all tended to wear the same suit—a gray flannel one; but no one would dream of saying that everybody wore numerically the identical suit. Nor, according to the skeptic, would we dream of saying that two people could ever have, numerically, the identical pain. *Whatever* may be the circumstances in which we find ourselves, your pain is yours and mine is mine—we can not imagine it otherwise. But Wittgenstein notes that this move from "same" to "identical" is a typical philosophical expedient which gets us no further; for the question of the principle of identity is still unanswered.

Wittgenstein's question "Which are *my* pains?" is clarified in *Philosophische Bemerkungen.* He asks there, "What in my experience justifies the 'my' in 'I feel *my* pains'? Where is the multiplicity of feeling that this word justifies?" [7] What he is driving at here is the mistaken picture of a pile of experiences which have to be assigned to their respective owners—like the pile of hats which must be sorted out at the end of the party. And it is at this point, according to Wittgenstein, that we get to the heart of the problem about possession. To say that I can not feel your pains must assume that it makes sense to speak of my feeling my own pains. But "I feel *my* pain" (or "You feel *your* pain") makes no sense; and thus "I feel your pains" is also senseless. That is, Wittgenstein is pointing out that we individuate sensations by the persons who have them—that is the criterion of identity. And once it is clear that "No one can have (experience, feel) another's pain" is only ɩ confused way of trying to point out that "I feel your pains" makes no sense, the

[7] Ludwig Wittgenstein, *Philosophische Bemerkungen* (Oxford: Basil Blackwell, 1964), p. 93 (my translation). Though recently published, this book was composed in 1930.

temptation to move to the skeptic's conclusion vanishes: "No one can have another's pain" is like "No one can have (frown) another's frowns." And nobody would think of concluding from this latter case that one can not know when someone else is frowning, or what the characteristics of his frown are.

In his second argument, Wittgenstein attempts to show that the "I" in the skeptical argument does not refer to an owner of experiences; and he presents two reasons in support of his conclusion. First, no criteria of personal identity are applied in my avowing my thoughts and feelings. For example, when I say "I am in pain," I do not first look at my body, at the characteristics of my behavior, or at my memories to determine that it *is* I who have the pain. It is indifferent to me whether my body, personality, or memories remain the same. Nor can the *I* be pointed out ostensively, for what would be pointed at? Thus Wittgenstein says that I am not talking about any particular entity *I*, but just about the experience of feeling pain itself. He does not maintain that all uses of "I" or "my" are nonreferential, but only what he calls the use of "I" as subject. In "I" 's other use as object, it clearly refers. Examples of this kind are "My arm is broken," "I've grown six inches," "I have a bump on my forehead," and "The wind blows my hair about." [8] In all of these cases, there is the possibility that I am wrong that it is I or mine. On the other hand, in the case of speaking of my pains or images, there is no chance of my referring to the wrong person. And here we come to his second reason for holding that "I" does not refer to an owner of experiences: he says that where there is no chance of referring to the wrong person, it does not make sense to speak of referring to a person at all.

Now the question naturally arises as to why a word which seems to refer but apparently does not is used at all in sentences such as "I have a pain" or "I have a mental image." Wittgenstein thinks that such a question comes from the inclination to think that since "I" can not be replaced by "this body" (as perhaps it might in the object use), it must be talking about or referring to something bodiless—the kind of thing that

---

[8] These examples are from Wittgenstein's *The Blue and Brown Books*, p. 66.

Descartes thought he was referring to when he said "I think, therefore I am." But, Wittgenstein says, this does not follow any more than "the numeral '3' refers to a mind" follows from the fact that this numeral does not refer to a body. Wittgenstein points out that like "It" in "It is raining," "I" is simply needed as a grammatical filler here.

Wittgenstein's two arguments dealing with the ownership of experiences may be contrasted in the following way: the first argues against the skeptical position by reminding us that we individuate sensations by the persons who have them, and in this way attacks both P_1 and P_2; while the second points out that a sentence like P_1 is not even talking about two *persons* who can't have each other's thoughts and feelings. As we noted from the beginning, the skeptical argument grows out of a self-centered perspective and is characteristically formulated in terms of first-person psychological sentences. According to Wittgenstein, the skeptic makes the mistake of thinking that such sentences are on the same logical level as second- and third-person psychological sentences. In particular in this case, the skeptic is under the linguistic illusion that "I" refers to a person in P_1 and in C.

The skeptical reasoning proposes that others can not know—or at least can not know with the certainty that I have—what I am thinking or feeling. But Wittgenstein's reply to this is that this sense of "know" is no sense of the word at all, for it makes sense to speak of knowledge only where it also makes sense to speak of doubt and uncertainty. If someone does not know what the word "pain" means, he can certainly be in doubt as to whether or not he is in pain. But it is unintelligible to suppose that someone who has mastered the correct use of the English word "pain" could wonder or doubt that what he was feeling was a pain. In other words, Wittgenstein argues, the expression of doubt has no place in such first person avowals as "I am in pain"; and since doubt is logically excluded, so is knowledge.

Furthermore, on page 221 in the *Investigations* Wittgenstein says that in cases where one can speak of knowing, it makes sense to speak of learning or finding out. But it makes no sense to speak of finding out or verifying that "I am in pain" since the question "How do you know that you're in pain?" is nonsensical. In the Moore selection we find his reasoning succinctly expressed:

> He criticized two answers which might be given to this last question by people who think it is not nonsensical, by saying (1) that the answer "Because I feel it" won't do, because "I feel it" means the same as "I have it," and (2) that the answer "I know it by inspection" also won't do, because it implies that I can "look to see" whether I have it or not, whereas "looking to see whether I have it or not" has no meaning.[9]

"Because I feel it" will not do because "feel" in this context is not an observation word as it is in this exchange: "How do you know there's a hat in the closet?"—"Because I feel it there." It doesn't matter whether I say I have a pain or that I feel it, whereas it does make a difference if I say I have a hat in the closet or that I feel it there. And the kind of reasoning behind his criticism of the second answer is that if I am in doubt that it is a three-legged frog, I can take a closer look; but it makes no sense to speak of my getting myself into a more favorable position to observe my toothache. Furthermore, while it would be absurd to speak of an "unfelt pain," no one would dream of suggesting that the existence of the frog depends upon my observing it.

In short, the skeptic argues that no one can know about the existence and character of my thoughts and feelings with the certainty that I do. But if Wittgenstein is right, this use of "know" is a spurious one. Since this use is contained in both P_2 and C, the skeptical argument would collapse.

When the skeptic thinks about the relationship between an inner experience such as pain and its outward manifestations, he

---

[9] P. 121 below.

feels that one can not justify attributing a pain to another person on the basis of that person's behavior, and in this way he gets to P_2. On the one hand, it seems obvious that a pain is not a piece of behavior; i.e., pain and pain behavior are two different things. On the other hand, he feels that I cannot attribute a pain to another person on the basis of an analogical inference from my own case, for this alternative appears incurably weak. When I make such an inference, I notice that in my own case my experiences are correlated with certain patterns of behavior and from this I conclude that when others behave in similar ways, they are having similar experiences. To mention only the most obvious difficulty here, how can I generalize on the basis of only a single case, my own? Consequently the skeptic thinks there is only one other alternative for justifying pain ascriptions to other people—namely, P_2. And of course he denies that the condition P_2 states can ever possibly be met. But we have seen Wittgenstein argue that P_2 is incoherent, as is the conclusion which it supposedly helps lead to.

Returning to Wittgenstein's arguments, if he is right so far, we *do* as a matter of fact often know what other people are thinking and feeling. But what is the justification for this claim to knowledge? Wittgenstein points out that there is a middle ground between behaviorism on the one hand, and the argument from analogy on the other: pain and pain behavior are two different things, but this does not entail denying that there are logical or conceptual connections between them such that statements about others' behavior can give support or justification for statements about their states of mind. For, Wittgenstein says, contrary to the skeptical point of view—and in particular, the private language thesis—we learn words for our thoughts and feelings in contexts in which we and those around us behave in certain characteristic ways; and once learned, we can not divorce the meanings of the words from their original contexts: the idea of a "pure" thought or feeling which carries with it not the slightest inclination to do or say anything is unintelligible. Surely it is impossible to conceive of an itch which would not carry with it *any* tendency to scratch.

This is not to say that a person's scratching entails his having an itch; nor that his itching entails that he actually scratch himself. Rather, our concept of an itch is that of a kind of sensation which is *characteristically* or *normally* manifested in certain behavior—and the same is true for our other states of consciousness. It is in this sense that Wittgenstein says behavior is a *criterion* for an inner process. Therefore we have a guarantee for the overall success of the passage (if we may even speak here of a passage) from others' behavior to their thoughts and feelings. The skeptic can raise a doubt about what someone else is thinking or feeling only in a *particular* case; and he can not even do this unless he produces reasons for showing the case to be abnormal or unusual.

These then are Wittgenstein's main ways of arguing against the skeptical view of other minds. These ways as well as others will be explicated in much greater detail and scrutinized critically in the essays that follow. It is hoped that this brief outline will assist the reader in relating the issues considered in these essays to the overall pattern of Wittgenstein's thoughts about the other-minds problem.

GENERAL INTRODUCTION
TO WITTGENSTEIN'S LATER PHILOSOPHY

I

Critical Notice of Wittgenstein's
Philosophical Investigations

P. F. Strawson

THIS BOOK IS a treatment, by a philosopher of genius, of a number of intricate problems, intricately connected. It also presents in itself an intricate problem: that of seeing clearly what the author's views are on the topics he discusses, and how these views are connected. The difficulty of doing this arises partly from the structure and style of the book. Wittgenstein himself describes the former accurately in the preface: "The best I could write could never be more than philosophical remarks"; "Thus this book is really only an album". It would, however, be a very strong prejudice against this disregard of the ordinary conventions of exposition, which could survive a careful reading of the whole book. Wittgenstein did not gloss his thoughts; but he arranged them. And the gains in power and concentration are great. It might even be thought that there were good reasons why no attempt at all should be made to present his views in a

Ludwig Wittgenstein, *Philosophical Investigations*. German text and English translation by G. E. M. Anscombe (Oxford: Basil Blackwell, 1953).

more conventional form. But this could be true only in a very specialised view of the nature of philosophical understanding. In what follows, I try to trace and connect the main lines of his thought, conscious that, at best, the result must involve a great impoverishment of his rich and complex thinking. I refer to passages in Part I of the book simply by paragraph number (*e.g.* 500); to passages in Part II by section and/or page number (*e.g.* II, xi, p. 200). Quotations from the text are in double quotation marks. Comment and criticism will be interspersed with exposition.

Meaning and Use

In the first thirty-seven or thirty-eight paragraphs of Part I, which are concerned with meaning, Wittgenstein is anxious to make us see "the multiplicity of kinds of words and sentences" (23). We are prone to assimilate different kinds. In particular, we are prone to work with a certain idea of language as consist- ing of words each correlated with something for which it stands, an object, the meaning of the word (1). This picture, though philosophically misleading for all words, is better suited to some than to others. When we have it in mind, we are primarily thinking of common nouns like 'chair' and 'bread' and of people's names; even primitive reflection shows that it does not fit, say, logical connectives. So not only is there a general tendency to assimilate different kinds of words to each other; there is also a particular direction which this assimilation tends to take. Per- haps the general tendency is in part explained by the fact that words look or sound much alike: from their uniform appearance on the printed page one would never guess at their diversity of function (11). But there are more complex reasons both for the general tendency and for its particular direction. The central point is this: *the picture with which we are inclined to work derives essentially from the instruction-setting of someone who has already mastered in part the technique of using the lan- guage; i.e.* from the situation in which someone is being taught the place of one word, of which he is ignorant, in a way of using language with which he is familiar (*cf.* 10, 27, 30, 32). In this situation, the instructor may well proceed by saying something like 'the word x means (is the name of, stands for, signifies, etc.) y' where the place of 'y' is taken by, *e.g.* 'this' 'this number' 'a number' 'this colour' 'the colour which . . .'; or simply by a synonym or translation of the word in question. In some, though not all, cases, he may accompany these words by pointing. Or he may just answer the question 'What is y (this, this colour, this thing) called?' by pronouncing the word. These procedures may give us the impression of a relation of a unique kind being established between two items, a word and something else; and the further impression that the essence of meaning is to be grasped by the contemplation of this unique relation. To counter this impression, to remind ourselves that the efficacy of these procedures depends on the existence of a prepared framework of linguistic training, we should bear in mind such points as these two: that an ostensive definition (*many* kinds of words can be taught by indicating situations in which they are in some sense applicable) can always be variously interpreted (28); and that the process of asking the names of things and being told them is itself one language-game [1] among others, and a comparatively sophisticated one.

Two minor comments. (1) Perhaps Wittgenstein does not here sufficiently emphasize the point that the *natural* place for the word 'meaning' and its derivatives in ordinary use is in just such instruction-situations as those referred to. One might get the impression that he was saying: 'In philosophy you want the meaning of the word. Don't look for the mythical, uniquely related term, but look at the use; for *that* is the meaning' (*cf.* 43). But in view of the natural place of 'meaning', it might be better to say: 'In doing philosophy, it can't be that you are ignorant of the meaning: what you want to know is the use.' (2) Wittgenstein does not seek to give a complete explanation of why, among all the kinds of names there are, it is substance-names that tend to be taken as the model for meaning. A suggestion which can

---

[1] Wittgenstein uses this phrase to refer to any particular way, actual or invented, of using language (*e.g.* to a particular way of using a certain sentence, or a certain word); and also to "the whole consisting of language and the actions into which it is woven" (7).

perhaps be extracted from the text is that (*a*) pointing figures largely both in ostensive explanation of words, and in that more primitive training in the naming-game which a child goes through before it actually uses words for any more practical purpose; and (*b*) pointing is more naturally used to discriminate the individual man or horse than any other kind of item. But there remains a question here.

Instead, then, of gazing at this over-simple picture of language, with its attendant assimilations, we are to look at the elements of language as instruments. We are to study their use. Only so can we solve our conceptual problems. Variants on 'use' in Wittgenstein are 'purpose' 'function' 'role' 'part' 'application'. It is not a complaint to say that this central notion is not immediately and wholly clear. The general aim is clear enough: to get us away from our fascination with the dubious relation of naming, of meaning, and to make us look at the speaking and writing of language as one human activity among others, interacting with others; and so to make us notice the different parts that words and sentences play in this activity. But here I inevitably re-introduce one of the variants: 'the parts they play'. Perhaps seeing what sorts of things count as *differences* of use will help one to get clear about the central notion. And here it will seem that there are differences between differences which Wittgenstein might have made more explicit.

Consider first what he says of different kinds of sentences. He makes the point that a formal (grammatical) likeness may cover a functional difference (21–22). Then (23): "But how many kinds of sentence are there? Say assertion, question, and command?—There are *countless* kinds: countless different kinds of use of what we call 'symbols' 'words' 'sentences'." There follows a list of activities which involve the use of language. When we look at the items in the list, it becomes clear that the shift from 'kinds of sentence' in the question to 'kinds of use' in the answer was an important one. The list includes, for example, as separate uses, the activities of reading a story, play-acting, and translating from one language to another. The sentence 'It was raining' might occur in the course of any one of these activities; as it

might in a factual narration. It would be absurd to speak of
different *sentences* here, let alone of different kinds of sentences.
We *might* speak of different uses of the sentence, though it
would be better to speak of different linguistic activities in each
of which the sentence occurred. Similarly, I suppose, reading
aloud a story containing the sentence would involve a different
use from copying the story out; reading aloud a translation of
a story from reading aloud (*a*) an original, (*b*) a translated
factual narrative in all of which the sentence occurred; and
there is also the special use involved in sending an old man to
sleep by reading aloud from a translation of a play. Surely distinctions are needed here to save the whole notion from sliding
into absurdity. Such points as the following call for attention:
sometimes there is a formal (grammatical) distinction to correspond to (not to coincide with) a 'difference in use'; sometimes
there is not (in what cases would it be more or less natural to
have one, and why?); sometimes the existence of a formal distinction would be self-defeating. There is a class of interrogative
sentences (sentences of which the standard use is to ask questions); there is no class of translators' sentences; there *could
be* no class of copyists' sentences.

Consider next the point that we cannot in general talk about
the functions or uses of *words* in the same sort of way as we can
talk about the functions or uses of sentences.[2] (Of course, a word
may *sometimes* function as a sentence.) To suppose that we
could would be like supposing that we could talk of the function
of a numeral in the same way as we could talk of the purpose of
a calculation; or discuss a gambit and a piece in the same terms.
We might imagine a very simple language A, in which a limited
number of sentences could be formed from a limited number of
words; and a second language B, containing no distinction of
sentences and words, but consisting of unitary expressions such
that every sentence of A could be translated into a unitary ex-

---

[2] *Cf.* Ryle, 'Ordinary Language', *The Philosophical Review*, April, 1953, pp. 178–180. Perhaps
Professor Ryle puts too much weight on the fact (if it is a fact) that we do not speak of the
'use' of sentences. Certainly we use them. But it is at any rate true that there are some things we
might mean by 'the use of a word' which we could not mean by 'the use of a sentence'; and the
other way about.

pression of B. Then it might be the case that every remark we
could make about a use of a sentence in A would also be true
of a use of an expression in B. We could also discuss the uses of
the *words* of A; but there would be nothing to be said on this
subject in the case of B. What perhaps causes confusion here is
that very often when we (and Wittgenstein) discuss the use of
words of certain classes, what we are concerned with is the
criteria for their correct application; and this discussion is the
same as the discussion of the conditions in which it is correct
to use a *sentence* of a certain kind, namely, the sentence which
says that we have here a case of what the word in question
describes.

The fact that Wittgenstein is content to leave this central
notion of use so vague is a manifestation of his reluctance to
make distinctions and classifications which are not of direct
assistance to the fly in the flybottle (309). Underlying this reluctance is a general, and debatable, doctrine of the nature of
philosophy: to which I shall refer later.

Towards the end of these introductory paragraphs there enters
one of the main themes of the book (33–36). Wittgenstein im-
agines an objection to the view that understanding an ostensive
definition requires a mastery of the language. Someone might
say that all that is necessary to this understanding is for the
learner to know what the teacher is *pointing to* or *meaning* or
attending to, when he makes his gesture—*e.g.* to the shape or to
the colour of the object. Wittgenstein does not deny this; but
points out that though there may be characteristic experiences
(*e.g.* feelings) of 'meaning' or 'pointing to' the shape, which the
learner might share with the teacher, their occurrence is not
sufficient to make the situation one of 'meaning the shape'. Not
just because they do not always occur. Even if they did it would
still depend on the circumstances, the setting, on what happens
before and afterwards, whether the case is one of intending or
interpreting the definition in such and such a way. Seeing this
is helped by seeing that there are in fact many things which may
occur at the time, and none which must. It is in such cases, how-

ever, that we are apt to feign a *special* experience or mental act
or process to answer to such a description.

This single topic, of *meaning* or *understanding something* by,
say, a gesture, a word or a sentence, is the most persistently recurrent in the book. It is easy to see why. It is a place where two
major preoccupations overlap, where two principal enemies may
join hands. These enemies are psychologism in the philosophy
of meaning, and the doctrine of special experiences in the philosophy of mind. Against them stand Wittgenstein's ideas. To
grasp a meaning is to be able to practise a technique; while
'meaning, understanding something by a word' is itself a prime
instance of those psychological expressions which seem to refer
to something which happens at a point, or over a short period,
of time, and may indeed do so; but, when they do, it is to something which gains its significance and its claim to its special title
from what stretches before and after the point or the period.

But the main discussion of psychological concepts is deferred
until the end of a further discussion of language and logic.

Language, Analysis and Philosophy

(See 38–137). The general over-simple picture of meaning
which Wittgenstein examines at the beginning of his book takes
an intenser, tauter form in a certain special doctrine of the *real*
names of a language. This doctrine Wittgenstein now discusses;
and the discussion broadens into a general repudiation of the set
of philosophical ideas and ideals, roughly indicated by the
title of 'logical atomism'. He begins with a consideration of two
related notions: the idea of the genuine names of a language,
and the idea of the simple indestructible elements of reality
which can only be named, not described or defined, and which
are the meanings of the genuine names. These are the primary
elements referred to by Socrates in the *Theaetetus,* and are identified by Wittgenstein with Russell's 'individuals' and his own
'objects' of the *Tractatus* (46). Both ideas are subjected to de-
structive criticism and diagnosis in 39–59. First Wittgenstein
attacks the notion of the word of which the meaning is the

object it applies to: he instances the ordinary proper name and distinguishes between its bearer and its meaning (40); in this case, too, the meaning is the use (41–43). (Wittgenstein here gives the wrong reason for objecting to the identification of the, or a, meaning of a proper name with its bearer, or one of its bearers. If we speak at all of the meaning of proper names, it is only in quite *specialised* ways, as when we say that 'Peter' means a stone, or 'Giovanni' means 'John'. This is not an accident of usage, but reflects a radical difference between proper names and other names. But here, as elsewhere, Wittgenstein neglects the use of 'meaning'.)

The antithesis 'simple-composite' is next examined and shown to have application only in a particular context, and to have different applications in different contexts: the *philosophical* question whether something is composite or simple is only too likely to lack a suitable context and hence a sense (47). Next (48–49) a simple model-language is constructed which might be held to answer to the specifications given in the *Theaetetus;* an arrangement of coloured squares is 'described' by an arrangement of letters, one letter for each square, the letters varying with the colour of the squares. We might perhaps say, in the context of this language-game, that the 'simple elements' were the individual squares. But then the assertion that the simple elements can only be named, not described, is at best, perhaps, a misleading way of saying that in the case of an arrangement consisting of one single square, the description consists of a single letter, the name of the coloured square; or of saying that *giving* a name to an element is different from *using* the name to describe a complex. Wittgenstein next considers the doctrine of the indestructibility, the necessary existence, of elements named by genuine names: the doctrine that the very meaningfulness of the name guarantees the existence of the item named. He is rightly not content to rely on a general repudiation of the notion of meaning-as-object, but produces answers to arguments in the doctrine's favour, and further explanations of its sources. The interest of the answers is weakened by the indescribable badness of the arguments (*cf.* 55, 56, 57). The explanations remain. If I understand them rightly, they run as follows. (1) We are inclined to get muddled over sentences like 'Turquoise exists'. This might be used to mean 'There are things which are turquoise'—an ordinary empirical proposition, which could be false—or 'There is such a colour as turquoise' [*i.e.* ' "Turquoise" does have meaning as a colour-word']. Taken the second way, it is again an empirical proposition, this time about a word. The muddle begins when we both take it this way and at the same time inconsistently take it as a proposition *using* the word 'turquoise' with the meaning it has, and thus as saying something about the colour, turquoise. Then we seem to be saying something necessary (for a word couldn't be used with, *i.e.* have, a meaning, and not have one), and also seem to be saying something about the colour, *viz.* that it necessarily exists (58). Wittgenstein does not remark that this account might apply to the abstract-noun form of *any* descriptive word (*e.g.* healthiness), and not merely to those which philosophers are prone to take as the names of ultimate elements. Perhaps this account should be regarded simply as a supplement to the other (2) which is summed up in the epigram, "What looks as if it *had* to exist is a part of the language" (50). If it were a necessary part of the activity of using a word 'W' that we, say, consulted a sample of W, then we might say that a sample of W must exist in order for the word to have meaning. From this *recherché* possibility, I take it we are to move to the truism that we could not teach a word by naming a sample unless there were a sample to name (*cf.* 50), and to join this to the reflection that there are at any rate some words which it is tempting to suppose could not be learnt except by means of an ostensive definition. Then we have the makings of a tautology which might be misconstrued as an assertion of metaphysically necessary existence.

The doctrine of elements is obviously connected with the belief in *analysis* as the inevitable method of philosophical clarification: the belief that the philosophical elucidation of an ordinary sentence is achieved when it is replaced by another, which makes explicit the complexity of the proposition expressed and reflects exactly the form of the fact described (91).

This belief is an illusion, engendered by confusions about language and logic, and to be dispelled only by a clear view of the actual functioning of language. How exactly does the illusion arise? (Here Wittgenstein's answer has a kind of passionate obscurity which it is difficult to penetrate.) In logic, which is at once completely pure, exact, and general, we seem to have the clue to the essential nature of thought and language, and with this, the clue to the general *a priori* order of the world, of things empirical (97). For do not thought and language mirror the world? (The *thought* that it is raining is the thought *that it is raining:* the propositions fit the facts (95–96).) Somehow the exactness and order of which logic gives us the ideal must (we think) be hidden in every, even the vaguest-looking, sentence of ordinary language: the *sense* of each must be definite. Logic shows us in advance what the structure of language and the world is—so this structure must be found hidden, to be revealed by analysis, in what we actually say (98 *et seq.*). Wittgenstein does not suggest that what philosophers have called 'analysis' is, in fact, useless. Sometimes "misunderstanding concerning the use of words, caused, among other things, by certain analogies between the forms of expression in different regions of language . . . can be removed by substituting one form of expression for another" (90). But this fact itself contributes to the illusion that there is "something like a final analysis of our forms of language, and so a *single* completely resolved form of every expression" (91).

To dispel this illusion, we are to give up looking for the essence of language and instead are to look at what is all the time before our eyes: the actual functioning of language. Then we see that linguistic activities are as diverse as all the things which we call 'games', and which are so called not because of any single common element, but because of "family resemblances"—a "complicated network of similarities, overlapping and criss-crossing" (66). (The sub-class of linguistic formations that we call 'propositions' is also just such a family. We are apt to think we have a clue to the general nature of the *proposition* in the idea of *whatever is true or false.* But one of these ideas cannot be used to elucidate the other: they move too closely together, they share each other's ambiguities (134–137).) Wittgenstein here makes an ingenious double use of his examination of the word 'game'. He not only uses the concept 'game' to cast light on the concept 'language' by means of direct *comparison:* games form a family, and so do the various activities which come under the general description of 'using language'. He also uses it as an *illustration,* to cast light on language in another way: by showing the parts which the notions of rules, and of exactness of meaning, play there. Thus the application of the word 'game' is not limited by any precise boundary; though a boundary could be fixed for a special purpose. We could say it was an *inexact* concept, that there was an indeterminacy in the rules for its use. But the important thing to notice is that this does not detract from its usefulness for ordinary purposes (and for extraordinary purposes, special rules can be devised). So that it would not even be *correct* in general, to speak of inexactness here; for 'inexact' is a word of dispraise, signifying that what is so-called falls short of a standard required for some particular purpose (88); and here no such special purpose has been specified. Moreover: (1) in whatever detail we give the rules for the use of a word (or for the playing of a game), cannot we always imagine a case in which there might be a doubt as to whether the rule applied to this case or not? and (2) is there not always the possibility of someone's not knowing how to interpret the rules or the explanations we give him of them, or the explanations of those explanations? The point Wittgenstein is making here is that the demand for absolute precision in the rules (a fixed meaning) or for absolute finality in their interpretation, their explanation, is senseless. What determines whether there is enough precision in the rules, or a sufficient explanation of them, is whether the concept is used successfully, with general agreement (84–87).

(One of the illustrations which Wittgenstein uses here is unfortunate. He wishes to say that I could use a proper name "without a fixed meaning", without its losing its usefulness; "asked what I understand by 'N'", he says, I might adduce various descriptions some of which I might later be prepared to abandon as false of N (79). Of course, I never should be asked *what* I understand by, but *whom* I mean by, 'N'; and in answering, I should not be defining 'N', but identifying N.).

With what conception of philosophy is this revised view of the nature of language associated? The key to the solution of our problems still lies in their source, *viz.* language itself. But we are not to try to improve on, to tamper with, language; only to describe its workings. For the confusions we are troubled by arise not when language is doing its work, but when it is idling, on holiday; it is when we consider words and sentences in abstraction from their linguistic and non-linguistic contexts that they seem to conceal a mystery and invite a myth. So we are to "assemble reminders" of obvious facts about their uses; not at random, nor yet systematically; but on each occasion with some particular purpose in view, the purpose of dispelling some particular confusion. And to make clear the ways in which words actually function, it will sometimes be helpful to consider ways in which they do not, but might, function; invented language-games will be useful objects of comparison with actual language-games (109–133).

Many philosophers would agree with much of this: it is difficult not to share the conception of philosophy held by the first philosopher of the age. Yet there are at least two very different directions in which it may seem unduly restrictive. First, there is the idea that the *sole* purpose of the distinctions we draw attention to, the descriptions we give of the different ways in which words function, is to dispel particular metaphysical confusions; and, associated with this, an extreme aversion from a systematic exhibition of the logic of particular regions of language. Now, even if we *begin* with a therapeutic purpose, our interest might not exhaust itself when that purpose is achieved; and there can be an investigation of the logic of sets of concepts, which starts with no purpose other than that of unravelling and ordering complexities for the sake of doing so. The desire to present the facts systematically here becomes important in proportion as therapeutic aims become secondary. The other direction might be suggested by what Wittgenstein himself says of certain metaphysical doctrines such as solipsism. The inventor of such a doctrine has discovered "a new way of looking at things"—something like "a new way of painting . . . or a new kind of song" (401). It is surely over-puritanical to hold that, just because the claims made for such new ways were too large, we should be concerned solely with preventing ourselves from seeing the world afresh. We might make room for a purged kind of metaphysics, with more modest and less disputable claims than the old. But one does not need to have an equal sympathy with both these possibilities in order to ask: could not the activities we call 'doing philosophy' also form a family?

Meaning and Understanding

(See first: 132–242, 319–326, 357–358, 431–436, 454. Further references are given later in this section.) Wittgenstein next reverts to the themes of *meaning* and *understanding* something by an expression—a theme announced, but not developed, at the end of the introductory paragraphs (33–36). The main sections which he devotes to this topic are of great brilliance and clarity. He begins with the point that the fundamental criteria for whether someone has understood an expression lie in the application which he makes of it. Of course, he may correctly be said to 'grasp the meaning in a flash'. A picture or a paraphrase may come before his mind; he may produce them to us. But neither picture nor paraphrase dictates the use that is to be made of it: they can be *variously* applied, and if we are inclined to forget this, it is because we are inclined to think of only one application. So the production of the picture or paraphrase, though normally (and rightly) enough to satisfy us, is not the final test: *that* resides in the application. Now this may seem acceptable enough so long as we are considering the criteria we employ for someone else's understanding. But do we not often and correctly say of *ourselves,* when, *e.g.* someone is trying to teach us how to develop a series, things like: 'Now I understand!', 'Now I can go on!'? It is obvious that we are not here applying to ourselves the criterion of application: we seem to be reporting something which "makes its appearance in a moment". No doubt there

usually is some momentary experience: *e.g.* a formula for the
series may occur to us, or we may just experience a feeling of
release of tension. But, though in certain cases, a remark such as
'The formula has occurred to me' might have the same force,
serve the same purpose as 'Now I understand' etc., it will not do
to say that in general these expressions have the same meaning
(183). In any case it is clear that *the understanding* is not to be
identified with any such characteristic experience. (This will
seem only too clear; and is the point at which we are tempted
to look for a special experience.) If we ask what, *in the eyes of
others*, "justifies" me in using the words 'Now I understand' etc.,
what shows my use of them to be "correct", it is not the occurrence of the experience, whatever it may be, but the circumstances under which I have it (*e.g.* that I have worked with these
formulae before, that I now continue the series, etc.) (153–155).
This obviously does not mean that the words 'Now I can go on!'
are short for a description of all these circumstances, or that
they mean 'I have had an experience which I know empirically
to lead to the continuation of the series' (179); my certainty
that I shall be able to go on is not a matter of induction (*cf.*
324–328). What we need (here I interpret a little) is to look at
such first-person utterances in a radically different way from the
way in which we look at the corresponding third-person utterances: to see them not as reports about myself for giving which
I have to apply criteria, but rather as "exclamations" (323) or
"signals" (180, p. 218), naturally and appropriately made or
given in certain circumstances. Such an exclamation could even
be compared with "an instinctive sound" or "a glad start" (323).
Failure to perform successfully after the signal had been given
would not necessarily mean that it had been incorrectly given.
In some cases (*e.g.* if there had been an unforeseen interruption
or disturbance) we should accept the plea: 'When I said I knew
how to go on, I did know' (323).

Two minor comments. (1) Wittgenstein does not enlarge on
the suggestion given by the word 'signal'. One might take as a
typical case that in which a teacher turns from the blackboard,
proffers the chalk to the class with the question 'Who can go

on?'. Here the answer '*I* can' would have the same function as a silent acceptance of the chalk. (2) Wittgenstein's continual use of phrases like 'gave him the right to say', 'made it a correct use of', 'justified him in saying' in connexion with these first-person utterances might tend to obscure a little his own doctrine. The essential point is that a person does *not* have (or need) grounds or reasons (does not apply criteria) for saying correctly that he himself understands, in the sense in which others must have them to say it of him. Of course, he may himself have, or lack, reasons or justifications in another (a social) sense.

Grasping the meaning (understanding it) should be compared with intending the meaning (meaning it). The two are connected in this way. We may be inclined to think that the purpose of the explanations we give (of, *e.g.* the rule for the development of the series) is really to get the learner to catch hold of something essential, the meaning we *intend* (210); and that the correct application he then makes of the rule is somehow a consequence of his catching hold of this essential thing. And here we have the idea of the mental act of *intending, meaning* this expression of the rule in a certain way, as somehow anticipating and pre-determining all the steps of its application before they are taken. Or the connexion may be approached in another way. The criterion for the learner's having understood the rule aright is his application of it. But not *any* application (anything that could possibly be represented as an application of the expression of the rule) will do. It must be the *correct* application. But what are the criteria for correctness? Here again one is inclined to answer that the correct application is the one that was meant: and this answer may once more give us the picture of all the steps being somehow covered in advance by the act of meaning. This idea is *very* compelling. For does not the *sense* of the rule (of the expression) determine what is to count as the correct application of it? What does the determining here is not just the words or the symbols themselves. They are dead, inert (432, 454); they could be applied, and applied systematically, in indefinitely numerous different ways. And the same goes for any paraphrase or picture (433), the substitution of one expression

or symbol for another: "interpretations (in this sense) by themselves do not determine meaning" (198). It is natural to suppose
that only the intention, "the psychical thing", can do that.
Natural, but of course wrong; (or at least misleading). The
criterion for the correct application of the rule is *customary
practice* (199–201); the customary practice of those who have
received a certain training; the way we are taught to use the
rule and do always use it. It is, too, in the existence of this
customary practice, and nowhere else, that we may find the way
in which the steps are "determined in advance", and the way in
which a certain application is "meant", or "intended" by the
ordinary instructor who has mastered that practice. (Of course;
for 'the rule determines this application' means 'the rule is not
correctly understood unless used in this way'.) What gives us the
illusion of some other mysterious determinant is the fact that,
having received a certain training, we find it so *utterly natural*
to make a certain application of the expression. We draw the
consequences of the rule *"as a matter of course"*; and cannot
understand how anyone can make a wholly different application
of the expression. [" 'But surely you can see . . . ?' That is
just the characteristic expression of someone who is under the
compulsion of a rule" (231).] Of course, in the instructor-pupil
situation, explanations are in place; but the purpose of the
explanations is to get the pupil to do as we do, and find it
equally natural. "Explanations come to an end somewhere";
then we just act. But equally, of course, "the pupil's capacity to
learn may come to an end".

Among resistances to his views Wittgenstein notes the tendency
to fall back on the words 'the same': the tendency, *e.g.* to say
'But when we explain a rule to someone by giving him examples
of its application, all we want him to see is that he is *to do the
same* in other cases'. In answer to this, Wittgenstein points out
that the idea of a single, generally sufficient criterion of 'what is
the same' is nonsense. The criteria for 'doing the same' in *the
case of a particular rule* are just the criteria, whatever they may
be, for the correct observance of that rule. The concepts of 'rule'
and 'identity' are as closely related to each other as the word

'proposition' to the phrase 'true or false'. (See 185, 208, 215–216, 223–227.)

Now although Wittgenstein, in the sections here discussed, is directly concerned mainly with the topics of meaning or understanding something by an expression of a rule, what he says is taken by him to have much wider implications about language in general. These implications give the meaning-use equation a new significance, of the utmost importance in relation to the topics of experience and sensation which he next discusses. Roughly speaking: what he says about obeying what we would ordinarily call 'rules' is applied to obeying what philosophers are apt to call 'the rules for the use' of all expressions, whether or not they are the expressions of rules. Obeying a rule is conforming to an agreed common practice; "it is impossible to obey a rule 'privately'" (202). The emphasis is on the *agreed common practice* in the use of expressions, and this carries with it, in cases where it is appropriate to speak of criteria, the existence of *agreed common criteria* for their application. Wittgenstein notes that this in its turn demands the existence of general agreement in *judgments* (242). The great importance of these points emerges rapidly in what follows.

Before turning to Wittgenstein's discussion of his next topic, it is in place to notice some of the further things he says about 'meaning something by an expression'. To this he reverts at intervals, in a rich succession of examples, arguments and suggestions throughout the rest of the book (see especially 503–510, 525–534, 540–546, 592–598, 607, 661–693, II. ii, II. vi, II. xi, pp. 214–219). As before, the main doctrine attacked is the doctrine that what gives an expression, in use, its meaning and its life, is the user's special experience, or act, of meaning something by it. I select some principal points.

(*a*) One of the sources of the doctrine is the difference we feel between using words in an ordinary, and in an abnormal, context (*e.g.* repeating a sentence mockingly, or as a quotation, or in elocution practice, etc.). Aware of a difference of feeling in these latter cases, we are apt to suppose it consists in the absence of the normal experience of meaning what we say. Just so might we suppose, until we remember the facts, that everything that does not feel strange, feels familiar (592–598, 607; *cf.* also, on 'being influenced', 169–170).

(*b*) In II. vi (*cf.* also 592), Wittgenstein analyses brilliantly the idea of a special atmosphere or feeling carried by each particular word. (So some philosophers have spoken, for example of an 'if-feeling'.) Whatever feeling-accompaniment the reading or uttering of a certain word may have, it is only *as so accompanying the word* that we are tempted to invest it with this special significance. Any such feeling or sensation might occur in a different context and not be recognised at all. But a feeling or atmosphere which loses its identity (its identity as, say, the 'if-feeling') when separated from a certain object, is *not* a special feeling or atmosphere associated with that object at all. Contrast it with a genuine case of separately identifiable but closely associated things. Here a different association would shock and surprise us.

(*c*) Wittgenstein does not deny that a sense can be given to the notion of *experiencing* the meaning of a word. (See II. ii and II. xi, pp. 214–216. *Cf.* also 526–534.) This phrase might reasonably be used in connexion with many experiences which we do have, and which profoundly affect our *attitude* to language. Among these are: finding the *mot juste* after rejecting a number of candidates; reading with *expression;* saying a word again and again until it seems to 'lose its meaning'. In particular Wittgenstein notes the game of pronouncing a word like 'March', now with one, now with another of its meanings. We can comply with the instruction to do this, and can perhaps report a different experience of the word. But this very game shows how unimportant the experience is in relation to meaning the word now in this way and now in that in the ordinary course of events; for then we may not be able to report any such experience. In general, the word 'meaning' may be said to acquire a secondary use in connexion with all these experiences which are of such significance in relation to the way we *feel* about our language. But this use *is* secondary. Words could still have their meanings, language be used as a means of communication, in the absence of these phenomena.

(*d*) The most important of these later discussions (661–693, and pp. 216–217) is concerned with meaning in the sense it has in such a question as 'Whom (which one) did you mean?', *i.e.* with an intended reference as opposed to an intended sense. But there are close analogies between the two. When, with reference to an earlier remark, I say 'I meant him' I refer to a definite time (the time at which I made the remark); but not to an experience which I had at that time. There may sometimes be characteristic accompaniments, looks, movements of attention; but these are not what 'meaning him' consists in. Compare 'I meant him' with the phrase 'I was speaking of him'. What makes it true that I was speaking of him is the set of circumstances in which the original remark was made, and in particular, the general set or direction of my actions, of which the explanation ('I meant him') is itself one. What is apt to confuse us here is that of course I do not discover whom I meant by studying those circumstances. But nor do I report an indubitable special experience. It is rather (here I interpret a little) that in giving the explanation of whom I meant I continue a certain chain of actions; as I might, in pointing things out on a complex diagram, discard a blunt pointer in favour of a finer one, more serviceable for my purpose. Or I might *dis-continue* that chain of action, think better of it; and substitute another name; and then I shall be said to have lied. The question *not* to ask is: How do I know whom I meant? For I have no *way* of knowing, I apply no criteria. (Wittgenstein suggests that the words 'know' and 'doubt' are both out of place here. But of course, one can in fact be said to forget whom one was speaking of, and thus to be in doubt, to be 'not sure'; and then to remember. But this is an unimportant qualification; for Wittgenstein discusses elsewhere the question of *remembering* one's intentions.)

Pain and Persons

(See 142, 243–315, 350–351, 384, 390, 398–421, II. iv, II. v.) Studying the sections in which Wittgenstein deals with sensations, one may well feel one's capacity to learn coming to an end. Wittgenstein's case against saying that the phrases 'meaning/understanding something by an expression' stand for or name special experiences seems to me thoroughly made out. But even the significance of this denial comes into question if it then appears that no word whatever stands for or names a special experience. (Experiences which characteristically accompany 'I understand!' are not to be identified with understanding. Try substituting " 'I am in pain' " and 'pain' in the appropriate places here.) Wittgenstein seems to me to oscillate in his discussion of this subject between a stronger and a weaker thesis, of which the first is false and the second true. These may be described, rather than formulated, as follows. (I attach no importance to their descriptions: their significance must emerge later.) The stronger thesis says that no words name sensations (or 'private experiences'); and in particular the word 'pain' does not (*cf.* 293). The weaker thesis says that certain conditions must be satisfied for the existence of a common language in which sensations are ascribed to those who have them; and that certain confusions about sensations arise from the failure to appreciate this, and consequently to appreciate the way in which the language of sensations functions. The oscillation between the two theses is to be explained by the fact that the weaker can be made to yield to the stronger by the addition of a certain premise about language, *viz.* that all there is to be said about the descriptive meaning of a word is said when it is indicated what *criteria* people can use for employing it or for deciding whether or not it is correctly employed.

The stronger thesis is first developed by an attack on the idea of a private language (243 *et seq.*). By a 'private language' we are here to understand a language of which the individual names (descriptive words) refer solely to the sensations of the user of the language. He may be imagined as keeping a record of the occurrence of certain sensations. The main point of the attack is that the hypothetical user of the language would have no check on, no criterion of, the *correctness* of his use of it. We might be inclined to say that his memory provides a check. But what check has he on his memory? Suppose in the case of one particular word he keeps on misremembering its use. What difference will it make? There will be no way in which he can distinguish between a correct and an incorrect use. So the idea of a correct use is empty here: and with it the idea of such a language. Now the interesting thing about the attack is that Wittgenstein presents it as if it applied only or peculiarly to the idea of a private language in which all the descriptive words were supposed to stand for sensations. But of course, if it has any validity at all, it has an equal validity for the case of a private language (here this means 'a language used by only one individual') in which the words stand not for sensations at all, but for things like colours or material objects or animals. Here again the individual will have no external check on the correctness of his use of the names. (It is no good saying that he can, in this case, though not in the case of the sensation-language, make himself a physical dictionary, *e.g.* a table with names opposite pictures. Wittgenstein's own arguments in other places are here decisive. The interpretation of the table depends on the use that is made of it.) But if this is so, then Wittgenstein's arguments would at most tend to show that the idea of a language *of any kind* used only by one person was an absurdity: and this conclusion would have no special immediate relevance to the case of sensation.

But it is clear that Wittgenstein intends his arguments to have special relevance to this case. So let us look at the differences between the two supposed private languages. We may suppose (following Wittgenstein) that in the case of the first private language, the one for sensations only, there are no particular characteristic overt expressions of the sensations, manifested by the hypothetical user of the language. Now we introduce observers, studying the behaviour and surroundings of the language users. The observer (B) of the user of the second language observes a correlation between the use of its words and sentences and the speaker's actions and environment. The observer of the user of the first language does not. Observer B is thus able to form hypotheses about the meanings (the regular use) of the words of his subject's language. He might in time come to be able to speak it: then the practice of each serves as a check on the correctness of the practice of the other. But

shall we say that, before this fortunate result was achieved
(before the use of the language becomes a *shared* "form of
life"), the words of the language had no meaning, no use? And
if we do not say this of the case where this result can be
achieved, why should we say it of the hypothetical case where it
cannot? In each case, while the language is used by one person
alone (let us say as in one of Wittgenstein's examples, to record
occurrences), the meaning of the words is a matter of the customary practice of the user: in each case the only check on this
customary practice is memory. But (it might be said), the hypothesis that someone was using a language of the first kind
could never be tested. But what is to count as a test here?
Suppose he also mastered the ordinary common language, and
then *told us* that he had been (or was still) using a private
language. It is also *just* worth asking, in connexion with some
of Wittgenstein's arguments here: Do we ever in fact find ourselves misremembering the use of very *simple* words of our common language, and having to correct ourselves by attention to
others' use?—Wittgenstein gives himself considerable trouble
over the question of how a man would *introduce* a name for a
sensation into this private language. But we need imagine no
special ceremony. He might simply be struck by the recurrence
of a certain sensation and get into the habit of making a certain
mark in a different place every time it occurred. The making
of the marks would help to impress the occurrence on his
memory. One can easily imagine this procedure being elaborated
into a system of dating. (The purpose of these remarks is to
indicate the place the sensation-name might play in the private
language-game.)

Another of Wittgenstein's main arguments is basically a vari-
ant on the first. He notes two associated points, which one is not
inclined to dispute: (1) "the expression of doubt has no place in
the language-game" (288), *i.e.* in the language-game with 'I am
in pain'; [3] and (2) "what I do (when I say 'I am in pain') is not
to identify my sensation by criteria" (290). Wittgenstein seems

[3] Even this is not quite true as it stands. There is no place for one kind of doubt, the kind that
might be expressed in 'Am I interpreting the facts of this situation aright?' But there is sometimes
place for another kind, which might be expressed in 'Does this quite deserve the *name* of "pain" '?

to think that these facts can only be accommodated if we regard 'I am in pain' as an *expression* or manifestation of pain, along-side such natural expressions as crying or groaning, but of course, one which, unlike these, is the result of training (244, 288, etc.). So regarded, 'pain' ceases to appear as the name or the description of a sensation. If we do *not* so regard it, then we shall require criteria of identity for the sensation; and with these there would enter the possibility of error (288). (Here one is, of course, reminded of the discussion of understanding. There are criteria of understanding, as of pain, which we apply in the case of others. But a man does not apply them to himself when he says 'I understand'—and his saying this is to be compared with an exclamation, a glad start, not a report of a mental occurrence.) Wittgenstein here seems to me to be in a muddle: the weaker thesis is being muddled with the stronger. What he has committed himself to is the view that one cannot sensibly be said to recognise or identify anything, unless one uses *criteria*; and, as a consequence of this, that one cannot recognise or identify sensations. But of course this is untrue. Consider cases where the rival pull of 'expression' or 'manifestation' is weaker or non-existent. Consider, for example, tastes; and such phrases as 'the taste of onions', 'a metallic taste'. Here we have one thing (a taste) associated with another (a material substance), but quite certainly recognisable and identifiable in itself. Only, of course, one does not use *criteria* of identity for *the taste*. If the question 'What is the criterion of identity here?' is pushed, one can only answer: 'Well, the taste itself' (*cf.* 'the sensation itself'). Of course, the phrases by which we *refer* to such tastes involve allusions to what can be seen and touched; for we speak a common language. But we do not identify the taste by means of the associated substance by allusion to which we name it. Consider also that we discriminate and recognise different particular pains (I do not mean pains in different places)—aches and throbs, searing and jabbing pains, etc. In many cases, there are not, or not obviously, different characteristic natural expressions of pain to correspond to these differences in quality. The phrases by which we name these particular pain-experiences are commonly analogical; and this too for the reason that we want a common language.[4] All the time Wittgenstein is driving at the conditions that are necessary for a common language in which pain can be ascribed to persons, the consequent need for *criteria for the ascription* of pain, and the effects of this upon the use of the word 'pain' of our common language. Hence his obsession with the *expression* of pain. But he errs through excess of zeal when this leads him to deny that sensations can be recognised and bear names. Rather the case is that these names must always contain in a more or less complex way, within their logic, some allusion to what is not sensation, to what can be seen and touched and heard.

Why is this? The answer illuminates the nature of Wittgenstein's mistake, and also the great extent to which he is right.

(1) To deny that 'pain' is the name of a (type of) sensation is comparable with denying that 'red' is the name of a colour.

(2) It is just the difference between the ways colours and pains enter into our lives that accounts for the fact (i) that we call the latter and not the former sensations (or, alternatively, that accounts for the very special status we assign to sensations); it is just this difference that accounts for the fact (ii) that we *ascribe* pains to those who suffer them and not colours to those who see them; and which accounts for the fact (iii) that *without* criteria for ascribing pains to persons, we could have no common language of pain. Finally, it is because our common language-game must be that of ascribing pains to persons that symptoms, expressions, of pain assume such overwhelming importance.

(3) Fact (iii), misunderstood, is reflected (upside down) in all the usual philosophers' confusions about sensations; and, over emphasised, is reflected (rightside up, but obscuring the rest of the picture) in Wittgenstein's.

To understand at least part of what is meant by 'the difference between the ways colours and pains enter our lives', it will be helpful to consider some unrealised possibilities. Let us suppose

---

[4] The fact that there are characteristic natural expressions of pain but not (or not obviously) characteristic differences between natural expressions of different kinds of pain (I do not mean different degrees or locations) is the explanation of the fact that the descriptions of the different kinds tend to be analogical, whereas the word 'pain' is not analogical. See below.

first that we feel pain only and always under the condition that our skin is in contact with the surfaces of certain bodies. (*Cf.* Wittgenstein's 'pain-patches', 312. But he does not exploit this fully.) The pain begins and ends with the contact. Then our pain-language might have a logic wholly different from that which it does have. Instead of ascribing pains to sufferers, we might ascribe painfulness to surfaces, much as we at present call them rough, smooth, hard, soft, etc. Another possibility is this. We say things like 'It's hot in here', 'It's cold out there', and so on, ascribing temperatures (I do not mean in degrees Fahrenheit or Centigrade) to regions. Let us suppose that any person felt pain if and only if every other normal person in the same region (which could be the size of a room or a continent) at the same time also felt pain. Then we might ascribe painfulness to regions instead of pain to persons; saying, *e.g.* 'It's painful today', or 'It's painful in here'. The point of both examples is that in each case we should have as *impersonal* a way of describing pain-phenomena as we have of describing colour-phenomena. But of course the incidence of physical pain is not like this. The causes of pain are often internal and organic. Even when pain is caused by contact, it generally requires a special kind of contact rather than contact with any special kind of thing; and it generally does not cease when contact ceases. If you have a pain and I come to the place where you are, or touch or look at what you are touching or looking at, this will not in general result in my having a pain. As Wittgenstein not infrequently points out, it is such very obvious general facts of nature which determine the logic of our concepts. I may put the point very roughly as follows. A set of people together in certain surroundings will be in general agreement on 'what it looks like here, what it feels like (to the touch) here, what it sounds like here'. In this possibility of a general agreement in judgments lies the possibility of a common impersonal language for describing what we see and hear and touch (*cf.* 242). But there is no such general agreement as to whether or not 'it's painful here', as to what it feels like (as we misleadingly say) *within*. In the absence of general agreement in judgment, a common language is impossible; and this is why a common impersonal pain-language is impossible. But if (to speak absurdly) we are prepared to make our pain-language a language for ascribing pain to persons, then we have something (*i.e.* people's pain-behaviour) which we see and hear, and on which, in consequence, general agreement in judgment is possible. Because of certain general facts of nature, therefore, the only possible common pain-language is the language in which pain is ascribed to those who talk the language, the criteria for its ascription being (mainly) pain-behaviour. And because of *this* fact it is necessarily empty and pointless (I will *not* say meaningless) either (*a*) to speculate about the ascription of pain to anything which does not exhibit behaviour comparable in the relevant respects with human behaviour (*i.e.* the behaviour of those who use the concept), or (*b*) to raise generalised doubts about other people's experience of pain, or about one's own knowledge of this. It is the above points which I take Wittgenstein essentially to be making. (He sees (142) that, as things are, the possibility of the language-game rests on there being characteristic expressions of pain.) But the way in which he makes them is, in part at least, misleading. For from none of these facts does it follow that 'pain' is not the name of a sensation. On the contrary. It is only in the light of the fact that 'pain' is the name of a sensation that *these* facts are intelligible; or, better, to say that 'pain' is the name of a sensation is (or ought to be) just to begin to draw attention to these facts. One could say: that pain is a sensation (or, that sensations have the special status they have) is a *fact of nature* which dictates the logic of 'pain'.

This outline is of course extremely crude. What a proper treatment of the topic above all requires is extensive and detailed *comparisons* between the different types of sensible experience we have.

Thoughts and Words

(316–394, 427, 501, 540, 633–637, II. xi. pp. 211, 216–223.) Wittgenstein's treatment of this topic has close connexions with his account of 'meaning/understanding something by an expression'; and presents certain analogies with the account of pain. It should first be noted that Wittgenstein is not primarily concerned with certain rather specialised applications of the word 'thinking' which are apt to come first to mind. We sometimes contrast the thinker and the active man; or may speak of having spent a fortnight's holiday without having a single thought. But Wittgenstein is not especially concerned with the thoughts which come only to the reflective. Again, we sometimes use 'thinking' in the sense of 'thinking out how to do something', or 'solving, or trying to solve, a problem', when the problem may indeed be as practical a one as you please. But Wittgenstein is not especially concerned with the thinking that overcomes difficulties. His concern is not restricted in either of these ways. He is quite as much interested in the most ordinary case of 'having a thought' or 'thinking something', in the sense in which, for example, someone who, talking neither at random nor insincerely, says that p, may be said to have had the thought that p, or to think that p, or to have said what he thought. The close connexion between Wittgenstein's discussions of 'meaning something' and 'thinking' should now be clear. For if a man satisfies the criteria for meaning a sentence in a certain way (and is not insincere in uttering it), then he also satisfies the criteria for having thought something and said what he thought. So much of the argument on the former topic bears directly on the latter.

There is a certain once common view of the nature of thinking against which Wittgenstein's arguments are mainly directed. It is this. Thinking or having a thought is a special event or process which may accompany and be expressed in speech or writing or relevant action, and may also occur in the absence of these. No one can ever know what another's thoughts are in just the way he knows what his own are; for each man is directly cognisant only of his own internal processes. Wittgenstein's general counter-thesis runs as follows. It is true that having a thought is not to be identified with any particular outward process of speech or writing or action; nor with inner speech or other imagery. The having of a thought is not the occurrence of any of these; but nor is it any other occurrence. It is the occurrence of one of these in a certain context, in certain circumstances. To see what sort of context, what sort of circumstances are relevant here, one must consider what criteria are used in ascribing thoughts to people. A man's actions may show his thought (*cf.* 330), or his remarks may tell it; but if a monkey imitated the actions, or a parrot repeated the words, we should not ascribe the same thought to the monkey or the parrot. The difference does not lie in what went on inside them, but in the difference between the rest of their behaviour. Of course, a man does not, in telling his own thoughts, apply to himself the criteria for ascription of thoughts which he applies to others. But neither, when he says what he is or has been thinking, does he report on any concurrent or antecedent inner process. It is rather that he takes, or continues, a certain line of linguistic action, much as he might take or continue, in other circumstances, a certain line of non-linguistic action; and of course, he might 'think better of it', *change* his line.

It is quite clear and very important that Wittgenstein does not deny the existence of those occurrences, whether observable, like an exclamation, or unobservable, like what we call a flash of insight, or inward speech, by reference to which we may *date* the occurrence of a thought. What he is most concerned to stress is the fact that these occurrences do not owe their significance or their claim to the titles they bear, to their own peculiar nature or that of some psychical accompaniment; but to their place in a general pattern of actions and events. The concept of thinking demands such a general pattern as a setting for the occurrence of thoughts. In this, which I shall call his hostility to the doctrine of immediacy, Wittgenstein is surely right. Another factor in his treatment of thinking which is, I think, quite distinct from this, and also more questionable, might be called his hostility to the doctrine of privacy. It is because of this factor that I speak of analogies with his treatment of pain. I shall try to illustrate this from some of the things he says about inward speech, *i.e.* about saying something to oneself in imagination. (I would emphasise that the hostility to the doctrine of privacy is not of peculiar importance in connexion with *thinking*. It has more general application. It is merely that it can be very clearly illustrated by some things that Wittgenstein says in the course of his discussion of thinking.)

II. xi, pp. 220–223 are largely concerned with telling or confessing what one 'has been saying to oneself in one's thoughts'. Wittgenstein says: (1) that what I say to myself in my thoughts is hidden from others only in the sense in which my thoughts are hidden from one who does not understand the language in which I speak out loud (pp. 220, 222); and (2) that when I tell another what I was saying to myself, or acknowledge that he has guessed aright, I do not describe what went on inside me: I do not tell what I was thinking from inspection of the inner process (p. 222). Now it seems to me that Wittgenstein is here equivocating with 'what I say to myself'; and that his motive for doing so is his hostility to the idea of what is not observed (seen, heard, smelt, touched, tasted), and in particular to the idea that what is not observed can in any sense be recognised or described or reported. The equivocation is made possible by the fact that 'what I was saying to myself in my thoughts' can mean either 'what I was thinking' or 'what words were going through my mind'. Now it is true that in saying what I was thinking, I do not report on 'what went on within me' (p. 222). In just the same way I do not tell what I am imagining by inspecting my image (II, iii). But also in just the same way I do not, in the case where I am talking or thinking aloud, discover what I am or have been thinking by listening to my words or their echo. As far as this goes, audible and inner speech are on the same level. (This fact indicates both the respect in which remark (1) above is justified and also the respect in which it is false.) They are on the same level in another way too. I may tell what I was saying to myself, not in the sense of telling what I was thinking, but in the sense of reporting what words were going through my mind. And here 'what went on within me' is just as much to the point, as 'what went on audibly' is when I am asked not to say what I meant when I spoke aloud, but to *repeat my words*. Of course, the difference between *these* two cases is that there is, and can be, no check (except the general reliability of my short-term memory) on my report of what words were going through my mind, whereas there can very well be a check on the correctness of my repetition of my audibly spoken words. But only a prejudice against 'the inner' would lead anyone, on the strength of this difference, to deny the possibility of the first

kind of report. Only the same prejudice would lead anyone to
deny that I can sometimes say something by way of description
of my experiences of having imagery, as well as describing to
people what I am imagining. (Having a confused and jumpy or
intermittent image is not the same as imagining something as
confused and jumpy or intermittent.) It is very likely true that
some have not distinguished describing or reporting such experiences from telling what one is thinking, or describing what one
is imagining. That a fact can be misconstrued is not, however,
a reason for denying it. It is also true that when we describe
'private' or 'inner' or 'hidden' experiences, our descriptions of
them (like our descriptions of their status) are often *analogical*;
and the analogies are provided by what we *do* observe (*i.e.* hear,
see, touch, etc.). This is in itself an important fact. It throws
light once more on the conditions necessary for a common
language. One could almost say that it is this fact which Wittgenstein is often stressing, often in a perverse way. But a description is none the worse for being analogical, especially if it
couldn't be anything else.[5] Moreover, some of the analogies are
very good ones. In particular the analogy between saying certain
words to oneself and saying them out loud is very good. (One
can even be unsure whether one has said them out loud or to
oneself.) The analogy between mental pictures and pictures
is, in familiar ways, less good.

Perhaps what is really operating here is the old verificationist
horror of a claim that cannot be checked. Elsewhere in his treatment of thinking, Wittgenstein manifests the more intelligible
aversion from a hypothesis or supposition that cannot be checked
(344, 348–349).

States of Mind and Introspection

(572–587, II. i, ix, x; also 437, 465.) Wittgenstein writes on
expectation, hope, belief, wishes, grief and fear. As in other
cases, the main hostility is to the doctrine of immediacy. Expectation, hope, grief are forms of human life, each with many

---

[5] If one were *very* anxious to appease here, one *could* say they were only 'descriptions' in an
analogical sense. But I think this would be being over-anxious.

variations. What the subject of these states is at any given moment doing or experiencing, gets its significance, its importance, from its surroundings (583–584), its context of situation and behaviour. The isolated occurrences could not claim these names. The falsity of the doctrine of immediacy is indeed, in some of these cases, a great deal more evident than it is in the cases of thinking or understanding. For a man may be said to expect or to believe or to be grieving over something when no thought of that thing is in his mind. There is therefore an *a fortiori* character about the non-immediacy of the states that these words name.

Among the criteria that we use for the ascription of certain of these states to another person, the *verbal* behaviour of the subject of them assumes an overwhelming importance. Wittgenstein in fact suggests that a necessary condition of the ascription of, *e.g.* hopes, wishes and some beliefs to a subject is the subject's mastery of a language for the *expression* of these (see II. i, ix and 650). His reason for this is clear. A creature's non-linguistic behaviour may certainly provide adequate criteria for the ascription of *some* states; but where descriptions of states take on a slightly higher degree of complexity, it may be difficult or impossible to imagine what sort of complication of non-linguistic criteria would be adequate in the case of beings incapable of speech. ("We say a dog is afraid his master will beat him; but not, he is afraid his master will beat him to-morrow.") In the sections on thinking Wittgenstein placed an analogous and obviously connected restriction on the ascription of thoughts. It seems that one ought here to distinguish between the thesis that there are certain *kinds* of state (say, wishing or hoping) which cannot even in their simplest forms be ascribed to beings without the power of linguistically expressing them; and the weaker thesis that there are more complex forms of certain kinds of states (wishing, believing, hoping) which cannot be ascribed to beings without this power. The weaker thesis seems to me obviously true. Still more obviously, the stronger thesis must, on *one* interpretation, be false. Words like 'wish' and 'hope' could never acquire a use at all unless there were *some* circumstances or range of circumstances, other than that of their being uttered, in and because of which it was correct to use them; and since wishes and hopes are ascribed to others, these circumstances must include *criteria*, must include the observable. Wittgenstein's general principles here refute his particular thesis. I may, however, very likely be mistaken in ascribing the stronger thesis in this form to Wittgenstein. His position may rather be the intermediate one that *some* linguistic capacities are required in the subject to whom wishes and hopes are ascribed, not the specific linguistic capacity for the conventional expressions of wishes and hopes. So amended, the doctrine cannot, of course, be refuted in this way.

What in general of the roles of first-person utterances about states of mind? Wittgenstein here draws an admirable distinction between those first-person utterances which are correctly called reports of the results of introspection, or descriptions of states of mind, on the one hand, and those which are only misleadingly so called (and only so called by philosophers), on the other. We can *come to conclusions* about our own hopes, fears, expectations, even beliefs; and in doing so we use much the same criteria as we use in coming to conclusions about others, though we may (or may not) have certain advantages in our own case. But first-person utterances about states of mind are more commonly not of this kind, but of another: not conclusions about, but conventional expressions of, states of mind, taking their (special) place among the other criteria which are used in ascribing them. I think Wittgenstein does not perhaps give quite enough weight to the *very* special nature of this place, that he tends to exaggerate a little the degree to which, or the frequency with which, these utterances are, so to speak, forced from us. We use them very often pretty deliberately, and to inform; to show others where we stand, what we may be expected to do and for what reasons. And this may safely be admitted—without either returning to the doctrine of reported special experiences, or advancing to the absurdity that *all* such utterances are *conclusions* about ourselves—just so long as we acknowledge, what Wittgenstein elsewhere examines, the nature of our certainties about our own deliberate behaviour. The utterance of 'I am embarrassed/ amazed/shocked/confident/very glad', etc. may be a social *act* (by this I mean something comparable with a polite greeting, a move to help someone, an offer of resistance, etc.) ; it may be a piece of deliberate self-revelation (compare exaggerating a *natural* facial expression) or an explanation of one's behaviour; it may be simply an embarrassed (amazed, etc.) *response;* it may be a conclusion about oneself, based on introspection (and only in this case does the question how one knows, arise) ; or it may be some, though not *any,* combination of these. I am not suggesting that Wittgenstein would dispute this diversity of function. On the contrary, much that he says (*cf.* especially II. ix on 'I am afraid') tends to emphasize it. It is rather that in his anxiety to stress the difference between most uses of these sentences on the one hand, and descriptions based on observation on the other, he tends perhaps to minimise their aspect as *deliberate exhibitions* of states of mind.

Immediately after the discussion of 'I am afraid', Wittgenstein reverts briefly to 'I am in pain' (p. 198). These words "may be a cry of complaint and may be something else". It looks as if he were almost prepared to acknowledge here that they may be just a report of my sensations. Pain is not, like grief, a pattern of life. And a report can *also* be a complaint; or a request.

Voluntary Action and Intention

(611–660, II. viii, I. xi, pp. 223–224.) What Wittgenstein says on these difficult topics is immensely suggestive and interesting —but elusive and incomplete. He begins with a brilliant short account (611–620) of our temptation, under the pressure of such a question as 'How do you raise your arm?' and of obvious analogies, to think of willing as a special act of which the phenomenal features of ordinary actions are consequences; a very special act, for the obvious difficulties of this model then force us to think of it not as an act which we perform, but as one which just occurs, of the will as "only a mover, not a moved". Then, abruptly, the problem is stated: "what is left over if I subtract the fact that my arm goes up from the fact that I raise

my arm?" This is sunk in the other question: "How do you know
(when your eyes are shut) that you have raised your arm?" The
answer is "I feel it", and this answer is correct, but misleading.
For it suggests that you recognise the special feelings (the kinaesthetic sensations) *and can tell from recognising them* that
their constant accompaniment, the raising of the arm, has occurred. And this is wrong. In fact, the certainty that you have
raised your arm is itself a criterion of recognising the feeling
here (625). It is important to note two things that Wittgenstein
is *not* saying. He is not saying that one would have this certainty
in the absence of any feeling, or in the presence of an unaccus-
tomed feeling. It is no doubt *because* of the kinaesthetic sensations that I know; but it is not *from* them that I tell (II. viii).
Nor is he saying that I could never (say, if suitably stimulated)
be mistaken about this (624). Here is a case where I know, but
don't have a *way* of knowing, of telling. Now he reverts to the
former question, and suggests: "voluntary movement is marked
by absence of surprise" (628). As a *sufficient* condition (he
neither says nor denies that he means it as one), this will not
do. Experience of involuntary movements in certain circumstances might lead me to be quite unsurprised by their occurrence. The answer suggested by his own remarks about knowing
may be more useful. Voluntary movements are characterised by
a certainty of their having been made, which neither has *nor*
needs a ground; though it may both have and, in another sense,
need a cause. It is still far from clear that we have a sufficient
condition; for this seems true of many compelled or involuntary
movements of parts of the body. But for the purposes of Wittgenstein's enquiry, I do not think a sufficient condition is required. For his purpose, I think, is to throw light from 'knowing
what one has done' on 'knowing what one is going to do (intends)' and on 'knowing what one *was* going to do (intended)'.
For there is no more reason to suppose that we need a *way* of
knowing, of telling, in these cases than in that one. Of course, an
announcement of a present intention, or a recalling of a past un-
executed intention is helped by, arises naturally from, the situation "in which it is (or was) embedded". But we do not read off

or infer our intentions from these situations, any more than we tell what limb-movements we have just made from recognition of the accompanying sensations. (Nor in announcing or recalling our intentions do we report a current or remembered special experience. Look for this and it vanishes (645–6).) The point is that knowing what we intend to do is no more mysterious than knowing what we are going to do. (We as often make announcements of intention in the form 'I shall . . .' as in the form 'I intend to . . .'.) And a man may very well know what he is going to do (*be able to say*, if he is asked or if it should otherwise become desirable), and do it, without having raised the question to himself at all, without indeed having thought about it. The purpose—or one purpose—of announcing intentions is obvious: others have an interest in knowing what we will do. Remembering and telling a past unfulfilled intention is a less obvious case. An intention might be unfulfilled because I abandoned it or was interrupted or forestalled, etc.; or because my action failed of its effect. In no such case am I reporting something else that happened at the time. (This is particularly clear where my telling could be described as 'telling what I nearly did'.) It is rather that I exhibit *now* a response to the past situation; and my purpose in doing this may be to reveal to my auditor "something of *myself*, which goes beyond what happened at the time" (659).

Evidently this topic—of doing and intending—could be pursued into refinements and elaborations which Wittgenstein, with his fixed polemical purpose, neglects. But rarely has a subject been treated so powerfully and suggestively in so few pages.

Seeing and Seeing as

(II. xi, pp. 193–214.) By means of a series of examples and comments, Wittgenstein seeks to bring out some of the complexities of the concept of seeing. The cases he mostly considers are very special ones; and it is consequently difficult to see just how far his conclusions reach. One thing at least which gives under the strain of his examples is the doctrine of the purely sensory given on the one hand, and our interpretation of it on the other, as two ever-present but distinguishable elements in visual perception.

The examples of which Wittgenstein writes are examples of "the 'dawning of' (noticing of) an aspect". Sometimes when we look at a thing, we suddenly *see* it *as* something different from what we saw it as before, while also seeing that it has not in any way changed. Easily the best cases of this are provided by certain schematic pictures or diagrams; but we may also, *e.g.* suddenly recognize a face, or suddenly see its likeness to another. In none of these cases is it to be supposed that we 'get a better (or different) view'. These cases, then, are to be sharply distinguished from those in which we suddenly see something because, say, a light has been switched on, or a screen removed. They are also to be distinguished from cases in which a man is able in certain ways to *treat*, say, a figure as a such-and-such or as a picture of a so-and-so, but does not have the experience of its suddenly assuming for him the aspect of a such-and-such or of a picture of a so-and-so. The difference from the first of these contrasted cases is that when a man *sees* something *as* x and then *as* y, there is a perfectly good sense in which it looks the same to him as it did before: *viz.* that drawings showing it as it looked to him before and after the change of aspect would be indistinguishable. The difference from the second contrasted case is that a man on whom an aspect dawns is not merely prepared to make different applications of what he sees, but also sees it differently, has the 'visual experience' of a change of aspect.

Wittgenstein notes an ambiguity in 'seeing as', which it is important to mention since it emphasises the special character of the experience he is concerned with. Suppose we have a visually ambiguous object such as Wittgenstein's duck-rabbit—a picture which can be seen as a picture of a duck or again as a picture of a rabbit. Then a man who never has the experience of the change of aspects, the dawning of an aspect, may nevertheless be said by those who know of its visual ambiguity to see it as, say, (a picture of) a rabbit. So a person may in an unimportant sense see something as something without having the experience in which Wittgenstein is interested. In neither sense is something which is not visually ambiguous—say, a conventional picture of a lion—normally said to be 'seen as' anything.

Why is the experience of the dawning of an aspect of such particular interest to Wittgenstein? He suggests that its importance resides in an analogy with 'experiencing the meaning of a word' (p. 214). Perhaps we might say that when an aspect of a figure dawns on us, we are 'experiencing an interpretation of the figure'. What we have here is something instantaneous, a visual experience; but it is also true that a *logical* condition of our having the experience is our being capable of making such-and-such applications of the figure, of reacting to it in certain ways, of *treating* it as what we *see* it as (p. 208). If we are to describe the experience correctly, we cannot isolate a 'pure visual element' in it and say that that and that alone is the momentary experience (*cf.* p. 193); we can describe the experience correctly only by referring to what does not relate to the moment. (Wittgenstein is helped in making this point by the fact that the figure in one sense presents exactly the same visual appearance—does not look different—before and after the dawning of the aspect.) We have here, Wittgenstein says, a modified concept of experience, of seeing.

What Wittgenstein is essentially opposed to is the conjunction of the three propositions: (1) that we have here (*a*) a pure sensory element, and (*b*) an interpretation (a tendency to treat what we see in certain ways); (2) that (*a*) and (*b*) are simply associated or conjoined; and (3) that (*a*) alone is the visual experience proper. What may at first seem odd is not this opposition, nor the remark that we have here a modified concept of experience (contrast for example with pains), but the remark that we have here a modified concept of seeing (209). For surely ordinary instantaneous visual experiences, such as we have when the light is switched on and we suddenly see the room and its contents, can also be correctly described only by a description which entails our possession of concepts of certain kinds, and which thus refers beyond the moment. So in what way is the concept of seeing *modified* in the special case of seeing as? I think the *difference* between the cases, which leads Wittgenstein to speak of a modification of the concept, is the presence in the case where the light is switched on of just such an instantaneous change in the way things look, in the visual appearance of things, as is absent from the case where the aspect changes. But if this is right, it is not very happy to speak of a modification of the concept of seeing in a way which suggests that a certain feature which is common to both seeing and 'seeing as' is peculiar to the latter.

Conclusion

Wittgenstein has penetrating and illuminating things to say on other subjects: for example, identity and difference of meaning, meaninglessness, negation, induction, dreams and memory. But the topics which I have selected are those which receive most extensive treatment. On these I have tried to summarise and criticise his main arguments and conclusions, aware that much of the power, vividness and subtlety with which, by means of example, comment and epigram, these conclusions are presented, must in this way be lost. For this there is no remedy but study of the book itself.

Three cardinal elements in his thought, as presented in this book, may perhaps be epitomised in these quotations:

(1) "To imagine a language is to imagine a form of life" (19) and "What has to be accepted, the given, is—so one could say—forms of life" (p. 226).
(2) "What is happening now has significance—in these surroundings. The surroundings give it its importance" (583).
(3) "An 'inner process' stands in need of outward criteria" (580).

The first may serve to remind us of a general prescription for doing philosophy: to understand a concept, a word, put the word in its linguistic context and the whole utterance in its social context and then describe, without preconceptions, what you find; remembering that each word, each utterance, may figure in *many* contexts.

The second epitomises what I earlier called the hostility to the doctrine of immediacy. It has analogies with the first. Just as a word gets its significance from the context of its use, so those elements of our experience which we are tempted to isolate (or, failing this, to fabricate) and make the self-sufficient bearers of certain names get their significance too from their setting, from the form of life to which their titles allude.

The third, though it contains much that is true, contains also the germ of mistakes. It epitomises the hostility to the doctrine of privacy. For the worn and dangerous 'outward' and 'inner' we may substitute 'shared' and 'unshared'. Then what is right and wrong in Wittgenstein here begins from the insight that a common language for describing and reporting requires general agreement in judgments. So for a (descriptive) word or phrase to belong to a common language, it is essential that *the occasions on which it is right to apply it should provide shared experiences of a certain kind,* the existence of which is connected with the rightness of applying the word. The experiences need not be connected with the rightness of applying the word or phrase as *criteria* for its application. No one has *criteria* for something's looking red, though this is something on which we commonly agree. (Wittgenstein is perhaps misled here by temporarily confusing criteria which justify one in applying a word or phrase with criteria which justify one in saying that it is correctly applied. That there is a distinction is clear from much else that Wittgenstein says. For *every* expression of a common language (I speak here of non-analogical uses) there must exist, in the common practice of the use of the expression, criteria for determining whether a given use of it is correct or not. This will be so even where the expression in question has no descriptive use at all. So the existence of criteria for the correctness of the use of an expression does not entail that using it correctly is applying it on the strength of certain criteria. Wittgenstein would agree that the entailment does not *generally* hold; and there is no reason for thinking that it holds in the *special* case of descriptive or reporting uses of expressions. Moreover it could be independently argued that it *could* not hold here.) Now, when a word is not applied on the strength of shareable experiences, Wittgenstein is inclined to say that it is not applied in the way of report or description at all, but is used in some other way, is something else: *e.g.* a response, the habit of which is acquired by training, an action, a signal and so on. Sometimes, often, this is right: it is right in just those cases where the relevant shareable experiences count as criteria in the full, *logical* sense of that word. But there are other cases for which, taken as a general rule, it is wrong. For sometimes a person applies a word or phrase not on the strength of shareable experiences but on the strength of non-shareable experiences, and *is* publicly reporting or describing those experiences; and this he is enabled to do either by the existence of shared experiences which count as signs (criteria in the weaker sense) of the occurrence of the unshared experiences (the case of 'I am in pain'), or by the adoption or invention of analogical modes of description, where the analogy is with shareable experiences (*e.g.* reporting the words that pass through my mind).[6] What misleads Wittgenstein here is, I think, partly the belief that criteria are always essential to a report or description, a belief in its turn based, perhaps, on the confusion, mentioned above, between criteria for application and criteria for correctness; and partly the fear of legitimising certain metaphysical doubtings and wonderings. As for these, they are, if you like, senseless: but in their own way, and not in any other. They are pointless and unreal and you can do nothing with them (unless you strip them of their form and use them to point a contrast); and that is condemnation enough.

Right or wrong, Wittgenstein's particular doctrines are of the greatest interest and importance. But the value of the book as a model of philosophical method is greater still. (Here I do *not* refer to idiosyncracies of style and form.) It will consolidate the philosophical revolution for which, more than anyone else, its author was responsible.

---

[6] Of course (*a*) the antithesis 'shared' and 'unshared' which I have used here, is a shorthand no more immune from misunderstanding than any other; and (*b*) I do not suggest that it represents a sharp division: tastes, for example, might count as an intermediate case, since one has to do something rather special to get them shared on a given occasion.

THE ATTACK
ON THE SKEPTICAL VIEW
OF OTHER MINDS

II

Wittgenstein's *Philosophical Investigations*
Norman Malcolm

*Ein Buch ist ein Spiegel; wenn ein Affe hineinguckt, so kann freilich
kein Apostel heraussehen.*

Lichtenberg

AN ATTEMPT TO SUMMARIZE the *Investigations* would be
neither successful nor useful. Wittgenstein compressed his
thoughts to the point where further compression is impossible.
What is needed is that they be unfolded and the connections
between them traced out. A likely first reaction to the book will
be to regard it as a puzzling collection of reflections that are
sometimes individually brilliant, but possess no unity, present no
system of ideas. In truth the unity is there, but it cannot be perceived without strenuous exertion. Within the scope of a review
the connectedness can best be brought out, I think, by concentrating on some single topic—in spite of the fact that there are
no separate topics, for each of the investigations in the book

Ludwig Wittgenstein, *Philosophical Investigations*, German and English on facing pages. Tr. by
G. E. M. Anscombe (New York: The Macmillan Company, 1953).

criss-crosses again and again with every other one. In the following I center my attention on Wittgenstein's treatment of the problem of how language is related to inner experiences—to sensations, feelings, and moods. This is one of the main inquiries of the book and perhaps the most difficult to understand. I am sufficiently aware of the fact that my presentation of this subject will certainly fail to portray the subtlety, elegance, and force of Wittgenstein's thinking and will probably, in addition, contain positive mistakes.

References to Part I will be by paragraph numbers, e.g. (207), and to Part II by page numbers, e.g. (p. 207). Quotations will be placed within double quotation marks.

Private Language

Let us see something of how Wittgenstein attacks what he calls "the idea of a private language." By a "private" language is meant one that not merely is not but *cannot* be understood by anyone other than the speaker. The reason for this is that the words of this language are supposed to "refer to what can only be known to the person speaking; to his immediate private sensations" (243). What is supposed is that I "*associate* words with sensations and use these names in description" (256). I fix my attention on a sensation and establish a connection between a word and the sensation (258).

It is worth mentioning that the conception that it is possible and even necessary for one to have a private language is not eccentric. Rather it is the view that comes most naturally to anyone who philosophizes on the subject of the relation of words to experiences. The idea of a private language is presupposed by every program of inferring or constructing the 'external world' and 'other minds.' It is contained in the philosophy of Descartes and in the theory of ideas of classical British empiricism, as well as in recent and contemporary phenomenalism and sense-datum theory. At bottom it is the idea that there is only a contingent and not an *essential* connection between a sensation and its outward expression—an idea that appeals to us all. Such thoughts as these are typical expressions of the idea of a private language:

that I know only from my *own* case what the word 'pain' means (293, 295); that I can only *believe* that someone else is in pain, but I *know* it if I am (303); that another person cannot have *my* pains (253); that I can undertake to call *this* (pointing inward) 'pain' in the future (263); that when I say 'I am in pain' I am at any rate justified *before myself* (289).

In order to appreciate the depth and power of Wittgenstein's assault upon this idea you must partly be its captive. You must feel the strong grip of it. The passionate intensity of Wittgenstein's treatment of it is due to the fact that he lets this idea take possession of him, drawing out of himself the thoughts and imagery by which it is expressed and defended—and then subjecting those thoughts and pictures to fiercest scrutiny. What is written down represents both a logical investigation and a great philosopher's struggle with his own thoughts. The logical investigation will be understood only by those who duplicate the struggle in themselves.

One consequence to be drawn from the view that I know only from my *own* case what, say, 'tickling' means is that "I know only what *I* call that, not what anyone else does" (347). I have not *learned* what 'tickling' means, I have only called something by that name. Perhaps others use the name differently. This is a regrettable difficulty; but, one may think, the word will still work for me as a name, provided that I apply it consistently to a certain sensation. But how about 'sensation'? Don't I know only from my *own* case what *that* word means? Perhaps what I call a "sensation" others call by another name? It will not help, says Wittgenstein, to say that although it may be that what I have is not what others call a "sensation," at least I have *something*. For don't I know only from my own case what "having something" is? Perhaps my use of *those* words is contrary to common use. In trying to explain how I gave 'tickling' its meaning, I discover that I do not have the right to use any of the relevant words of our common language. "So in the end when one is doing philosophy one gets to the point where one would like just to emit an inarticulate sound" (261).

Let us suppose that I did fix my attention on a pain as I pro-

nounced the word 'pain' to myself. I think that thereby I established a connection between the word and the sensation. But I
did not establish a connection if subsequently I applied that
word to sensations other than pain or to things other than
sensations, e.g., emotions. My private definition was a success
only if it led me to use the word correctly in the future. In the
present case, 'correctly' would mean '*consistently* with my own
definition'; for the question of whether my use agrees with that
of others has been given up as a bad job. Now how is it to be
decided whether I have used the word consistently? What will
be the difference between my having used it consistently and its
seeming to me that I have? Or has this distinction vanished?
"Whatever is going to seem right to me is right. And that only
means that here we can't talk about 'right' " (258). If the distinction between 'correct' and 'seems correct' has disappeared,
then so has the concept *correct*. It follows that the 'rules' of my
private language are only *impressions* of rules (259). My impression that I follow a rule does not confirm that I follow the
rule, unless there can be something that will prove my impression correct. And the something cannot be another impression—
for this would be "as if someone were to buy several copies of
the morning paper to assure himself that what it said was true"
(265). The proof that I am following a rule must appeal to
something *independent* of my impression that I am. If in the
nature of the case there cannot be such an appeal, then my
private language does not have *rules*, for the concept of a rule
requires that there be a difference between 'He is following
a rule' and 'He is under the impression that he is following a
rule'—just as the concept of understanding a word requires that
there be a difference between 'He understands this word' and 'He
thinks that he understands this word' (cf. 269).

  'Even if I cannot prove and cannot know that I am correctly
following the rules of my private language,' it might be said,
'still it *may* be that I am. It has *meaning* to say that I am. The
supposition makes sense: you and I *understand* it.' Wittgenstein
has a reply to this (348–353). We are inclined to think that we
know what it means to say 'It is five o'clock on the sun' or 'This
congenital deaf-mute talks to himself inwardly in a vocal lan-

guage' or 'The stove is in pain.' These sentences produce pictures in our minds, and it *seems* to us that the pictures tell us how to *apply* them—that is, tell us what we have to look for, what we have to do, in order to determine whether what is pictured is the case. But we make a mistake in thinking that the picture contains in itself the instructions as to how we are to apply it. Think of the picture of blindness as a darkness in the soul or in the head of the blind man (424). There is nothing wrong with it *as a picture.* "But *what* is its application?" What shall count for or against its being said that this or that man is blind, that the picture applies to him? The *picture* doesn't say. If you think that you understand the sentence 'I follow the rule that *this* is to be called "pain" ' (a rule of your private language), what you have perhaps is a picture of yourself checking off various feelings of yours as either being *this* or not. The picture appears to solve the problem of how you determine whether you have done the 'checking' right. Actually it doesn't give you even a hint in that direction; no more than the picture of blindness provides so much as a hint of *how* it is to be determined that this or that man is blind (348–353, 422–426, p. 184).

One will be inclined to say here that one can simply *remember* this sensation and by remembering it will know that one is making a consistent application of its name. But will it also be possible to have a *false* memory impression? On the private-language hypothesis, what would *show* that your memory impression is false—or true? Another memory impression? Would this imply that memory is a court from which there is no appeal? But, as a matter of fact, that is *not* our concept of memory.

Imagine that you were supposed to paint a particular colour "C," which was the colour that appeared when the chemical substances X and Y combined.—Suppose that the colour struck you as brighter on one day than on another; would you not sometimes say: "I must be wrong, the colour is certainly the same as yesterday"? This shews that we do not always resort to what memory tells us as the verdict of the highest court of appeal [56].

There is, indeed, such a thing as checking one memory against another, e.g., I check my recollection of the time of departure of a train by calling up a memory image of how a page of the time-table looked—but "this process has got to produce a memory which is actually *correct*. If the mental image of the time-table could not itself be *tested* for correctness, how could it confirm the correctness of the first memory?" (265).

If I have a language that is really private (i.e., it is a logical impossibility that anyone else should understand it or should have any basis for knowing whether I am using a particular name consistently), my assertion that my memory tells me so and so will be utterly empty. 'My memory' will not even mean —my memory *impression*. For by a memory impression we understand something that is either accurate or inaccurate; whereas there would not be, in the private language, any *conception* of what would establish a memory impression as correct, any conception of what 'correct' would mean here.

The Same

One wants to say, 'Surely there can't be a difficulty in knowing whether a feeling of mine is or isn't the *same* as the feeling I now have. I will call this feeling "pain" and will thereafter call the *same* thing "pain" whenever it occurs. What could be easier than to follow that rule?' To understand Wittgenstein's reply to this attractive proposal we must come closer to his treatment of rules and of what it is to follow a rule. (Here he forges a remarkably illuminating connection between the philosophy of psychology and the philosophy of mathematics.) Consider his example of the pupil who has been taught to write down a cardinal number series of the form 'o, n, 2n, 3n . . .' at an order of the form '+n,' so that at the order '+1' he writes down the series of natural numbers (185). He has successfully done exercises and tests up to the number 1,000. We then ask him to continue the series '+2' beyond 1,000; and he writes 1,000, 1,004, 1,008, 1,012. We tell him that this is wrong. His instructive reply is, "But I went on the same way" (185). There was nothing in the previous explanations, examples and exer-

cises that made it *impossible* for him to regard that as the continuation of the series. Repeating *those* examples and explanations won't help him. One must say to him, in effect, 'That isn't
what we *call* going on in the *same* way.' It is a fact, and a fact
of the kind whose importance Wittgenstein constantly stresses,
that it is *natural* for human beings to continue the series in the
manner 1,002, 1,004, 1,006, given the previous training. But that
is merely what it is—a fact of human nature.

One is inclined to retort, 'Of course he can misunderstand the
instruction and misunderstand the order '+2'; but if he *understands* it he must go on in the right way.' And here one has the
idea that "The understanding itself is a state which is the *source*
of the correct use" (146)—that the correct continuation of the
series, the right application of the rule or formula, springs from
one's understanding of the rule. But the question of whether one
understands the rule cannot be divorced from the question of
whether one will go on in that one particular way that we call
'right.' The correct use is a criterion of understanding. If you say
that knowing the formula is a state of the mind and that making
this and that application of the formula is merely a *manifestation* of the knowledge, then you are in a difficulty: for you are
postulating a mental apparatus that explains the manifestations,
and so you ought to have (but do not have) a knowledge of the
construction of the apparatus, quite apart from what it does
(149). You would like to think that your understanding of the
formula determines in advance the steps to be taken, that when
you understood or meant the formula in a certain way "your
mind as it were flew ahead and took all the steps before you
physically arrived at this or that one" (188). But how you
meant it is not independent of how in fact you use it. "We say,
for instance, to someone who uses a sign unknown to us: 'If by
'*x*!2' you mean x^2, then you get *this* value for y, if you mean $2x$,
that one!—Now ask yourself: how does one *mean* the one thing
or the other by '*x*!2'?" (190). The answer is that his putting
down *this* value for y shows whether he meant the one thing and
not the other: "*That* will be how meaning it can determine the
steps in advance" (190). How he meant the formula determines

his subsequent use of it, only in the sense that the latter is a criterion of how he meant it.

It is easy to suppose that when you have given a person the order 'Now do the *same* thing,' you have pointed out to him the way to go on. But consider the example of the man who obtains the series 1, 3, 5, 7 . . . by working out the formula $2x + 1$ and then asks himself, "Am I always doing the same thing, or something different everytime?" (226). One answer is as good as the other; it doesn't matter which he says, so long as he continues in the right way. If we could not observe his work, his mere remark 'I am going on in the same way' would not tell us what he was doing. If a child writing down a row of 2's obtained '2, 2, 2' from the segment '2, 2' by adding '2' once, he might deny that he had gone on in the *same* way. He might declare that it would be doing the same thing only if he went from '2, 2' to '2, 2, 2, 2' in *one* jump, i.e., only if he *doubled* the original segment (just as it doubled the original single '2'). That could strike one as a *reasonable* use of 'same.' This connects up with Wittgenstein's remark: "If you have to have an intuition in order to develop the series 1 2 3 4 . . . you must also have one in order to develop the series 2 2 2 2 . . ." (214). One is inclined to say of the latter series, 'Why, all that is necessary is that you keep on doing the *same* thing.' But isn't that just as true of the other series? In both cases one has already *decided* what the correct continuation is, and one calls that continuation, and no other, 'doing the same thing.' As Wittgenstein says: "One might say to the person one was training: 'Look, I always do the same thing: I . . .'" (223). And then one proceeds to show him what 'the same' *is*. If the pupil does not acknowledge that what you have shown him is the *same*, and if he is not persuaded by your examples and explanations to carry on as you wish him to— then you have reached bedrock and will be inclined to say "This is simply what I do" (217). You cannot give him more reasons than you yourself have for proceeding in that way. Your reasons will soon give out. And then you will proceed, without reasons (211).

Private Rules

All of this argument strikes at the idea that there can be such a thing as my following a rule in my private language—such a thing as naming something of which only I can be aware, 'pain,' and then going on to call the same thing, 'pain,' whenever it occurs. There is a charm about the expression 'same' which makes one think that there cannot be any difficulty or any chance of going wrong in deciding whether *A* is the *same* as *B*—as if one did not have to be *shown* what the 'same' is. This may be, as Wittgenstein suggests, because we are inclined to suppose that we can take the identity of a thing *with itself* as "an infallible paradigm" of the *same* (215). But he destroys this notion with one blow: "Then are two things the same when they are what *one* thing is? And how am I to apply what the *one* thing shows me to the case of two things?" (215).

The point to be made here is that when one has given oneself the private rule 'I will call this same thing "pain" whenever it occurs,' one is then free to do anything or nothing. That 'rule' does not point in any direction. On the private-language hypothesis, no one can teach me what the correct use of 'same' is. I shall be the sole arbiter of whether this is the *same* as that. What I choose to call the 'same' will *be* the same. No restriction whatever will be imposed upon my application of the word. But a sound that I can use *as I please* is not a *word*.

How would you teach someone the meaning of 'same'? By example and practice: you might show him, for instance, collections of the same colors and same shapes and make him find and produce them and perhaps get him to carry on a certain ornamental pattern uniformly (208). Training him to form collections and produce patterns is teaching him what Wittgenstein calls "techniques." Whether he has mastered various techniques determines whether he understands 'same.' The exercise of a technique is what Wittgenstein calls a "practice." Whether your pupil has understood any of the rules that you taught him (e.g., the rule; this is the 'same' color as that) will be shown in his practice. But now there cannot be a 'private' practice, i.e., a

practice that cannot be exhibited. For there would then be no
distinction between believing that you have that practice and
having it. 'Obeying a rule' is itself a practice. "And to *think* one
is obeying a rule is not to obey a rule. Hence it is not possible
to obey a rule 'privately'; otherwise thinking one was obeying
a rule would be the same thing as obeying it" (202. cf. 380).

If I recognize that my mental image is the 'same' as one that I
had previously, how am I to know that this public word 'same'
describes what I recognize? "Only if I can express my recognition in some other way, and if it is possible for someone else to
teach me that 'same' is the correct word here" (378). The notion
of the private language doesn't admit of there being 'some other
way.' It doesn't allow that my behavior and circumstances can
be so related to my utterance of the word that another person,
by noting my behavior and circumstances, can discover that my
use of the word is correct or incorrect. Can I discover this for
myself, and how do I do it? That discovery would presuppose
that I have a conception of correct use which comes from outside
my private language and against which I measure the latter. If
this were admitted, the private language would lose its privacy
and its point. So it isn't admitted. But now the notion of 'correct' use that will exist within the private language will be such
that if I *believe* that my use is correct then it is correct; the
rules will be only impressions of rules; my 'language' will not
be a language, but merely the impression of a language. The
most that can be said for it is that I *think* I understand it
(cf. 269).

Sensations of Others

The argument that I have been outlining has the form of
reductio ad absurdum: postulate a 'private' language; then
deduce that it is not *language.* Wittgenstein employs another
argument that is an external, not an internal, attack upon
private language. What is attacked is the assumption that once I
know from my *own* case what pain, tickling, or consciousness is,
then I can transfer the ideas of these things to objects outside
myself (283). Wittgenstein says:

If one has to imagine someone else's pain on the model of one's own, this is none too easy a thing to do: for I have to imagine pain which I *do not feel* on the model of the pain which I *do feel*. That is, what I have to do is not simply to make a transition in imagination from one place of pain to another. As, from pain in the hand to pain in the arm. For I am not to imagine that I feel pain in some region of his body. (Which would also be possible.) [302]

The argument that is here adumbrated is, I think, the following: If I were to learn what pain is from perceiving my own pain then I should, necessarily, have learned that pain is something that exists only when *I* feel pain. For the pain that serves as my paradigm of pain (i.e., my own) has the property of existing only when *I* feel it.[1] That property is essential, not accidental; it is nonsense to suppose that the pain I feel could exist when I did not feel it. So if I obtain my *conception* of pain from pain that I experience, then it will be part of my conception of pain that *I* am the only being that can experience it. For me it will be a *contradiction* to speak of *another's* pain. This strict solipsism is the necessary outcome of the notion of private language. I take the phrase "this is none too easy" to be a sarcasm.

One is tempted at this point to appeal to the 'same' again: "But if I suppose that someone has a pain, then I am simply

[1] [This is an error. Apparently I fell into the trap of assuming that if two people, A and B, are in pain, the pain that A feels must be *numerically* different from the pain that B feels. Far from making this assumption, Wittgenstein attacks it when he says: "In so far as it makes *sense* to say that my pain is the same as his, it is also possible for us both to have the same pain" (*op. cit.*, 253). There is not some sense of "same pain" (*numerically* the same) in which A and B *cannot* have the same pain. "Today I have that same backache that you had last week" is something we say. "Same" means here, answering to the same description. We attach no meaning to the "question" of whether the backache you had and the one I have are or are not "numerically" the same.

A more correct account of Wittgenstein's point in sec. 302 is the following: A proponent of the privacy of sensations rejects circumstances and behavior as a criterion of the sensations of others, this being essential to his viewpoint. He does not need (and could not have) a criterion for the existence of pain that he feels. But surely he will need a criterion for the existence of pain that *he does not feel.* Yet he cannot have one and still hold to the privacy of sensation. If he sticks to the latter, he ought to admit that he has not the faintest idea of what would count for or against the occurrence of sensations that he does not feel. His conclusion should be, not that it is a contradiction, but that it is unintelligible to speak of the sensations of others. (There is a short exposition of Wittgenstein's attack on the idea that we learn what sensation is *from our own case,* in "Knowledge of Other Minds," see pp. 136–138 [in Malcolm's *Knowledge and Certainty—Ed.*].)]

supposing that he has just the same as I have so often had"
(350). I will quote Wittgenstein's brilliant counterstroke in full:

> That gets us no further. It is as if I were to say: "You surely know
> what 'It is 5 o'clock here' means; so you also know what 'It's 5
> o'clock on the sun' means. It means simply that it is just the same
> time there as it is here when it is 5 o'clock."—The explanation by
> means of *identity* does not work here. For I know well enough that
> one can call 5 o'clock here and 5 o'clock there "the same time,"
> but what I do not know is in what cases one is to speak of its
> being the same time here and there.
>
> In exactly the same way it is no explanation to say: the supposi-
> tion that he has a pain is simply the supposition that he has the
> same as I. For *that* part of the grammar is quite clear to me: that
> is, that one will say that the stove has the same experience as I,
> *if* one says: it is in pain and I am in pain [350].

Expressions of Sensation

Wittgenstein says that he destroys "houses of cards" ("Luft-
gebäude": 118) and that his aim is to show one how to pass
from disguised to obvious nonsense (464). But this is not all he
does or thinks he does. For he says that he changes one's *way
of looking at things* (144). What is it that he wishes to substitute
for that way of looking at things that is represented by the idea
of private language? One would *like* to find a continuous exposition of his own thesis, instead of mere hints here and there.
But this desire reflects a misunderstanding of Wittgenstein's
philosophy. He rejects the assumption that he should put for-
ward a *thesis* (128). "We may not advance any kind of theory"
(109). A philosophical problem is a certain sort of confusion. It
is like being lost; one can't see one's way (123). Familiar surroundings suddenly seem strange. We need to command a view
of the country, to get our bearings. The country is well known
to us, so we need only to be *reminded* of our whereabouts.
"The work of the philosopher consists in assembling reminders
for a particular purpose" (127). "The problems are solved,
not by giving new information, but by arranging what we have
always known" (109). When we describe (remind ourselves

of) certain functions of our language, what we do must have a definite bearing on some particular confusion, some "deep disquietude" (111), that ensnares us. Otherwise our work is irrelevant—to *philosophy*. It is philosophically pointless to formulate a general theory of language or to pile up descriptions for their own sake. "This description gets its light, that is to say its purpose—from the philosophical problems" (109). Thus we may not complain at the absence from the *Investigations* of elaborate theories and classifications.

Wittgenstein asks the question "How do words *refer* to sensations?" transforms it into the question "How does a human being learn the meaning of the names of sensations?" and gives this answer: "Words are connected with the primitive, the natural expressions of the sensation and used in their place. A child has hurt himself and he cries; and then the adults talk to him and teach him exclamations and, later, sentences. They teach the child new pain-behaviour" (244). Wittgenstein must be talking about how it is that a human being learns to refer with words to his *own* sensations—about how he learns to use 'I am in pain'; not about how he learns to use 'He is in pain.' What Wittgenstein is saying is indeed radically different from the notion that I learn what 'I am in pain' means by fixing my attention on a 'certain' sensation and calling it 'pain.' But is he saying that what I do instead is to fix my attention on my *expressions* of pain and call them 'pain'? Is he saying that the word 'pain' means crying? "On the contrary: the verbal expression of pain replaces crying and does not describe it" (244). My words for sensations are used *in place of* the behavior that is the natural expression of the sensations; they do not *refer* to it.

Wittgenstein does not expand this terse reminder. He repeats at least once that my words for sensations are "tied up with my natural expressions of sensation" (256) and frequently alludes to the importance of the connection between the language for sensations and the behavior which is the expression of sensation (e.g., 288, 271). The following questions and objections will arise:

(1) What shows that a child has made this 'tie up'? I take Witt-

genstein to mean that the child's utterances of the word for a sensation must, in the beginning, be frequently concurrent with some nonverbal, natural expression of that sensation. This concomitance serves as the criterion of his understanding the word. Later on, the word can be uttered in the absence of primitive expressions. ('It hurts' can be said without cries or winces.)

(2) In what sense does the verbal expression 'replace' the non-verbal expression? In the sense, I think, that other persons will react to the child's mere words in the same way that they previously reacted to his nonverbal sensation-behavior; they will let the mere words serve as a *new* criterion of his feelings.

(3) I feel inclined to object: 'But has the child *learned* what the words *mean?* Hasn't he merely picked up the *use* of the word from his parents?' My objection probably arises from assimilating the learning of the meaning of words to the labeling of bottles—a tendency that is easily decried but not easily resisted. 'Learning *ought* to consist in attaching the right name to the right object,' I should like to say (cf. 26). The example of 'the beetle in the box' is pertinent here (see 293). The aim of this fantasy is to prove that attending to a private object can have nothing to do with learning words for sensations. Suppose you wanted to teach a child what a tickling feeling is. You tickle him in the ribs, and he laughs and jerks away. You say to him, 'That's what the feeling of tickling is.' Now imagine he felt something that you can't know anything about. Will this be of any interest to you when you decide from his subsequent use of the word 'tickling' whether he understands it? Others understand the word too. If each one has something that only he can know about, then all the somethings may be different. The something could even be nothing! Whatever it is, it can have no part in determining whether the person who has it understands the word. "If we construe the grammar of the expression of sensation on the model of 'object and name' the object drops out of consideration as irrelevant" (293, cf. 304).

My previous objection could be put like this: the teaching and learning of names of sensations cannot stop at the mere expressions of sensation; the names must be brought *right up* to the

sensations themselves, must be applied *directly* to the sensations!
Here we can imagine Wittgenstein replying, "Like *what*, e.g.?"
as he replies to an analogous objection in a different problem
(191). In *what* sense is Wittgenstein denying that names are applied directly to sensations? Do I have a model of what it would
be to apply the name 'directly'? No. I have this picture—that
learning the meaning of 'pain' is applying the sign 'pain' to pain
itself. I have that picture, to be sure, but what does it teach me,
what is its "application"? When shall I say that what it pictures
has taken place, i.e., that someone has learned the meaning of
'pain'? It doesn't tell me; it is *only* a picture. It cannot conflict
with, cannot refute, Wittgenstein's reminder of what it is that
determines whether a child has learned the word for a sensation.
(4) Wittgenstein says that the verbal expressions of sensation can
take the place of the nonverbal expressions and that in learning
the former one learns "new pain-behavior." This seems to mean
that the words (and sentences) for sensations are related to
sensations in the same way as are the primitive expressions of
sensations. I am inclined to object again. I want to say that the
words are used to *report* the occurrence of a sensation and to
inform others of it. The natural expressions, on the contrary, are
not used to inform others; they are not 'used' at all; they have
no purpose, no function; they *escape* from one. But I have over-
simplified the difference, because (a) a sentence can be forced
from one, can escape one's lips ('My God, it hurts!'), and (b) a
natural expression of sensation can be used to inform another,
e.g., you moan to let the nurse know that your pain is increasing
(you would have suppressed the moan if she hadn't entered the
room), yet the moan is genuine. Perhaps my objection comes to
this: I don't *learn* to moan; I do learn the words. But this is the
very distinction that is made by saying that moaning is a "natural," a "primitive," expression of sensation.

   It is a mistake to suppose that Wittgenstein is saying that the
utterance 'My leg hurts' is *normally called* an 'expression of sensation.' (Of course it isn't. For that matter, only a facial expression, not a groan, is called an *'expression* of pain.' But this is of
no importance.) He is not reporting ordinary usage, but drawing

our attention to an *analogy* between the groan of pain and the utterance of those words. The important similarity that he is trying to bring to light (here I may misinterpret him) is that the verbal utterance and the natural pain-behavior are each (as I shall express it) 'incorrigible.' [2] A man cannot be in *error* as to whether he is in pain; he cannot say 'My leg hurts' by mistake, any more than he can groan by mistake. It is senseless to suppose that he has wrongly identified a tickle as pain or that he falsely believes that it is in his leg when in fact it is in his shoulder. True, he may be undecided as to whether it is best described as an 'ache' or a 'pain' (one is often hard put to give satisfactory descriptions of one's feelings); but his very indecision *shows* us what his sensation is, i.e., something between an ache and a pain. His hesitant observation, 'I'm not sure whether it is a pain or an ache,' is itself an *expression* of sensation. What it expresses is an indefinite, an ambiguous sensation. The point about the incorrigibility of the utterance 'I'm in pain' lies behind Wittgenstein's reiterated remark that 'I *know* I'm in pain' and 'I don't know whether I'm in pain' are both senseless (e.g., 246, 408).[3] Wherever it is *meaningless* to speak of 'false belief,' it is also meaningless to speak of 'knowledge'; and wherever you cannot say 'I don't know . . .' you also cannot say 'I know . . . .' Of course, a philosopher can say of me that I *know* I am in pain. But "What is it supposed to mean—except perhaps that I *am* in pain?" (246).[4]

There are many 'psychological' sentences, other than sentences about sensations, that are incorrigible, e.g., the *truthful* report of a dream is a criterion for the occurrence of the dream and, unless some other criterion is introduced, "the question cannot arise" as to whether the dreamer's memory deceives him (pp. 222–223). If one who has a mental image were asked whom the

---

[2] [I try to explain the notion of "incorrigibility," as I understand it, in "Direct Perception" (see pp. 77–86 in *Knowledge and Certainty*). I concentrate there on the seeing of after-images, but with appropriate changes the notion carries over to bodily sensations.]

[3] It is interesting to note that as long ago as 1930 Wittgenstein had remarked that it has no sense to speak of *verifying* "I have a toothache." (See G. E. Moore, "Wittgenstein's Lectures in 1930–33," *Mind*, LXIII, January 1954, 14. [See Selection V in this anthology.—*Ed.*]

[4] [In "A Definition of Factual Memory," I mention a sense in which an adult person (but not an infant or a dog) can be said to know that he has a pain (see p. 239 in *Knowledge and Certainty*).]

image is of, "his answer would be decisive," just as it would be if he were asked whom the drawing represents that he has just made (p. 177). When you say 'It will stop soon' and are asked whether you *meant* your pain or the sound of the piano-tuning, your truthful answer *is* the answer (666–684).

When Wittgenstein says that learning the words for sensations is learning "new pain-behavior" and that the words "replace" the natural expressions, he is bringing to light the arresting fact that my sentences about my present sensations have the same logical status as my outcries and facial expressions. And thus we are helped to "make a radical break with the idea that language always functions in one way, always serves the same purpose: to convey thoughts—which may be about houses, pains, good and evil, or anything else you please" (304).

This is not to deny that first-person sentences about sensations may, in other respects, be more or less like natural expressions of sensation. Wittgenstein's examples of the use of 'I am afraid' (pp. 187–188) show how the utterance of that sentence can be a cry of fear, a comparison, an attempt to tell someone how I feel, a confession, a reflection on my state of mind, or something in between. "A cry is not a description. But there are transitions. And the words 'I am afraid' may approximate more, or less, to being a cry. They may come quite close to this and also be *far* removed from it" (p. 189). The words 'I am in pain' "may be a cry of complaint, and may be something else" (p. 189); and 'it makes me shiver' may be a "shuddering reaction" or may be said "as a piece of information" (p. 174). If we pursue these hints, it is not hard to construct a list of examples of the use of the words 'My head hurts,' in which the variety is as great as in Wittgenstein's list for 'I am afraid.' E.g., compare 'Oh hell, how my head hurts!' with 'If you want to know whether to accept the invitation for tonight then I must tell you that my head hurts again.' In one case the sentence 'My head hurts' belongs to an exclamation of pain, not in the other. In saying that in *both* cases it is an 'expression' of pain, Wittgenstein stretches ordinary language and in so doing illuminates the hidden continuity between the utterance of that sentence and—expressions of pain.

Criterion

That the natural pain-behavior and the utterance 'It hurts'
are each incorrigible is what makes it possible for each of them
to be a criterion of pain. With some reluctance I will undertake
to say a little bit about this notion of 'criterion,' a most difficult region in Wittgenstein's philosophy. Perhaps the best way to
elucidate it is to bring out its connection with *teaching* and
learning the use of words. "When I say the ABC to myself, what
is the criterion of my doing the same as someone else who
silently repeats it to himself? It might be found that the same
thing took place in my larynx and in his. (And similarly when
we both think of the same thing, wish the same, and so on.) But
then did we learn the use of the words, 'to say such-and-such to
oneself,' by someone's pointing to a process in the larynx or the
brain?" (376). Of course we did not, and this means that a
physiological process is not our 'criterion' that *A* said such-and-
such to himself. Try to imagine, realistically and in detail, how
you would teach someone the meaning of 'saying the ABC silently to oneself.' This, you may think, is merely psychology.
But if you have succeeded in bringing to mind what it is that
would show that he *grasped* your teaching, that he *understood*
the use of the words, then you have elicited the 'criterion' for
their use—and that is not psychology. Wittgenstein exhorts us,
over and over, to bethink ourselves of how we learned to use
this or that form of words or of how we should teach it to a
child. The purpose of this is not to bring philosophy down to
earth (which it does), but to bring into view those features of
someone's circumstances and behavior that *settle* the question
of whether the words (e.g., 'He is calculating in his head')
rightly apply to him. Those features constitute the 'criterion'
of calculating in one's head. It is logically possible that someone
should have been born with a knowledge of the use of an
expression or that it should have been produced in him by a
drug; that his knowledge came about by way of the normal
process of teaching is not necessary. What is necessary is that
there should be something on the basis of which we *judge*

whether he *has* that knowledge. To undertake to describe this may be called a 'logical' investigation, even though one should arrive at the description by reflecting on that logically inessential process of teaching and learning.

If someone says, e.g., 'I feel confident . . . ,' a question can arise as to whether he understands those words. Once you admit the untenability of 'private ostensive definition' you will see that there must be a *behavioral* manifestation of the feeling of confidence (579). There must be behavior against which his words 'I feel confident . . . ,' can be checked, if it is to be possible to judge that he does not understand them. Even if you picture a feeling of confidence as an "inner process," still it requires "outward criteria" (580).

Wittgenstein contrasts 'criterion' with 'symptom,' employing both words somewhat technically. The falling barometer is a 'symptom' that it is raining; its looking like *that* outdoors (think how you would teach the word 'rain' to a child) is the 'criterion' of rain (354). A process in a man's brain or larynx might be a symptom that he has an image of red; the criterion is "what he says and does" (377, 376). What makes something into a symptom of y is that experience teaches that it is always or usually associated with y; that so-and-so is the criterion of y is a matter, not of experience, but of "definition" (354). The satisfaction of the criterion of y establishes the existence of y beyond question. The occurrence of a symptom of y may also establish the existence of y 'beyond question'—but in a different sense. The observation of a brain process may make it certain that a man is in pain—but not in the same way that his pain-behavior makes it certain. Even if physiology has established that a specific event in the brain accompanies bodily pain, still it *could* happen (it makes sense to suppose) that a man was not in pain although that brain event was occurring. But it will not make sense for one to suppose that another person is not in pain if one's criterion of his being in pain is satisfied. (Sometimes, and especially in science, we *change* our criteria: "what to-day counts as an observed concomitant of a phenomenon will to-morrow be used to define it" [79].)

The preceding remarks point up the following question: Do the propositions that describe the criterion of his being in pain *logically imply* the proposition 'He is in pain'? Wittgenstein's answer is clearly in the negative. A criterion is satisfied *only in certain circumstances.* If we come upon a man exhibiting violent pain-behavior, couldn't something show that he is not in pain? Of course. For example, he is rehearsing for a play; or he has been hypnotized and told, 'You will act as if you are in pain, although you won't be in pain,' and when he is released from the hypnotic state he has no recollection of having been in pain; or his pain-behavior suddenly ceases and he reports in apparent bewilderment that it was as if his body had been possessed— for his movements had been entirely involuntary, and during the 'seizure' he had felt no pain; or he has been narrowly missed by a car and as soon as a sum for damages has been pressed into his hand, his pain-behavior ceases and he laughs at the hoax; or . . . , etc. The expressions of pain are a criterion of pain in *certain* "surroundings," not in others (cf. 584).

Now one would like to think that one can still formulate a logical implication by taking a description of his pain-behavior and conjoining it with the negation of every proposition describing one of those circumstances that would count against saying he is in pain. Surely, the conjunction will logically imply 'He is in pain'! But this assumes there is a *totality* of those circumstances such that if none of them were fulfilled, and he were also pain-behaving, then he *could not but* be in pain (cf. 183). There is no totality that can be exhaustively enumerated, as can the letters of the alphabet. It is quite impossible to list six or nine such circumstances and then to say 'That is all of them; no other circumstances can be imagined that would count against his being in pain.' The list of circumstances has no 'all,' in that sense; the list is not infinite, but *indefinite.* Therefore, entailment-conditions cannot be formulated; there are none.

The above thought is hard to accept. It is not in line with our *ideal* of what language should be. It makes the 'rules' for the use of 'He is in pain' too vague, too loose, not really *rules.* Wittgenstein has deep things to say about the nature of this 'ideal': "We want to say that there can't be any vagueness in logic. The idea now absorbs us, that the ideal '*must*' be found in reality. Meanwhile we do not as yet see *how* it occurs there, nor do we understand the nature of this 'must.' We think it must be in reality; for we think we already see it there" (101). "The strict and clear rules of the logical structure of propositions appear to us as something in the background—hidden in the medium of the understanding" (102). "The more narrowly we examine actual language, the sharper becomes the conflict between it and our requirement. (For the crystalline purity of logic was, of course, not a *result of investigation:* it was a requirement.)" (107). What we need to do is to remove from our noses the logical glasses through which we look at reality (103). We must study our language as it is, without preconceived ideas. One thing this study will teach us is that the criteria for the use of third-person psychological statements are not related to the latter by an entailment-relation.

Wittgenstein suggests that propositions describing the fulfillment of behavioral criteria are related to third-person psychological statements in the way that propositions describing sense-impressions are related to physical-object statements (compare 486 and p. 180). It does not *follow* from the propositions describing my sense-impressions that there is a chair over there (486). The relation cannot be reduced to a *simple* formula (p. 180). *Why* doesn't it follow? Wittgenstein does not say, but the reason would appear to be of the same sort as in the example of 'He is in pain.' The propositions describing my sense-impressions would have to be conjoined with the proposition that I am not looking in a mirror, or at a painted scenery, or at a movie film, or . . . , etc. Here too there cannot be an exhaustive enumeration of negative conditions that would have to be added to the description of sense-impressions *if* 'There's a chair over there' *were* to be logically implied.

The puzzling problem now presents itself: if it does not *follow* from his behavior and circumstances that he is in pain, then how can it ever be *certain* that he is in pain? "I can be as *certain* of someone else's sensations as of any fact," says Witt-

genstein (p. 224). How can this be so, since there is not a
definite set of six or eight conditions (each of which would
nullify his pain-behavior) to be checked off as not fulfilled? It
looks as if the conclusion ought to be that we cannot 'completely
verify' that he is in pain. This conclusion is wrong, but it is not
easy to see why. I comprehend Wittgenstein's thought here only
dimly. He says:

> A doctor asks: "How is he feeling?" The nurse says: "He is
> groaning." A report on his behaviour. But need there be any ques-
> tion for them whether the groaning is really genuine, is really the
> expression of anything? Might they not, for example, draw the
> conclusion "If he groans, we must give him more analgesic"—
> without suppressing a middle term? Isn't the point the service to
> which they put the description of behaviour [p. 179]?

One hint that I take from this is that there can be situations of
real life in which a question as to whether someone who groans
is pretending, or rehearsing, or hypnotized, or . . . , simply does
not exist. "Just try—in a real case—to doubt someone else's fear
or pain" (303). A doubt, a question, would be rejected as absurd
by anyone who knew the actual surroundings. 'But might there
not be still further surroundings, unknown to you, that would
change the whole aspect of the matter?' Well, we go only *so* far
—and then we are certain. "Doubting has an end" (p. 180).
Perhaps we can *imagine* a doubt; but we do not take it seriously
(cf. 84). Just as it becomes certain to us that there is a chair
over there, although we can imagine a *possible* ground of doubt.
There is a concept of certainty in these languages-games only
because we stop short of what is conceivable.

" 'But, if you are *certain,* isn't it that you are shutting your
eyes in face of doubt?'—They are shut" (p. 224). This striking
remark suggests that what we sometimes do is draw a boundary
around *this* behavior in *these* circumstances and say 'Any additional circumstances that might come to light will be irrelevant
to whether this man is in pain.' Just as we draw a line and say
'No further information will have any bearing on whether there

is a chair in the corner—that is settled.' If your friend is struck
down by a car and writhes with a broken leg, you do not think:
Perhaps it was prearranged in order to alarm me; possibly his
leg was anesthetized just before the 'accident' and he isn't
suffering at all. Someone *could* have such doubts whenever
another person was ostensibly in pain. Similarly: "I can easily
imagine someone always doubting before he opened his front
door whether an abyss did not yawn behind it; and making sure
about it before he went through the door (and he might on
some occasion prove to be right)—but that does not make me
doubt in the same case" (84).

The man who doubts the other's pain may be neurotic, may
'lack a sense of reality,' but his reasoning is perfectly sound. *If*
his doubts are true then the injured man is *not* in pain. His reaction is abnormal but not illogical. The certainty that the injured
man is in pain (the normal reaction) ignores the endless doubts
that *could* be proposed and investigated.

And it is important to see that the abnormal reaction *must* be
the exception and not the rule. For if someone *always* had
endless doubts about the genuineness of expressions of pain, it
would mean that he was not using *any criterion* of another's being in pain. It would mean that he did not accept anything as an
expression of pain. So what could it mean to say that he even
had the *concept* of another's being in pain? It is senseless to
suppose that he has this concept and yet always doubts.

Third-Person Sensation-Sentences

Wittgenstein assimilates first-person, not third-person, sensation-sentences to *expressions* of sensation. I will say one or two
things more about his conception of the use of third-person
sensation-sentences.

(1) "Only of a living human being and what resembles (behaves
like) a living human being can one say: it has sensations; it
sees; is blind; hears; is deaf; is conscious or unconscious" (281).
The *human* body and *human* behavior are the *paradigm* to
which third-person attributions of consciousness, sensations,
feelings are related. (The use of first-person sensation-sentences

is governed by *no* paradigm.) Thus there cannot occur in ordinary life a question as to whether other human beings ever possess consciousness, and I can have this question when I philosophize only if I forget that I use that paradigm in ordinary life. It is by analogy with the human form and behavior that I attribute consciousness (or unconsciousness) to animals and fish: the more remote the analogy the less sense in the attribution. (Just as it is by analogy with our ordinary language that anything is called 'language.') (494). In order to imagine that a pot or a chair has thoughts or sensations one must give it, in imagination, something like a human body, face, and speech (282, 361). A child says that its doll has stomach-ache, but this is a "secondary" use of the concept of pain. "Imagine a case in which people ascribed pain *only* to inanimate things; pitied *only* dolls!" (282; cf. 385, p. 216). Wittgenstein means, I think, that this is an impossible supposition because we should not want to say that those people *understood* ascriptions of pain. If they did not ever show pity for human beings or animals or expect it for themselves, then their treatment of dolls would not be *pity*.

(2) My criterion of another's being in pain is, first, his behavior and circumstances and, second, his words (after they have been found to be connected in the right way with his behavior and circumstances). Does it follow that my interest is in his behavior and words, not in his pain? Does 'He is in pain' *mean* behavior? In lectures Wittgenstein imagined a tribe of people who had the idea that their slaves had no feelings, no souls—that they were automatons—despite the fact that the slaves had human bodies, behaved like their masters, and even spoke the same language. Wittgenstein undertook to try to give sense to that idea. When a slave injured himself or fell ill or complained of pains, his master would try to heal him. The master would let him rest when he was fatigued, feed him when he was hungry and thirsty, and so on. Furthermore, the masters would apply to the slaves our usual distinctions between genuine complaints and malingering. So what could it mean to say that they had the idea that the slaves were automatons? Well, they would *look* at the slaves in a

peculiar way. They would observe and comment on their movements *as if* they were machines. ('Notice how smoothly his limbs move.') They would discard them when they were worn and useless, like machines. If a slave received a mortal injury and twisted and screamed in agony, no master would avert his gaze in horror or prevent his children from observing the scene, any more than he would if the ceiling fell on a printing press. Here is a difference in 'attitude' that is not a matter of believing or expecting different facts.

So in the *Investigations*, Wittgenstein says, "My attitude towards him is an attitude towards a soul. I am not of the *opinion* that he has a soul" (p. 178). I do not *believe* that the man is suffering who writhes before me—for to what facts would a 'belief' be related, such that a change in the facts would lead me to alter it? I *react* to his suffering. I look at him with compassion and try to comfort him. If I complain of headache to someone and he says 'It's not so bad,' does this prove that he believes in something *behind* my outward expression of pain? "His attitude is a proof of his attitude. Imagine not merely the words 'I am in pain' but also the answer 'It's not so bad' replaced by instinctive noises and gestures" (310). The thought that behind someone's pain-behavior is the pain itself does not enter into our use of 'He's in pain,' but what does enter into it is our sympathetic, or unsympathetic, reaction to him. The fact that the latter does enter into our use of that sentence (but might not have) gives sense to saying that the sentence 'He is in pain' does not just *mean* that his behavior, words, and circumstances are such and such—although these are the criteria for its use.

When he groans we do not *assume*, even tacitly, that the groaning expresses pain. We fetch a sedative and try to put him at ease. A totally different way of reacting to his groans would be to make exact records of their volume and frequency—and do nothing to relieve the sufferer! But our reaction of seeking to comfort him does not involve a presupposition, for, "Doesn't a presupposition imply a doubt? And doubt may be entirely lacking" (p. 180).

Form of Life

The gestures, facial expressions, words, and activities that constitute pitying and comforting a person or a dog are, I think, a good example of what Wittgenstein means by a "form of life." One could hardly place too much stress on the importance of this latter notion in Wittgenstein's thought. It is intimately related to the notion "language-game." His choice of the latter term is meant to "bring into prominence the fact that the *speaking* of language is part of an activity, or of a form of life" (23; cf. 19). If we want to understand any concept we must obtain a view of the human behavior, the activities, the natural expressions, that surround the words for that concept. What, for example, is the concept of *certainty* as applied to *predictions?* The nature of my certainty that fire will burn me comes out in the fact that "Nothing could induce me to put my hand into a flame" (472). That reaction of mine to fire shows the *meaning* of certainty in this language-game (474). (Of course, it is *different* from the concept of certainty in, e.g., mathematics. "The kind of certainty is the kind of language-game" [p. 124].) But is my certainty justified? Don't I need reasons? Well, I don't normally think of reasons, I can't produce much in the way of reasons, and I don't feel a need of reasons (cf. 477). Whatever was offered in the way of reasons would not strengthen my fear of fire, and if the reasons turned out to be weak I still wouldn't be induced to put my hand on the hot stove.

As far as 'justification' is concerned, "What people accept as a justification—is shewn by how they think and live" (325). If we want to elucidate the concept of justification we must take note of what people *accept* as justified; and it is clearly shown in our lives that we accept as justified both the certainty that fire will burn and the certainty that this man is in pain—even without reasons. Forms of life, embodied in language-games, teach us what justification is. As philosophers we must not attempt to justify the forms of life, to give reasons for *them*—to argue, for example, that we pity the injured man because we believe, assume, presuppose, or know that in addition to the groans and writhing, there is pain. The fact is, we pity him! "What has to be accepted, the given, is—so one could say—*forms of life*" (p. 226). What we should say is: "*This language-game is played*" (654).

From this major theme of Wittgenstein's thought one passes easily to another major theme—that "Philosophy simply puts everything before us, and neither explains nor deduces anything" (126). "It leaves everything as it is" (124).

Strawson's Criticism

Mr. Peter Strawson's critical notice [5] of the *Investigations* contains misunderstandings that might obtain currency. To Strawson it appears that, for Wittgenstein, "no word whatever stands for or names a special experience," [6] "no words name sensations (or 'private experiences'); and in particular the word 'pain' does not." [7] Wittgenstein "has committed himself to the view that one cannot sensibly be said to recognize or identify anything, unless one uses *criteria*; and, as a consequence of this, that one cannot recognize or identify sensations." [8] His "obsession with the *expression* of pain" leads him "to deny that sensations can be recognized and bear names." [9] Wittgenstein is hostile to "the idea of what is not observed (seen, heard, smelt, touched, tasted), and in particular to the idea that what is not observed can in any sense be recognized or described or reported" [10]— although at one place in the book (p. 189) "it looks as if he were almost prepared to acknowledge" that 'I am in pain' "may be just a report of my sensations." [11] His "prejudice against 'the inner'" leads him to deny that it is possible for a person to report the words that went through his mind when he was saying something to himself in his thoughts.[12] Strawson attributes Wittgenstein's errors not only to prejudice and, possibly, to "the old verificationist horror of a claim that cannot be checked," [13] but also to various confusions and muddles.[14]

It is important to see how very erroneous is this account of

[5] "Critical Notice: *Philosophical Investigations*," *Mind*, LXIII, January 1954, 70–99. (References to Strawson will be placed in footnotes, references to Wittgenstein will remain in the text.) [See Selection I in this anthology. The page references in brackets are to Strawson's essay as it appears in the present volume.—*Ed.*]

[6] P. 83 [22].   [7] P. 84 [Ibid.].   [8] P. 86 [25].   [9] P. 87 [26].   [10] P. 90 [31].   [11] P. 94 [35].
[12] P. 91 [31f.].   [13] P. 92 [32].   [14] See p. 86 [25] and p. 98 [41].

Wittgenstein. The latter says, "Don't we talk about sensations
every day, and give them names?" and then asks, "How does a
human being learn the names of sensations?—of the word 'pain'
for example?" (244). So Wittgenstein does not deny that we
name sensations. It is a howler to accuse Wittgenstein of "hostility to the idea of what is not observed" ("observed" apparently means 'perceived by one of the five senses') and of
"hostility to the idea that what is not observed can in any sense
be recognized or described or reported." [15] Dreams and mental
pictures are not observed, in Strawson's sense; yet Wittgenstein
discusses *reports* of dreams (p. 222; also p. 184) and *descriptions*
of mental pictures (e.g., 367). Consider this general remark:
"Think how many different kinds of things are called 'description': description of a body's position by means of its co-
ordinates; description of a facial expression; *description of a
sensation of touch*; of a mood" (24, my italics). And at many
places in the *Investigations*, Wittgenstein *gives* descriptions of
various sensations, although sensations are not observed, in
Strawson's sense. Strawson's belief that Wittgenstein thinks that
"one cannot sensibly be said to recognize or identify anything,
unless one uses criteria," [16] is proved false by the remarks about
mental images: I have *no* criterion for saying that two images
of mine are the same (377); yet there is such a thing as
recognition here, and a correct use of 'same' (378). How can it
be maintained that Wittgenstein has a prejudice against 'the
inner' when he allows that in our ordinary language a man *can*
write down or give vocal expression to his "inner experiences
—his feelings, moods, and the rest—for his private use"? (243).
Wittgenstein does not deny that there are *inner* experiences any
more than he denies that there are *mental* occurrences. Indeed,
he gives examples of things that he calls "*seelische Vorgänge*,"
e.g., "a pain's growing more or less," and in contrast with which
a thing like *understanding a word* is not, he argues a "*seelischer
Vorgang*" (154). Either to deny that such occurrences exist or to
claim that they cannot be named, reported, or described is entirely foreign to Wittgenstein's outlook. For what would the de-

[15] P. 90 [31].   [16] P. 86 [25].

nial amount to other than an attempt to "reform language," which is not his concern? It may *look* as if he were trying to reform language, because he is engaged in "giving prominence to distinctions which our ordinary forms of language easily make us overlook" (132). For example, Wittgenstein suggests that when we think about the philosophical problem of sensation the word 'describe' *tricks* us (290). Of course he does not mean that it is a mistake to speak of 'describing' a sensation. He means that the similarity in "surface grammar" (664) between 'I describe my sensations' and 'I describe my room' may mislead, may cause us to fail "to call to mind the differences between the language-games" (290).

Strawson rightly avers, "To deny that 'pain' is the name of a (type of) sensation is comparable to denying that 'red' is the name of a colour." [17] I suppose that, conversely, to affirm that 'pain' is the name of a sensation is like affirming that 'red' is the name of a color, and also that '0' is the name of a number. This classification tells us nothing of philosophical interest. What we need to notice is the *difference* between the way that '0' and '2,' say, function, although both are 'names of numbers' (think how easily one may be tempted to deny that 0 is a number), and the difference between the way 'red' and 'pain' function, although both are 'names.' "We call very different things 'names'; the word 'name' is used to characterize many different kinds of use of a word, related to one another in many different ways" (38). To suppose that the use of 'pain' and 'red,' as *names*, are alike is just the sort of error that Wittgenstein wants to expose. If one thinks this, one will want to by-pass the *expression* of pain and will wonder at Wittgenstein's 'obsession' with it. Not that Strawson does by-pass it, but he seems to attach the wrong significance to it. He appears to think that the fact that there is a characteristic pain-behavior is what makes possible a *common* "language of pain," and he seems to imply that if we did not care to have a *common* language of pain each of us would still be able to name and describe his pains in "a private language-game," even if there were no characteristic pain-behavior.[18] It looks as if he

[17] P. 87 [26]. [18] See pp. 84–88 [22–28].

thinks that with his private language he could step between pain
and its expression, and apply names to the bare sensations themselves (cf. 245).

For Strawson the conception of a private language possesses no
difficulty. A man "might simply be struck by the recurrence of a
certain sensation and get into the habit of making a certain mark
in a different place every time it occurred. The making of the
marks would help to impress the occurrence on his memory." [19]
Just as, I suppose, he might utter a certain sound each time a
cow appeared. But we need to ask, what makes the latter sound
a *word*, and what makes it the word for *cow?* Is there no difficulty here? Is it sufficient that the sound is uttered when and
only when a cow is present? Of course not. The sound might
refer to anything or nothing. What is necessary is that it should
play a part in various activities, in calling, fetching, counting
cows, distinguishing cows from other things and pictures of cows
from pictures of other things. If the sound has no fixed place in
activities ("language-games") of this sort, then it isn't a word
for *cow*. To be sure, I can sit in my chair and talk about cows
and not be engaged in any of those activities—but what makes
my words *refer* to cows is the fact that I have already mastered
those activities; they lie in the background. The kind of way
that 'cow' refers is the kind of language-game to which it belongs. If a mark or sound is to be a word for a *sensation* it, too,
must enter into language-games, although of a very different
sort. What sort? Well, such things as showing the location of the
sensation, exhibiting different reactions to different intensities
of stimulus, seeking or avoiding causes of the sensation, choosing
one sensation in preference to another, indicating the duration
of the sensation, and so on. Actions and reactions of that sort
constitute the sensation-behavior. They are the "outward criteria" (580) with which the sign must be connected if it is to be
a sign for a sensation *at all*, not merely if it is to be a sign in a
common language. In the mere supposition that there is a man
who is "struck by the recurrence of a certain sensation" and who
gets into the habit of "making a certain mark in a different

19 P. 85 [24].

place every time it occurred," no ground *whatever* has been given for saying that the mark is a sign for a sensation. The necessary surroundings have not been supplied. Strawson sees no problem here. He is surprised that "Wittgenstein gives himself considerable trouble over the question of how a man would *introduce* a name for a sensation into this private language." [20] It is as if Strawson thought: There is no difficulty about it; the man just *makes* the mark refer to a sensation. How the man does it puzzles Strawson so little that he is not even inclined to feel that the connection between the name and the sensation is queer, occult (cf. 38)—which it would be, to say the least, if the name had no fixed place in those activities and reactions that constitute sensation-behavior, for that, and not a magical act of the mind, is what *makes* it refer to a sensation.

The conception of private language that Wittgenstein attacks is not the conception of a language that only the speaker does understand, but of a language that no other person *can* understand (243). Strawson thinks that Wittgenstein has not refuted the conception of a private language but has only shown that certain conditions must be satisfied if a common language is to exist. Strawson appears to believe (I may misunderstand him) that each of us not only can have but does have a private language of sensations, that if we are to understand one another when we speak of our sensations there must be criteria for the use of our sensation-words, and that therefore the words with which we *refer* to our sensations must, in addition, contain "allusions" either to behavior or to material substances that are "associated" with the sensations.[21] The allusions must be to things that can be perceived by us all. By virtue of this the use of sensation-words can be taught and misuses corrected, and so those words will belong to a common language. There is another feature of their use (namely, their reference) that cannot be taught. Thus sensation-words will have both a public and a private meaning. Strawson's view appears to be accurately characterized by Wittgenstein's mock conjecture: "Or is it like this: the word 'red' means something known to everyone; and in

[20] Ibid. [Ibid.].   [21] P. 86 [25].

addition, for each person, it means something known only to him? (Or perhaps rather: it *refers* to something known only to him.)" (273)

But if my words, *without* these allusions, can refer to my sensations, then what is alluded to is only *contingently* related to the sensations. Adding the "allusions to what can be seen and touched" [22] will not help one little bit in making us understand one another. For the behavior that is, for me, contingently associated with 'the sensation of pain' may be, for you, contingently associated with 'the sensation of tickling'; the piece of matter that produces in you what you call 'a metallic taste' may produce in me what, if you could experience it, you would call 'the taste of onions'; my 'sensation of red' may be your 'sensation of blue'; we do not know and cannot know whether we are talking about the same things; we cannot *learn* the essential thing about one another's use of sensation-words—namely, their reference. The language in which the private referring is done cannot be turned into a common language by having something grafted on to it. Private language cannot be the understructure of the language we all understand. It is as if, in Strawson's conception, the sensation-words were supposed to perform two functions—to refer and to communicate. But if the reference is incommunicable, then the trappings of allusion will not communicate it, and what they do communicate will be irrelevant.

Strawson's idea that expressions like 'jabbing pain,' 'metallic taste,' mean something known to everyone and, in addition, for each person, refer to something known only to him, is responsible, I believe, for his failure to understand Wittgenstein on the topic of recognizing and identifying sensations. There is *a* sense of 'recognize' and 'identify' with respect to which Wittgenstein does deny that we can recognize or identify our own sensations, feelings, images. Consider, for example, that although a man understands the word 'alcohol' he may fail to identify the alcohol in a bottle as alcohol, because the bottle is marked 'gasoline' or because the cork smells of gasoline; or, although he understands 'rabbit' and is familiar with rabbits, he may fail

[22] Ibid. [Ibid.].

to recognize a rabbit as a rabbit, taking it for a stump instead; or, he may be in doubt and say, 'I don't know whether this is alcohol,' 'I'm not sure whether that is a rabbit or a stump.' But can a man who understands the word 'pain' be in doubt as to whether he has pain? Wittgenstein remarks:

> If anyone said "I do not know if what I have got is a pain or something else," we should think something like, he does not know what the English word "pain" means; and we should explain it to him.—How? Perhaps by means of gestures, or by pricking him with a pin and saying: "See, that's what pain is!" This explanation, like any other, he might understand right, wrong, or not at all. And he will show which he does by his use of the word, in this as in other cases.
>
> If he now said, for example: "Oh, I know what 'pain' means; what I don't know is whether *this*, that I have now, is pain"—we should merely shake our heads and be forced to regard his words as a queer reaction which we have no idea what to do with [288].

That a man wonders whether what he has is pain can only mean that he does not understand the word 'pain'; he cannot both understand it and have that doubt. Thus there is a sense of 'identify' that has no application to sensations. One who understands the word 'alcohol' may fail to identify *this* as alcohol or may be in doubt as to its identity or may correctly identify it. These possibilities have no meaning in the case of pain. There is not over and above (or underneath) the understanding of the word 'pain' a further process of correctly identifying or failing to identify *this* as pain. There would be if Strawson's conception were right. But there is not, and this is why "That expression of doubt ['Oh, I know what 'pain' means; what I don't know is whether *this*, that I have now, is pain'] has no place in the language-game" (288). (Strawson does not have, but in consistency should have, an inclination to dispute this last remark of Wittgenstein's.) [23] The fact that there is no *further* process of identifying a particular sensation is a reason why "the object drops

[23] See p. 85 [24].

out of consideration as irrelevant" when "we construe the grammar of the expression of sensation on the model of 'object and
name' " (293)—a remark that Strawson misunderstands as the
thesis that "no words name sensations." [24] If my use of a sensa-
tion-word satisfies the normal outward criteria and if I truthfully
declare that I have that sensation, then I *have* it—there is not a
further problem of my applying the word right or wrong within
myself. If a man used the word 'pain' in accordance with "the
usual symptoms and presuppositions of pain" then it would have
no sense to suppose that perhaps his memory did not retain
what the word 'pain' refers to, "so that he constantly called different things by that name" (271). If my use of the word fits those
usual criteria there is not an added problem of whether I accurately pick out the objects to which the word applies. In this
sense of 'identify,' the hypothesis that I identify my sensations
is "a mere ornament, not connected with the mechanism at all"
(270).

It does not follow nor, I think, does Wittgenstein mean to
assert that there is *no* proper use of 'identify' or 'recognize' with
sensations. He acknowledges a use of 'recognize' with mental
images, as previously noted. It would be a natural use of language, I believe, if someone who upon arising complained of an
unusual sensation were to say, 'Now I can identify it! It is the
same sensation that I have when I go down in an elevator.' Wittgenstein, who has no interest in reforming language, would not
dream of calling this an incorrect use of 'identify.' He attacks
a philosophical use of the word only, the use that belongs to the
notion of the private object. In this example of a non-philo-
sophical use, if the speaker employed the rest of the sensation-
language as we all do, and if his behavior in this case was
approximately what it was when he was affected by the down-
ward motion of an elevator, then his declaration that he was
feeling the elevator-sensation would be decisive; and also his
declaration that it was *not* the elevator-sensation would be
decisive. It is *out of the question* that he should have made a
mistake in identifying the sensation. His identification of his

[24] P. 84 [22].

sensation is an *expression* of sensation (in Wittgenstein's extended sense of this phrase). The identification is 'incorrigible.' We have here a radically different use of 'identify' from that illustrated in the examples of alcohol and rabbit.

The philosophical use of 'identify' seems to make possible the committing of *errors* of identification of sensations and inner experiences. The idea is that my sensation or my image is an object that I cannot show to anyone and that I identify it and from it derive its description (374). But if this is so, why cannot my identification and description go wrong, and not just sometimes but always? Here we are in a position to grasp the significance of Wittgenstein's maneuver: "Always get rid of the idea of the private object in this way: assume that it constantly changes, but that you do not notice the change because your memory constantly deceives you" (p. 207). We are meant to see the *senselessness* of this supposition: for what in the world would *show* that I was deceived constantly or even once? Do I look again—and why can't I be deceived that time, too? The supposition is a knob that doesn't turn anything (cf. 270). Understanding this will perhaps remove the temptation to think that I have something that I cannot show to you and from which I derive a knowledge of its identity. This is what Wittgenstein means in saying that when I related to another what I just said to myself in my thoughts " 'what went on within me' is not the point at all" (p. 222). He is not declaring, as Strawson thinks, that I cannot report what words went through my mind.[25] He is saying that it is a report "whose truth is guaranteed by the special criteria of truthfulness" (p. 222). It is *that* kind of report. So it is not a matter of trying faithfully to observe something within myself and of trying to produce a correct account of it, of trying to do something at which I might unwittingly fail.

The influence of the idea of the private object on Strawson's thinking is subtly reflected, I believe, in his declaration that a metallic taste is "quite certainly recognizable and identifiable in itself" and in his remark that "if the question 'What is the criterion of identity here?' is pushed, one can only answer: 'Well,

---

[25] See pp. 90, 91 [30–32].

the taste itself" (cf. 'the sensation itself')." [26] Strawson realizes
that we don't identify a sensation by means of criteria (e.g., a
metallic taste by means of the metallic material that produces
it). He is inclined to add that we identify it by 'the sensation
itself.' This seems to me to misconstrue the 'grammar' of 'identify' here. It may be to the point to consider again the comparison of colors and sensations. Wittgenstein says, "How do I know
that this colour is red?—It would be an answer to say 'I have
learned English' " (381). One thing this answer does is to deny
that I have *reasons* for saying that this color before me is red.
We might put this by saying that I identify it as red by 'the
color itself,' not by anything else. The cases of red and pain (or
metallic taste) so far run parallel. Equally, I don't have reasons
for saying that this color is red or that this sensation is pain.
But it *can* happen that I should fail to identify this color correctly, even though I have learned English (e.g., the moonlight
alters its appearance). Here the parallel ends. Nothing can alter
the 'appearance' of the sensation. Nothing counts as mistaking
its identity. If we assimilate identifying sensations to identifying
colors, because in neither instance reasons are relevant, we conceal the philosophically more important difference. To insist
that the parallel is perfect, that one identifies sensations in the
same sense that one identifies colors, is like saying that "there
must also be something boiling in the pictured pot" (297).
Identifying one's own sensation is nothing that is either in error
or *not* in error. It is not, in *that* sense, *identifying.* When I
identify my sensation, I do not *find out* its identity, not even
from 'the sensation itself.' My identification, one could say,
defines its identity.

We use a man's identification of his sensation as a criterion of
what his sensation is. But this is a *dependent* criterion. His verbal reports and identifications would not *be* a criterion unless
they were grounded in the primitive sensation-behavior that is
the primary and independent criterion of his sensations. If we
cut out human behavior from the language-game of sensations
(which Strawson does in defending the 'private language-game')

26 P. 86 [25].

one result will be that a man's identifying a sensation as the 'same' that he had a moment before will no longer be a criterion of its being the same. Not only the speaker but *no one* will have a criterion of identity. Consequently, for no one will it have any meaning to speak of a man's being "struck by the *recurrence* of a certain sensation." [27]

[27] P. 85 [24], my italics.

III

Can There Be
A Private Language?

A. J. Ayer

IN A QUITE ordinary sense, it is obvious that there can be private languages. There can be, because there are. A language may be said to be private when it is devised to enable a limited number of persons to communicate with one another in a way that is not intelligible to anyone outside the group. By this criterion, thieves' slang and family jargons are private languages. Such languages are not strictly private, in the sense that only one person uses and understands them, but there may very well be languages that are. Men have been known to keep diaries in codes which no one else is meant to understand. A private code is not, indeed, a private language, but rather a private method of transcribing some given language. It is, however, possible that a very secretive diarist may not be satisfied with putting familiar words into an unfamiliar notation, but may prefer to invent new words: the two processes are in any case not sharply distinct. If he carries his invention far enough he can properly be said to be employing a private language. For all I know, this has actually been done.

From this point of view, what makes a language private is simply the fact that it satisfies the purpose of being intelligible only to a single person, or to a restricted set of people. It is necessary here to bring in a reference to purpose, since a language may come to be intelligible only to a few people, or even only to a single person, merely by falling into general disuse: but such 'dead' languages are not considered to be private, if the limitation of their use was not originally intended. One may characterize a private language by saying that it is not in this sense meant to be alive. There is, however, no reason, in principle, why it should not come alive. The fact that only one person, or only a few people, are able to understand it is purely contingent. Just as it is possible, in theory, that any code should be broken, so can a private language come to be more widely understood. Such private languages are in general derived from public languages, and even if there are any which are not so derived, they will still be translatable into public languages. Their ceasing to be private is then just a matter of enough people becoming able to translate them or, what is more difficult but still theoretically possible, not to translate but even so to understand them.

If I am right, then, there is a use for the expression 'private language' which clearly allows it to have application. But this is not the use which philosophers have commonly given it. What philosophers usually seem to have in mind when they speak of a private language is one that is, in their view, necessarily private, in as much as it is used by some particular person to refer only to his own private experiences. For it is often held that for a language to be public it must refer to what is publicly observable: if a person could limit himself to describing his own sensations or feelings, then, strictly speaking, only he would understand what he was saying; his utterance might indirectly convey some information to others, but it could not mean to them exactly what it meant to him. Thus, Carnap who gives the name of 'protocol language' to any set of sentences which are

used to give 'a direct record' of one's own experience argues, in
his booklet on *The Unity of Science*,[1] that if an utterance like
'thirst now', belonging to the protocol language of a subject S_1,
is construed as expressing 'only what is immediately given' to S_1,
it cannot be understood by anyone else. Another subject S_2 may
claim to be able to recognize and so to refer to S_1's thirst, but
'strictly speaking' all that he ever recognizes is some physical
state of S_1's body. 'If by "the thirst of S_1" we understand not the
physical state of his body, but his sensations of thirst, *i.e.* something non-material, then S_1's thirst is fundamentally beyond the
reach of S_2's recognition.'[2] S_2 cannot possibly verify any statement which refers to S_1's thirst, in this sense, and consequently
cannot understand it. 'In general,' Carnap continues, 'every
statement in any person's protocol language would have sense
for that person alone. . . . Even when the same words and
sentences occur in various protocol languages, their sense would
be different, they could not even be compared. Every protocol
language could therefore be applied only solipsistically: there
would be no intersubjective protocol language. This is the consequence obtained by consistent adherence to the usual view and
terminology (rejected by the author).'[3]

Since Carnap wishes to maintain that people can understand
one another's protocol statements, if only on the ground that
this is a necessary condition for statements made in what he
calls the physical language to be intersubjectively verifiable, he
draws the inference that 'protocol language is a part of physical
language'. That is, he concludes that sentences which on the face
of it refer to private experiences must be logically equivalent to
sentences which describe some physical state of the subject.
Other philosophers have followed him in giving a physicalist
interpretation to the statements that one makes about the experiences of others, but have stopped short of extending it to
all the statements that one may make about one's own. They
prefer to hold that certain sentences do serve only to describe
the speaker's private experiences, and that, this being so, they
have a different meaning for him from any that they can possibly have for anybody else.

[1] Pp. 76 ff.   [2] *The Unity of Science*, p. 79.   [3] *Ibid.* p. 80.

In his *Philosophical Investigations* Wittgenstein appears to go much further than this. He seems to take the view that someone who attempted to use language in this private way would not merely be unable to communicate his meaning to others, but would have no meaning to communicate even to himself; he would not succeed in saying anything at all. 'Let us', says Wittgenstein,[4] 'imagine the following case: I want to keep a diary about the recurrence of a certain sensation. To this end I associate it with the sign "E" and write this sign in a calendar for everyday on which I have the sensation.—I will remark first of all that a definition of the sign cannot be formulated.—But still I can give myself a kind of ostensive definition.—How? Can I point to the sensation? Not in the ordinary sense. But I speak or write the sign down, and at the same time I concentrate my attention on the sensation—and so, as it were, point to it inwardly.—But what is this ceremony for? for that is all it seems to be! A definition surely serves to establish the meaning of a sign.—Well, that is done precisely by the concentration of my attention; for in this way I impress on myself the connection between the sign and the sensation. But "I impress it on myself" can only mean: this process brings it about that I remember the connection *right* in the future. But in the present case I have no criterion of correctness. One would like to say: whatever is going to seem right to me is right. And that only means that here one can't talk about "right".'

Again, 'What reason have we for calling "E" the sign for a *sensation?* For "sensation" is a word of our common language, not of one intelligible to me alone. So the use of the word stands in need of a justification which everybody understands.'[5]

This point is then developed further: 'Let us imagine a table (something like a dictionary) that exists only in our imagination. A dictionary can be used to justify the translation of a word X into a word Y. But are we also to call it a justification if such a table is to be looked up only in the imagination?—"Well, yes; then it is a subjective justification."—But justification consists in appealing to something independent.—"But surely I can appeal from one memory to another. For example, I don't know

---

[4] *Philosophical Investigations*, i. 258.   [5] *Op. cit.* I. 261.

if I have remembered the time of departure of a train right, and to check it I call to mind how a page of the time-table looked. Isn't it the same here?"—No; for this process has got to produce a memory which is actually *correct*. If the mental image of the time-table could not itself be *tested* for correctness, how could it confirm the correctness of the first memory? (As if someone were to buy several copies of the morning paper to assure himself that what it said was true.)

'Looking up a table in the imagination is no more looking up a table than the image of the result of an imagined experiment is the result of an experiment.'[6]

The case is quite different, Wittgenstein thinks, when the sensation can be coupled with some outward manifestation. Thus he maintains that the language which we ordinarily use to describe our 'inner experiences' is not private because the words which one uses to refer to one's sensations are 'tied up with [one's] natural expressions of sensation',[7] with the result that other people are in a position to understand them. Similarly he grants that the person who tries to describe his private sensation by writing down the sign 'E' in his diary might find a use for this sign if he discovered that whenever he had the sensation in question it could be shown by means of some measuring instrument that his blood pressure rose. For this would give him a way of telling that his blood pressure was rising without bothering to consult the instrument. But then, argues Wittgenstein, it will make no difference whether his recognition of the sensation is right or not. Provided that whenever he thinks he recognizes it, there is independent evidence that his blood pressure rises, it will not matter if he is invariably mistaken, if the sensation which he takes to be the same on each occasion is really not the same at all. 'And that alone shows that the hypothesis that [he] makes a mistake is mere show.'[8]

Let us examine this argument. A point to which Wittgenstein constantly recurs is that the ascription of meaning to a sign is something that needs to be justified: the justification consists in there being some independent test for determining that the

[6] *Op. cit.* I. 265.   [7] *Op. cit.* I. 256.   [8] *Op. cit.* I. 270.

sign is being used correctly; independent, that is, of the subject's recognition, or supposed recognition, of the object which he intends the sign to signify. His claim to recognize the object, his belief that it really is the same, is not to be accepted unless it can be backed by further evidence. Apparently, too, this evidence must be public: it must, at least in theory, be accessible to everyone. Merely to check one private sensation by another would not be enough. For if one cannot be trusted to recognize one of them, neither can one be trusted to recognize the other.

But unless there is something that one is allowed to recognize, no test can ever be completed: there will be no justification for the use of any sign at all. I check my memory of the time at which the train is due to leave by visualizing a page of the timetable; and I am required to check this in its turn by looking up the page. But unless I can trust my eyesight at this point, unless I can recognize the figures that I see written down, I am still no better off. It is true that if I distrust my eyesight I have the resource of consulting other people; but then I have to understand their testimony, I have correctly to identify the signs that they make. Let the object to which I am attempting to refer be as public as you please, let the word which I use for this purpose belong to some common language, my assurance that I am using the word correctly, that I am using it to refer to the 'right' object, must in the end rest on the testimony of my senses. It is through hearing what other people say, or through seeing what they write, or observing their movements, that I am enabled to conclude that their use of the word agrees with mine.[9] But if without further ado I can recognize such noises or shapes or

---

[9] My use of a similar argument in my book *The Problem of Knowledge* has led Miss Anscombe to accuse me of committing a logical fallacy (*vide* her book *An Introduction to Wittgenstein's Tractatus*, pp. 138–9). She supposes that I argue 'from the fact that it is not possible, and a *fortiori* not necessary, that every identification or recognition should in fact be checked, to the innocuousness of the notion of an uncheckable identification'. I agree with her that this is a fallacy, but I do not think I have committed it. My argument is that since every process of checking must terminate in some act of recognition, no process of checking can establish anything unless some acts of recognition are taken as valid in themselves. This does not imply that these acts of recognition are uncheckable in the sense that their deliverances could not in their turn be subjected to further checks; but then these further checks would again have to terminate in acts of recognition which were taken as valid in themselves and so *ad infinitum*. If the inference drawn from this is that an act of recognition is worthless unless it is corroborated by other acts of recognition, the recognition of private sensations will not necessarily be excluded. For there is no reason in principle why such acts of recognition should not corroborate one another.

movements, why can I not also recognize a private sensation?
It is all very well for Wittgenstein to say that writing down the
sign 'E', at the same time as I attend to the sensation, is an idle
ceremony. How is it any more idle than writing down a sign,
whether it be the conventionally correct sign or not, at the same
time as I observe some 'public' object? There is, indeed, a
problem about what is involved in endowing any sign with
meaning, but it is no less of a problem in the case where the
object for which the sign is supposed to stand is public than
in the case where it is private. Whatever it is about my behaviour that transforms the making of a sound, or the inscrip-
tion of a shape, into the employment of a sign can equally well
occur in either case.

But, it may be said, in the one case I can point to the object
I am trying to name, I can give an ostensive definition of it; in
the other I cannot. For merely attending to an object is not
pointing to it. But what difference does this make? I can indeed
extend my finger in the direction of a physical object, while
I pronounce what I intend to be the object's name; and I cannot
extend my finger in the direction of a private sensation. But how
is this extending of my finger itself anything more than an idle
ceremony? If it is to play its part in the giving of an ostensive
definition, this gesture has to be endowed with meaning. But if
I can endow such a gesture with meaning, I can endow a word
with meaning, without the gesture.

I suppose that the reason why the gesture is thought to be
important is that it enables me to make my meaning clear to
others. Of course they have to interpret me correctly. If they are
not intelligent, or I am not careful, they may think that I am
pointing to one thing when I really intend to point to another.
But successful communication by this method is at least possible.
The object to which I mean to point is one that they can
observe. On the other hand, no amount of gesturing on my part
can direct their attention to a private sensation of mine, which
ex hypothesi they cannot observe, assuming further that this
sensation has no 'natural expression'. So I cannot give an ostensive definition of the word which I wish to stand for the sensa-

tion. Nor can I define it in terms of other words, for how are
they to be defined? Consequently I cannot succeed in giving it
any meaning.

This argument is based on two assumptions, both of which I
believe to be false. One is that in a case of this sort it is impossible, logically impossible, to understand a sign unless one
can either observe the object which it signifies, or at least
observe something with which this object is naturally associated.
And the other is that for a person to be able to attach meaning
to a sign it is necessary that other people should be capable of
understanding it too. It will be convenient to begin by examining
the second of these assumptions which leads on to the first.

Imagine a Robinson Crusoe left alone on his island while still
an infant, having not yet learned to speak. Let him, like
Romulus and Remus, be nurtured by a wolf, or some other
animal, until he can fend for himself; and so let him grow to
manhood. He will certainly be able to recognize many things
upon the island, in the sense that he adapts his behaviour to
them. Is it inconceivable that he should also name them? There
may be psychological grounds for doubting whether such a
solitary being would in fact invent a language. The development
of language, it may be argued, is a social phenomenon. But
surely it is not self-contradictory to suppose that someone,
uninstructed in the use of any existing language, makes up a
language for himself. After all, some human being must have
been the first to use a symbol. And even if he did so as a member
of a group, in order to communicate with the other members,
even if his choice of symbols was socially conditioned, it is at
least conceivable that it should originally have been a purely
private enterprise. The hypothesis of G. K. Chesterton's dancing
professor about the origin of language, that it came 'from the
formulated secret language of some individual creature', is very
probably false, but it is certainly not unintelligible.

But if we allow that our Robinson Crusoe could invent words
to describe the flora and fauna of his island, why not allow that
he could also invent words to describe his sensations? In
neither case will he be able to justify his use of words by draw-

ing on the evidence provided by a fellow creature: but while
this is a useful check, it is not indispensable. It would be difficult to argue that the power of communication, the ability even
to keep a private diary, could come to him only with the arrival
of Man Friday. His justification for describing his environment
in the way that he does will be that he perceives it to have just
those features which his words are intended to describe. His
knowing how to use these words will be a matter of his remembering what objects they are meant to stand for, and so of his
being able to recognize these objects. But why should he not
succeed in recognizing them? And why then should he not
equally succeed in recognizing his sensations? Undoubtedly, he
may make mistakes. He may think that a bird which he sees
flying past is a bird of the same type as one which he had
previously named, when in fact it is of a different type, sufficiently different for him to have given it a different name if
he had observed it more closely. Similarly, he may think that
a sensation is the same as others which he has identified, when
in fact, in the relevant aspects, it is not the same. In neither case
may the mistake make any practical difference to him, but to
say that nothing turns upon a mistake is not to say that it is not
a mistake at all. In the case of the bird, there is a slightly
greater chance of his detecting his mistake, since the identical
bird may reappear: but even so he has to rely upon his memory
for the assurance that it is the identical bird. In the case of the
sensation, he has only his memory as a means of deciding
whether his identification is correct or not. In this respect he is
indeed like Wittgenstein's man who buys several copies of the
morning paper to assure himself that what it says is true. But
the reason why this seems to us so absurd is that we take it for
granted that one copy of a morning paper will duplicate another; there is no absurdity in buying a second newspaper, of a
different type, and using it to check the first. And in a place
where there was only one morning newspaper, but it was so
produced that misprints might occur in one copy without occurring in all, it would be perfectly sensible to buy several
copies and check them against each other. Of course there re-

mains the important difference that the facts which the newspaper reports are independently verifiable, in theory if not always in practice. But verification must stop somewhere. As I have already argued, unless something is recognized, without being referred to a further test, nothing can be tested. In the case of Crusoe's sensation, we are supposing that beyond his memory there is no further test. It does not follow that he has no means of identifying it, or that it does not make sense to say that he identifies it right or wrong.

So long as Crusoe remains alone on the island, so long, that is, as he communicates only with himself, the principal distinction which he is likely to draw between 'external' objects and his 'inner' experiences is that his experiences are transient in a way that external objects are not. He will not be bound to draw even this distinction; his criteria for identity may be different from our own; but it is reasonable to suppose that they will be the same. Assuming, then, that his language admits the distinction, he will find on the arrival of Man Friday that it acquires a new importance. For whereas he will be able to teach Man Friday the use of the words which he has devised to stand for external objects by showing him the objects for which they stand, he will not, in this way, be able to teach him the use of the words which he has devised to stand for his sensations. And in the cases where these sensations are entirely private, in the sense that they have no 'natural expressions' which Man Friday can identify, it may well be that Crusoe fails to find any way of teaching him the use of the words which he employs to stand for them. But from the fact that he cannot teach this part of his language to Man Friday it by no means follows that he has no use for it himself. In a context of this sort, one can teach only what one already understands. The ability to teach, or rather the ability of someone else to learn, cannot therefore be a prerequisite for understanding.

Neither does it necessarily follow, in these circumstances, that Man Friday will be incapable of learning the meaning of the words which Crusoe uses to describe his private sensations. It is surely a contingent fact that we depend upon ostensive definitions, to the extent that we do, for learning what words mean. As it is, a child is not taught how to describe his feelings in the way he is taught to describe the objects in his nursery. His mother cannot point to his pain in the way that she can point to his cup and spoon. But she knows that he has a pain because he cries and because she sees that something has happened to him which is likely to cause him pain; and knowing that he is in pain she is able to teach him what to call it. If there were no external signs of his sensations she would have no means of detecting when he had them, and therefore could not teach him how to describe them. This is indeed the case, but it might easily be otherwise. We can imagine two persons being so attuned to one another that whenever either has a private sensation of a certain sort, the other has it too. In that case, when one of them described what he was feeling the other might very well follow the description, even though he had no 'external' evidence to guide him. But how could either of them ever know that he had identified the other's feeling correctly? Well, how can two people ever know that they mean the same by a word which they use to refer to some 'public' object? Only because each finds the other's reactions appropriate. Similarly one may suppose that Man Friday sympathizes when Crusoe's private sensation is painful, and congratulates him when it is pleasant, that he is able to say when it begins and when it stops, that he correctly describes it as being rather like such and such another sensation, and very different from a third, thereby affording proof that he also understands the words that stand for these sensations. Admittedly, such tests are not conclusive. But the tests which we ordinarily take as showing that we mean the same by the words which we apply to public objects are not conclusive either: they leave it at least theoretically open that we do not after all mean quite the same. But from the fact that the tests are not conclusive it does not, in either case, follow that they have no force at all. It is true also that such tests as the expressed agreement about the duration of the experience require that the two men already share a common language, which they have no doubt built up on the basis of common ob-

servations. It would indeed be difficult, though still, I think, not
necessarily impossible,[10] for them to establish communication
if all their experiences were private, in Wittgenstein's sense.
But even if their understanding each other's use of words could
come about only if some of the objects which these words described were public, it would not follow that they all must
be so.

It is not even necessary to make the assumption that Man
Friday comes to know what Crusoe's sensations are, and so to
understand the words which signify them, through having
similar sensations of his own. It is conceivable that he should
satisfy all the tests which go to show that he has this knowledge,
and indeed that he should actually have it, even though the
experience which he rightly ascribes to Crusoe is unlike any
that he has, or ever has had, himself. It would indeed be very
strange if someone had this power of seeing, as it were, directly
into another's soul. But it is strange only in the sense that it is
something which, on casual grounds, we should not expect to
happen. The idea of its happening breaks no logical rule. An
analogous case would be that of someone's imagining, or seeming to remember, an experience which was unlike any that he
had ever actually had. To allow that such things are possible is,
indeed, to admit innate ideas, in the Lockean sense, but that is
not a serious objection. The admission is not even inconsistent
with the prevalent varieties of empiricism. It can still be made
a rule that in order to understand a word which signifies a
sensation one must know what it would be like to have the sensation in question: that is, one must be able to identify the
sensation when one has it, and so to verify the statement which
describes it. The peculiarity of the cases which we are envisaging
is just that people are credited with the ability to identify experiences which they have not previously had. There may indeed
be causal objections to the hypothesis that this can ever happen.
The point which concerns us now is that these objections are no
more than causal. The ways in which languages are actually

---

[10] I have come to doubt this. See footnote to 'Privacy', p. 78 [in *The Concept of a Person and Other Essays*, by A. J. Ayer—*Ed.*].

learned do not logically circumscribe the possibilities of their being understood.

If the sort of insight which we have been attributing to Man Friday were commonly possessed, we might well be led to revise our concepts of publicity and privacy. The mistake which is made by philosophers like Carnap is that of supposing that being public or being private, in the senses which are relevant to this discussion, are properties which are somehow attached to different sorts of objects, independently of our linguistic usage. But the reason why one object is publicly and another only privately accessible is that in the one case it makes sense to say that the object is observed by more than one person and in the other it does not.[11] Tables are public; it makes sense to say that several people are perceiving the same table. Headaches are private: it does not make sense to say that several people are feeling the same headache. But just as we can assimilate tables to headaches by introducing a notation in which two different persons' perceiving the same table becomes a matter of their each sensing their own private 'tabular' sense-data, so we could assimilate headaches to tables by introducing a notation in which it was correct to speak of a common headache, which certain people only were in a condition to perceive. As things are, this notation would not be convenient. But if people were so constituted that they were communally exposed to headaches in the way that they are communally exposed to the weather, we might cease to think of headaches as being necessarily private. A London particular might come to be a local headache as well as, or instead of, a local fog. Certain persons might escape it, just as certain persons, for one reason or another, may fail to perceive the fog. But the fog exists for all that, and so, given this new way of speaking, would the public headache. The conditions which would make this way of speaking useful do not, indeed, obtain; but that they do not is, once again, a purely contingent fact.

---

[11] This is an over-simplification, see 'Privacy'.

The facts being what they are, we do not have a use for such expressions as 'S_2's feeling S_1's thirst' or 'S_2's observing the sensation of thirst which S_1 feels'. On the other hand, we do attach a meaning to saying that the same physical object, or process, or event, for instance a state of S_1's body, is observed by S_2 as well as by S_1. Does it follow, as Carnap thinks, that for this reason S_2 cannot understand a statement which refers to S_1's feeling of thirst, whereas he can understand a statement which refers to the condition of S_1's body? Suppose that we modified our rules for identity, in a way that many philosophers have proposed, and allowed ourselves to say that what was ordinarily described as S_1 and S_2's observing the same physical event was 'really' a case of each of them sensing his own sense-data which, while they might be qualitatively similar, could not be literally the same. Should we thereby be committed to denying that either could understand what the other said about this physical event? Surely not. And equally the fact that S_2 cannot feel, or inspect, S_1's feelings in no way entails that he cannot understand what S_1 says about them. The criteria for deciding whether two people understand each other are logically independent of the fact that we do, or do not, have a use for saying that literally the same objects are perceived by both.

I conclude, first, that for a person to use descriptive language meaningfully it is not necessary that any other person should understand him, and, secondly, that for anyone to understand a descriptive statement it is not necessary that he should himself be able to observe what it describes. It is not even necessary that he should be able to observe something which is naturally associated with what it describes, in the way that feelings are associated with their 'natural expressions'. If we insist on making it a necessary condition for our understanding a descriptive statement that we are able to observe what it describes, we shall find ourselves disclaiming the possibility of understanding not merely statements about other people's private sensations, but also statements about the past; either that, or reinterpreting them in such a way that they change their reference, as when philosophers substitute bodily states for feelings, and the future for the past. Both courses, I now think, are mistaken. No doubt it is a necessary condition for my understanding a descriptive statement that it should be, in some way, verifiable. But it need not be directly verifiable, and even if it is directly verifiable, it need not be directly verifiable by me.

IV

Two Arguments
Against a Private Language

Moreland Perkins

202. And hence also 'obeying a rule' is a practice. And to think one is obeying a rule is not to obey a rule. Hence it is not possible to obey a rule 'privately': otherwise thinking one was obeying a rule would be the same thing as obeying it.

258. Let us imagine the following case. I want to keep a diary about the recurrence of a certain sensation. To this end I associate it with the sign "E" and write this sign in a calendar for every day on which I have the sensation.—I will remark first of all that a definition of the sign cannot be formulated.—But still I can give myself a kind of ostensive definition.—How? Can I point to the sensation?—Not in the ordinary sense. But I speak, or write the sign down, and at the same time I concentrate my attention on the sensation—and so, as it were, point to it inwardly.—But what is this ceremony for? for that is all it seems to be! A definition surely serves to establish the meaning of a sign.—Well, that is done precisely by the concentration of my attention; for in this way I impress on myself the connexion between the sign and the sensation.—But "I impress it on myself" can only mean: this process brings it about that I remember the connexion right in the future. But in the present case I have no criterion of correctness. One would like to say: whatever is going to seem right to me is right. And that only means that here we can't talk about 'right'.

259. Are the rules of the private language impressions *of rules?—The balance on which impressions are weighed is not the* impression *of a balance.*

Ludwig Wittgenstein, Philosophical Investigations

IN WHAT FOLLOWS I shall first interpret Wittgenstein's argument against a private language as a formal deduction from more or less exactly stated premises. In this form the argument is rather abstract, and its scope, the range of its generalizations, is wide. I shall then move toward a more complete interpretation of the argument by posing a dilemma we confront when we set about construing the crucial word 'practice'. This dilemma is artificial in so far as there is an easy escape from it provided for us by Wittgenstein. But it is useful to pose, because by trying to escape from it we are led to see that to take the easy way out is to deny that the argument is novel, whereas the hard way out is impassable. After looking briefly at the hard way, I discuss the easy way out of the dilemma. Next I develop a revision of my interpretation in an attempt to generate an argument that is both persuasive and novel. This revision amounts to a serious restriction in the scope of the argument, but the restriction does no more than limit the argument's subject matter to what Wittgenstein was actually investigating when he introduced the argument in passages #258–#259 of *Philosophical Investigations*. There are, however, as I point out at the end, obstacles in the way of accepting the revised interpretation as a correct rendering of Wittgenstein's argument.

(The reader who would like to avoid studying the formal proof may, at this point, skip over to page 101 and begin with the abbreviated statement of that proof.)

Initially, I construe the argument against a private language as undertaking to show that the truth of 1′,

1′. Whenever Smith utters the word 'E' it is logically impossible for anyone else either to understand what object Smith means to speak of or how he means to characterize it.

entails the falsehood of A′,

A'. On some occasion of Smith's uttering 'E' Smith uses 'E' to characterize an individual object as of a certain kind.

(Here the word 'object' simply means anything that *can* be referred to, whether mental or physical or neither, and the word 'uttering' denotes an action that can be performed either out loud or by writing or silently.)

Three additional premises are needed (*2, *3, *5). In the proof these premises, together with a modified form of premise 1', are marked with an asterisk. 1' is changed into *1 in order to avoid problems posed for deductive inference by intensional objects. And A' is abbreviated, to save words, into A. Associated with this latter abbreviation is the shortening, throughout the essay, of the phrase "uses 'E' to characterize an individual object as of a certain kind," and its variants, into "uses 'E' to refer to something" or simply "uses 'E'," "the use of 'E'," and so on. A now reads:

A. On some occasion of Smith's uttering 'E' Smith uses 'E' to refer to something.

The proof that *1, below, entails the falsehood of A is this:

*1. In regard to no occasion O of Smith's uttering 'E' is it logically possible for any person P, other than Smith, to satisfy this description: P understands Smith's use of 'E' on occasion O.
*2. If what a person is doing on some occasion is using a particular word to refer to something, then what he is doing is either a case of correctly using that particular word to refer to something or a case of incorrectly doing so.
*3. If what a person does by uttering a particular word on some occasion is neither part of a *practice* of using that particular word to refer to something nor part of a *practice* of using words, generally, to refer to things, then what the person does on that occasion is neither a case of correctly nor a case of incorrectly using that particular word to refer to something.
∴4. If, when Smith utters 'E', what Smith does with 'E' is never

part of a *practice* of using words to refer to things, then on no occasion of Smith's uttering 'E' is Smith either correctly or incorrectly using 'E' to refer to something. (From *3.)

*5. Anything that a person does which is part of a practice can, in principle, be fully understood by some other person.

6. Assume that on some occasion O_1 what Smith does with 'E' by uttering 'E' is part of a practice of using words to refer to things.

∴7. In regard to occasion O_1 of Smith's uttering 'E' it is logically possible for some person P, other than Smith, to satisfy the description: P understands Smith's use of 'E' on occasion O. (From 6, using *5.)

8. But from *1 we know that 7 is false.

∴9′. Assumption 6 is false. (Since it entails false 7.)

Which is to say:

∴9. On no occasion is what Smith does by uttering 'E' part of a practice of using words to refer to things.

∴10. On no occasion of Smith's uttering 'E' is Smith either correctly or incorrectly using 'E' to refer to something. (From 9 and 4.)

∴11′. On no occasion of Smith's uttering 'E' is Smith using 'E' to refer to something. (From 10 and *2.)

Which is to say:

∴11. A is false.

Thus, if *2, *3, and *5 are true, the truth of *1 entails the falsehood of A, and the truth of A therefore entails the falsehood of *1. So, if *2, *3, and *5 are true, *1 and A are incompatible; that is to say, a private language cannot exist. And if *2, *3, and *5 are necessary truths, a private language is a logical impossibility.

We might call the *conclusion* of the argument "C":

C. *1 and A are incompatible. (By the rule of conditional proof, with *2,*3, and *5 assumed.)

Before discussing the argument I will abbreviate the proof. The abbreviation is formally defective, but it need not be misleading. At the end of each notable line, I put in brackets the number of the corresponding longer line in the full demonstration. The task is to show that i and (a) are incompatible under the assumption that ii, iv, and vi are true.

The proposition whose falsehood is to be proved is (a):

(a) Smith uses 'E' to refer. [A]

Proof:

    i. No one else can understand Smith's use of 'E'. [*1]

    ii. If Smith's use of 'E' *is* part of a practice, then someone else *can* understand his use of 'E'. [*5]

∴iii. Smith's use of 'E' is *not* part of a practice.

    iv. If Smith's use of 'E' is *not* part of a practice, then he neither uses 'E' correctly nor incorrectly. [*3]

∴v. Smith neither uses 'E' correctly nor incorrectly.

    vi. If Smith uses 'E' to refer, then he either uses it correctly or incorrectly. [*2]

∴vii. Smith does *not* use 'E' to refer. [11']

    viii. That is to say, (a) is false. [11]

Hence, if ii, iv, and vi are true, then if i is true (a) is false and if (a) is true i is false, or—then i and (a) are incompatible.

Two facts about the present statement of the Argument deserve immediate notice. First, the object to which Smith is alleged to refer in a private way is not characterized as a hidden mental event. Nothing is said explicitly in either *1 or A about what kind of object it is that Smith allegedly refers to in a private way. If it makes sense, one may suppose that it is a material object to which Smith tries to refer in a private way. Second, the following criticism of the Argument is inadequate: "It is logically possible that a man who has never been associated with other men should use words to characterize objects as being of a

certain kind. Therefore a private language is possible." The
implication of this criticism is that the conclusion of the Argument denies the possibility of a language that happens in fact to
be understood by no one except the man who uses it. But as *1
makes clear, this is mistaken. The conclusion of the Argument
rejects only a language which it is impossible that anyone but
the speaker should come to understand. And making a man
however solitary in the development and use of the language he
speaks does nothing to establish the impossibility of others'
learning to understand his language; so it goes no way toward
making his language private in the sense of the Argument.[1]

Nonetheless, although the conceivability of hermit monologue
would not directly contradict the Argument's conclusion, it
might place an obstacle in the way of accepting one or more of
the premises needed to prove the conclusion. And indeed I think
that it does. I shall try to show this by formulating a dilemma.

Call the concept we get when we take the word 'practice' to
mean a social custom or institution "Social Practice." Call the
concept of a certain sort of pattern in the activity of a single
person, which does not require association with other persons,
"Individual Practice." Now we encounter this dilemma: Either
we adopt the concept Social Practice in interpreting the Argument or we adopt the concept Individual Practice. If we adopt
Social Practice, then in all likelihood premise *3 is false. And, if
we adopt Individual Practice, then the Argument fails to make
clear what reason there is for accepting the premise numbered
*5. Both *3 and *5 are indispensable too the Argument. So it
appears that the Argument fails to be conclusive either because
premise *3 is false or because the reasons for accepting premise
*5 are unclear.

Let us examine the elements of this dilemma more closely.

[1] Both of these points have been made by Judith Jarvis Thomson in "Private Languages,"
American Philosophical Quarterly, 1, 1 (January, 1964) : 20–31. See pp. 26 and 20. In fact there is
a close resemblance between her interpretations of the argument against a private language (which
she, however, does not attribute to Wittgenstein) and the one I develop in the first two-thirds of
this essay. Much of what is common was present in drafts of this essay written before her article
was published. But in the several drafts written since, I am certain that I have been influenced by
her interesting article in ways that I cannot now pinpoint. There is, too, the common influence of
Malcolm's well-known treatment of the subject in his review of the *Investigations, Philosophical
Review*, 63 (1954) : 530–559. [See Selection II in this anthology.—*Ed.*]

If we adopt the concept Social Practice, then *5 is a necessary truth. It takes at least two persons to make a social practice, and a person cannot engage in a practice without understanding the practice; so some second person will always be capable in principle of understanding any particular action that is part of a social practice.

But if we adopt the concept Social Practice, then premise *3 is probably false. In order that we be entitled to speak of a person as sometimes using a sign correctly and sometimes using it incorrectly, it is not necessary to suppose that he participates in a *social* practice. Describing in detail the practice on the part of a born and lifelong hermit that would count as using words to refer, including those moments which would properly be counted as examples of making a mistake and of the hermit's recognizing that he has made a mistake, offers no extraordinary difficulty. It may be true that, in the ordinary use of the word 'language' and, hence, in the ordinary use of the word 'word', there is an implication that more than one person is involved. But the important question is not whether or not the word 'language' as customarily used can properly be applied with all its connotation to any wholly solitary practice. Rather, a question we need to ask in appraising this Argument is whether or not some significant portion of what individual persons who do belong to societies of word users manage to accomplish with words could conceivably be accomplished also by a person who had had no association whatever with other persons—in particular, of course, whether it is conceivable that such a naturally solitary person should make mistakes (and recognize that he had) with regard to his use of signs to refer to things. I see no way of proving that this is possible short of describing in detail the practice the natural hermit is imagined to have. Rather than do this here, I will simply point out that Wittgenstein admitted the conceivability of language that is not part of a social practice. In #243 of the *Investigations* he writes, ". . . we could imagine human beings who spoke only in monologue; who accompanied their activities by talking to themselves.—An explorer who watched them and listened to their talk might succeed in translating their language into ours." Since in this very passage Wittgenstein goes on to explain what he means by a private language we may not suppose that the impossibility of hermit monologue is necessary to Wittgenstein's argument for the impossibility of a private language. If, then, we use the concept Social Practice to interpret the Argument, premise *3 will probably be false, and it will, apparently, be rejected by Wittgenstein himself.[2]

Suppose, instead, that we adopt the concept, Individual Practice, in construing the Argument. Now our born hermit can qualify, under the rule of premise *3, as using words correctly and incorrectly; so the conceivability of hermit monologue no longer places an obstacle in the way of our accepting *3.

But what ground have we, employing the concept Individual Practice, for believing *5, which when Social Practice figured in it was self-evident? Why is it that every natural hermit's practice *must* be intelligible to someone other than the hermit?

It is here that we can expect to find an all too easy answer offered to us by Wittgenstein. So first let us try the hard way out.

Perhaps the Argument means to say that, since each word-using practice of every individual must consist of overt behavior, then always another person is capable in principle of understanding a given person's practice. But first, why *must* the activity that constitutes the practice be overt? If we admit that a hermit's practice can generate standards of correct and incorrect use, if unqualified solitude is no barrier, what is there that necessitates that the practice be a matter of *behavior?* That

---

[2] Wittgenstein sometimes appears to be almost deliberately elusive in his remarks on this subject. Consider #199:

"Is what we call "obeying a rule" something that it would be possible for only *one* man to do, and to do only *once* in his life?

"It is not possible that there should have been only one occasion on which someone obeyed a rule. It is not possible that there should have been only one occasion on which a report was made, an order given or understood; and so on.—To obey a rule, to make a report, to give an order, to play a game of chess, are *customs* (uses, institutions).

"To understand a sentence means to understand a language. To understand a language means to be master of a technique." Wittgenstein answers the second part of his opening question. But what answer does he here mean to suggest to the first part of that question?

Compare *Remarks on the Foundations of Mathematics*, p. 94e, #66, #67, especially: "But what about this consensus—dosen't it mean that *one* human being by himself could not calculate? Well, one human being could at any rate not calculate just *once* in his life."

seems relevant only in so far as it assures publicity. But what need has a *hermit* of publicity?

Suppose we pass that question by for now and think only of practices that do manifest themselves in behavior. Is each such practice *merely* a matter of behavior? Behavior is overt. But it does not appear that all action is—some decisions, trains of thought, and ways of trying to do something, for example, are forms of action that do not appear to be observable. And some such hidden actions as these might enter into a referring practice. In that case what ground is there for the doctrine that all solitary practices *must* be intelligible to other persons?

We might reply that there is in Wittgenstein's writings the view that apparently hidden mental actions are not really hidden (that this is a misleading way of characterizing them, anyhow, when it leads one to say that the actions are unobservable); rather they are, as we might say, too widely extended in space and time to come within any single view: each present and allegedly hidden mental action is what it is in virtue of the context in which what happens now—and is always a posture or movement of the body—is placed. And this context may have a very wide extent, in space and in time. Nonetheless this context is, at different times and places, observable—or it is comprised of observable elements. Let us attribute to the Argument this radical contextualism. We recall that we have decided that a referring practice need not be social. The practice of the natural hermit, who works and thinks alone, is genuine. Into this hermit's practice no human environment enters. It is possible, then, according to the Argument, for a man's use of signs to acquire its meaning through a context provided only by the rest of his behavior and by the nonhuman environment in which all his motions and postures are located. Now on what special ground does the Argument propose to justify the claim that we others *know* that we shall be capable of understanding exactly how the environment (and the rest of his behavior) figures in defining any natural hermit's practice of using signs to single out portions, states, and aspects of that environment? The Argument, as it stands, does not enable us to answer this question.

However, Wittgenstein does provide us with an all too easy answer. And this route of escape from our dilemma could be built into the original Argument. It is given in #206–#207:

> Suppose you came as an explorer into an unknown country with a language quite strange to you. (#206) . . . Let us imagine that the people in that country carried on the usual activities and in the course of them employed, apparently, an articulate language. If we watch their behavior we find it intelligible, it seems 'logical'. But when we try to learn their language we find it impossible to do so. For there is no regular connection between what they say, the sounds they make, and their actions. . . .
> Are we to say that these people have a language: orders, reports and the rest?
> There is not enough regularity for us to call it "language" (#207).
> . . . The common behavior of mankind is the system of reference by means of which we interpret an unknown language (#206).

What reason can we find in these remarks for saying that a born hermit's language cannot be private? The reason offered is that to characterize a person's use of a word as a private use is to stipulate that no evidence can ever be gathered by the rest of us that could justify us in saying that this person does mean something by his utterance. Consequently it is logically impossible that we should ever be in a position to say that something is privately meant by anyone, hermit or other. The indispensable marks of meaningful utterance will never show themselves when the alleged meaning is private—by the definition of 'private'. But a statement that attributes to a certain person's utterance a characteristic whose presence it is logically impossible for the public to verify is a "statement" that the public must count as saying nothing significant about that person's utterance. We are the public. So we say nothing significant when we say of a person's utterance that it means something private. And this is to say that it is impossible that anyone should ever mean something private by his utterances.

But this line of thought is surely not new. It can be understood as an application of the *public*-verifiability theory of meaning to those statements in which we assert that certain persons are, on certain occasions, using words to refer.[3] If, as the public-verifiability theory claims, it is true that only publicly verifiable statements characterize possible states of affairs, then when I make the statement, "Smith just now used a word to refer," my statement must say of Smith that he *behaved* in a certain way, and the way of behaving ascribed to him must be such as *we*, the public, can ascertain meets certain criteria whose use *we* can share; otherwise no possible state of affairs is characterized by my statement that Smith referred to something. Therefore any statement of the sort, "Smith just now made a *private* use of a word to refer to something," fails to characterize a possible state of affairs. So the public-verificationist's argument proceeds.

There is much that is original in the use Wittgenstein makes of the concept of a practice. So it is, of course, false that there is no novelty in his sometimes characterizing the absence of the usual marks of someone's meaning something by an utterance as the absence of the usual marks of a *practice*. But the fact that the usual marks of a person's meaning something by his utterance constitutes a species of the usual marks of a person's engaging in a practice plays no essential role at this point in *this* argument. We need only say that the publicly recognizable marks of someone's meaning something are in principle never forthcoming in the case of someone's privately meaning something, and we have all that the argument here relies upon in order to show that we have no right to speak of someone's meaning something at all in this case.

[3] This interpretation of the easy way out of the dilemma is very close to a principle Mrs. Thomson makes integral to the argument in her "Private Languages," referred to earlier. See section VI, pp. 26–29. However, the verifiability principle—she finds it unnecessary to appeal to the *public*-verifiability principle—does not, in her interpretation of the argument, play a role exactly analogous to the role the public-verifiability principle here plays in mine.

Certainly Wittgenstein emphasizes more consistently than either pragmatists or public-verificationists have done the fact that the sort of behavior we count as referring behavior is decided upon by reference to the *common* behavior of referring persons. But the *principle* involved here is not new, nor has acceptance of the principle involved been limited to philosophers who subscribe to the public-verifiability theory of meaning. The principle has, for example, been emphasized by C. I. Lewis and by other empiricists. We might call it the Principle of the Ubiquity of Classification (PUC) : to affirm that what you now see in front of you is a sheet of paper involves, according to this principle, classifying it with other sheets, and, in consequence, using the common appearance and "behavior" of sheets of paper as your system of reference. We judge *this* to be a rabbit running across the yard by appealing to the common appearance and behavior of running rabbits as our system of reference. And we judge *that* to be a person running across the yard by appealing to the common appearance and behavior of running persons. The same will hold, of course, according to the PUC, for our judgment that a person is using a word to refer to something: we compare his behavior to the common behavior of persons who are engaged in using words to refer to things. In espousing the PUC in conjunction with the public-verifiability theory of meaning one is, then, no more saying that a word user must be associated with others in a practice than one would be saying, in regard to the other two examples, that this individual sheet of paper must be associated in a practice with other sheets or that that rabbit must be associated in a practice with other running rabbits, in order to be a sheet of paper or a rabbit running across the yard. If we join the PUC to the public-verifiability theory of meaning, we arrive at the result that it must be publicly verifiable that this object resembles other objects that are sheets if it is to be a sheet; it must be publicly verifiable that this rabbit resembles other rabbits, engaged in running, if it is to be a running rabbit; and it must be publicly verifiable that this person resembles other persons engaged in referring-with-a-word, if he is to be a referring-with-a-word person. So, since it is, by the definition of 'privately', impossible to verify publicly that a *privately* referring-with-a-word person resembles other referring-with-a-word persons, a privately referring-with-a-word person is not a referring-with-a-word person at all. A person who is privately referring with a word is not a logical possibility. But this is all that Wittgenstein's Argument comes to, when appeal is made to #206–#207 to help us out of our dilemma.

I speak of this solution of our dilemma as all too easy, then, because if we accept it we divest Wittgenstein's argument against a private language of its interest as something originating with him.

Why this easy solution to our dilemma disappoints may be expressed in another way. In reading #258–#259 one forms an impression that the impossibility of privately referring is being demonstrated, as it were, from the inside, from the point of view of the alleged referrer. (I suppose that something of this sort is part of what is intended by Malcolm in labeling this the "internal" argument against a private language). It is as if we are being told that if we put ourselves in the position of the person imagined to refer in a private way, we will, by the Argument's aid, come to appreciate the impossibility of privately referring. And this, we gather, turns somehow upon the specific content of the idea of a practice—in particular, upon what exactly is needed in the way of a practice to make sense of correct and incorrect use of words. But as the Argument now stands analyzed, utilizing the thought of #206–#207, it does not provide us with this sort of internal demonstration. The obvious way of doing it has (in #243) been eliminated—namely, by showing that participation in a *social* practice is presupposed by all referring acts. Barred from that path and faced with the hermit's acknowledged capacity (in principle) to generate his own standards of correctness and incorrectness by means of his solitary practice, the Argument offers no reasoning that forces us to say that his practice *must* be intelligible to others, except the very "external" and comparatively old-fashioned consideration that, if we members of a communicating public are to speak of someone's meaning something, or of any*thing's* doing *any-thing*, we may not stipulate in advance that the indispensable and common marks of the presence of what we speak of *can*not in this case be publicly displayed.

I conclude that, if we construe practice as Social Practice, the Argument fails, because then it is false that in order to use a word either correctly or incorrectly one's use must be part of a practice: the natural hermit's use of words, implicitly admitted by Wittgenstein at #243, falsifies premise *3. And, if we take practice to be Individual Practice, then the Argument becomes persuasive (in so far as it does) only by losing its claim to novelty.

It remains to inquire whether or not there is a way of interpreting the argument against a private language so that it is at the same time persuasive and original. I think that there is. But first a word of caution. We shall now encounter a sense of the word 'private' that is sharply to be distinguished from the technical sense of that word introduced into the Argument in premise *1. In the technical sense, the word 'private' is applied to what may alternately be conceived as an alleged use of a word, an alleged case of referring by means of words, or an alleged meaning, any one of which is said to be in principle un-intelligible to any second person when it is characterized as "private." In the sense of 'private' that we now encounter, how-ever, the word 'private' is not applied to uses of words, cases of referring by means of words, or to meanings; it is applied rather to occurrences like itches, aches, pains, and tickles. And char-acterizing such occurrences as these as private in this new sense is so far from characterizing them as incommunicable that it is, I wish to suggest, rather a way of saying something about how we *do* communicate to one another experiences into which such occurrences enter. I shall speak of *sensations* as occurrences that are private in an ordinary way; and I shall suggest that this means that for every sensation there may be occasions on which a person P has a sensation of that kind and other persons, who are as well placed for observing what goes on in P as it is possible for others to be, can (and do) decide with complete assurance that P has that sensation solely on the basis of P's telling them that he has it. I shall also use the phrase 'inner event', in the sense of a mentally or psychologically inner event, to denote classes of occurrences that are, in the sense just explained, private. There may be other conditions that have to be fulfilled in order that an occurrence be in this ordinary sense private and in order that it be mentally inner; I am concerned here only to suggest one necessary condition.

First I present a revision of the Argument in a form which is useful as a first approximation of what is wanted but to which there is an objection on the ground that it does not exactly express Wittgenstein's doctrine. But since this first approximation to what is wanted is somewhat less esoteric than exactly what is wanted, I introduce it first, hoping thereby to render more persuasive to more persons the final result.

Though there is no insurmountable obstacle to a born hermit's inventing words which he uses to refer to and characterize portions and aspects of the material world, it is impossible for him to develop the concept of a sensation.[4] This is impossible because it is part of the concept of a sensation that on occasion a sensation can be, in the ordinary way, private: that is to say, it is part of the concept of a sensation that there may be occasions on which a second person can know one has a sensation only if one tells him. Consequently, it is a necessary condition for anyone's understanding the concept of a sensation that he understand something about how other persons may relate themselves to his own sensation reports; specifically, one must understand that other persons may on occasion be able to know that one has the sensation on the basis of one's saying one has, and on this basis alone. But a natural hermit is incapable of appreciating the fact that on some occasions other persons can know he has a sensation only if he tells them; he cannot appre-

---

[4] The line of reasoning I now introduce was worked out in response to criticism of an earlier draft of this paper by Lawrence Resnick.

ciate this fact because he has no comprehension of what it is to
have commerce with other people and, hence, of what it is
to tell them of his sensations. Therefore, a hermit cannot possess
the concept of a sensation. Indeed, in order for him to have the
concept of a sensation, more yet is required of the hermit that
is outside his power. A natural hermit cannot appreciate another, related fact: that the same sensation which others can
sometimes only know he has if he tells them, others have as
well, *and* that sometimes he can know that others have this
sensation only if *they* tell *him*. But one has to appreciate this
second fact in order to appreciate the first. For included within
the idea of the first fact was the idea of communicating to
someone else something about a sensation of one's own. And a
person cannot be sure he is communicating to others information
about a particular *kind* of sensation of his own when he "tells
them about his sensation" unless those others also tell him about
their experiences of having that same (kind of) sensation; nor
can a person know that it is a *sensation* he succeeds in telling
others about unless they too sometimes *tell* him they are having
it when otherwise he couldn't know they were. But a hermit
cannot appreciate this second sort of fact either, because he can
have no notion of what it would be like to accept others' reports
of their sensations.

Now it may be said that, although this argument proves that
a born hermit cannot have the concept of a sensation, it does not
prove that he cannot *refer* to a sensation, for a man may lack,
say, the concept of a carburetor and yet refer to one, by pointing
to it, or by speaking of "that thing on the floor in the garage." [5]
However, sensations cannot be referred to *merely* by pointing.
And there is a case for saying that a person cannot succeed in
referring to a carburetor unless use is made of the category,
"concrete physical object"; otherwise he might, as well, be
referring to the color or the illumination, the shadow or the
grease spot, which may also occupy the place he appears to indicate by his gesture or his place-description. A similar case

[5] This objection was called to my attention by Lawrence Resnick.

exists for the contention that a person cannot refer to a sensation (I do not here speak of whether or not he can *have* a sensation) without making use of the category, "something inner," which is to say, the category, "something (at least potentially) hidden or private"; otherwise, if a person "tries to refer" to the sensation by means of some such description as "what happened just now when that mosquito bit me" or by pointing to his elbow and saying, "that," he will succeed only in referring to the red spot or the disturbance in the skin caused by the mosquito's bite, and not to the itch—not to the sensation. So we have a case for saying that it is possible to refer to a sensation only if one can refer to something *as* inner, in the psychological sense of 'inner'. And it is precisely this that a born and lifelong hermit cannot do, for, in the psychological sense of the word, the "inner" in me is (at least partly defined as) that which others can sometimes know about only if I tell them and which may be inner in others, too, in the sense that I can sometimes know that others are having *it* only if *they* tell *me*.

If we accept this reasoning, and if we now *reconstrue Wittgenstein's argument against a private language as intended to apply ONLY to alleged acts of privately referring to SENSATIONS*, where to refer privately is to refer in such a way that no one else can understand what you are referring to or what you are saying about "it," then it turns out that one cannot privately refer to sensations, because to refer to a sensation is *necessarily* to participate in a social practice. This means that we shall now adopt the concept Social Practice in interpreting the Argument. So premise *5—the principle that anything that is part of a practice is intelligible to more than one person—becomes an evident necessary truth. And, despite our use of the concept Social Practice, we can now accept premise *3—the principle that 'correct' and 'incorrect' apply only to what is part of a practice— as true, because hermit talk *about sensations* is impossible and *it is only to facts concerning* talk *about sensations that the Argument (and so premise *3) now addresses itself.*

Indeed it would appear that we could enlarge the scope of the Revised Argument by allowing it to apply to *all* inner mental events, not merely to sensations, so long as a part of what is essential to an event's being inner is that sometimes others can know about it if and only if the person in whom it occurs tells the others about it.

One objection to this Revised Argument is the following: Wittgenstein did not think that when we say "I have an itch" we refer to sensations in the sense of 'refer' that figures in the true proposition, "A person sometimes refers to a book when he says 'I have a book',," whereas the line of reasoning I have just advanced supposes that we do refer, in that sense of 'refer', to sensations. But we can carry the whole argument through to the same conclusion using the conception of referring to a sensation which, I take it, one who makes this objection believes that Wittgenstein accepted.

Let us say that, roughly speaking, according to Wittgenstein one refers to one's own sensations primarily in the sense that one verbally "expresses" one's own sensations. *Now* the question becomes: Could a hermit use words to *express* a sensation? Sources for some of the following line of reasoning in support of a negative answer can be found in Wittgenstein's thought.

In order to use words to characterize a portion of the skin as a freckle a man must use words in some of the ways we do when we use them to label a spot as a freckle. But if we leave out of account the value we place upon freckles, there is still a substantial phenomenon left which need not be a social phenomenon In consequence, a good deal of what we do in labeling spots as freckles we can conceive done in natural solitude. The same goes for labeling something as a rash on the skin; the social content of the concept of a rash is secondary; so, to imagine a being labeling a rash on the skin can be, in significant part, to imagine something that need not be conceived as a social phenomenon— for we have granted that referring, merely *as such*, need not be social; the same goes for imagining someone *manifesting*, by his utterance, a condition of the skin, a rash, say: this we might call verbally "expressing" a skin rash. But an *itch* is distinguished from a skin rash as a *sensation;* and this is to say that it is distinguished as psychologically inner. And this makes expressing an itch necessarily a social phenomenon, for to express what is inner is to express what is private in an ordinary way, and to express what is private in this ordinary way is to express what can be expressed *only if* it is at least sometimes *expressed to other people.* So to think of a man as verbally expressing an itch —as distinguished from a skin rash—is to think of him as entering into a special relationship with other persons. To think of someone verbally expressing an itch is to think of a social phenomenon. Specifically, in order to think of a person as verbally expressing an itch we must think of him as at least sometimes being treated by others as having an itch when there is no visible rash on his skin and no mosquito has been observed to bite him and he has not been noticed scratching himself—when, in short, he has merely said "I have an itch"; *and* we must think of him as sometimes treating others as having itches under similar circumstances. It follows that one can verbally express an itch only by means of an action that is part of a social practice. (So a natural hermit cannot verbally express an itch.) Consequently a private language for expressing sensations is impossible.

One qualification is needed. It may be that if a person participates in *some* social practices of the kind mentioned, accepting and giving reports of *some* sensations, or possibly even only of some inner mental events, a sufficient foundation for regarding him on some occasion as verbally expressing a particular sensation is thereby provided even though he never fully participates in the social practice of reporting that particular sort of sensation.

What is there to be said for and against this Revised Interpretation of Wittgenstein's argument against a private language? In the end, both the case for and the case against it must rest upon #258–#259, supplemented by #202. Here, if anywhere, the structure of Wittgenstein's argument is sketched out for us.

We are told that " 'obeying a rule' is a practice" and that "it is not possible to obey a rule 'privately': otherwise thinking one was obeying a rule would be the same thing as obeying it"

(#202) ; we are told that if one's practice is private, then one
will "have no criterion of correctness"; "whatever is going to
seem right to me is right" (#258). Here is the heart of the argument. In favor of the Revised Interpretation is the fact that,
as in that interpretation, here Wittgenstein tells us that a man's
private use of a word is impossible not because *we others* can
have no justification for calling such a use a use (though this is
also true) but because the alleged *user* can have no standard of
correct use, and this *he* must have in order to use a word. (The
necessity, to be sure, springs from *our* concept of a use; but,
one might say, it generates in *him* a need which is peculiar to a
person "trying to" use words; and it is upon the impossibility of
satisfying this specific need of his that the impossibility of his
referring privately is here made to rest.)

Now why is it, according to #202 and #258–#259, that the
alleged private user of a word can have no standard of correct
use?

Here we interpret. We answer: because a community of persons is needed in order to provide a standard, and, if the word-
using practice is private, then communal standards cannot
govern it. Well, on our Revised Interpretation it is precisely the
requirement that every case of referring to a sensation be part
of a social practice that precludes the possibility that referring
to sensations should be private. So far so good. Now the argument is interesting; now it is novel. Now indeed it is "internal."
Not the concept of referring in general but at least the concept
of referring to sensations, to inner mental events, is the concept
of an "inherently" social phenomenon; looked at, *by* us of
course but in a sense, *from* within him, the alleged private
referrer fails, because it is as if we imagine him trying to play
a social game and imagine him at the same time barred from
the necessary connection with a society.

On the other hand, and I think this is decisive, as working
against the Revised Interpretation we must count the following
deviation in it from the thought of #202, #258–#259. The Revised Interpretation does *not*, as the thought of #202, #258–#259
does, ground itself upon the following contention: that I must

refer to my itch by means of actions that are part of a social practice *because* otherwise my referring to an itch would be indistinguishable from *my merely thinking that I am referring to an itch.* Rather, the Revised Interpretation grounds itself upon the following claim: that I must refer to my itch by means of actions that are part of a social practice *because* otherwise my referring to an itch would be indistinguishable from *my referring to a mere condition of the skin.* This difference in the structure of the two arguments seems to me to be sufficient to exclude the Revised Interpretation as a true rendering of what Wittgenstein has explicitly given us in the way of an argument against a private language.

I am inclined to draw the following conclusion. Wittgenstein does offer in his many discussions of what *I* have called inner mental events something both novel and extremely persuasive in the way of material for a demonstration of the impossibility of a language which is used by exactly one person, is intelligible to him alone, *and* is used to refer to inner mental events. For from these discussions one can certainly discover good reasons for saying that the concept of the inner is the concept of that which is communicated from one person to another in a special way and that therefore no one can be thinking of something inner who is thinking of what can be communicated in no way. On the other hand, Wittgenstein does not offer anything *new* in the way of a persuasive demonstration of the impossibility of *every* language which is defined simply as a language that it is possible for only the solitary "speaker" of that language to understand. And, finally, in those passages in the *Investigations* in which he seems to state explicitly and in succinct form, as in #258—#259, and in #202, a persuasive argument against the possibility of a private language, he does not in fact succeed, no matter how we construe the subject-matter of the imagined language.

Instead, however, of firmly drawing the negative portion of this conclusion, I will stop with a question. Suppose one accepts as the conclusion of the revised argument, treated as cogent, the proposition that it is impossible for a natural hermit to refer to *any* inner mental events. Can the hermit, then, form the concept of a self, specifically, the concept of himself? Can 'I' and 'my' and 'me' have a place in his language? If the answer to this question should be no, then can we sensibly suppose that the natural hermit has a language to refer to trees and deer, to arms and legs, to conditions of the skin, and to material things and their states generally? Could the hermit refer to *any* object if he could not refer to himself? And could he refer to himself if he lacked the capacity to refer to inner mental events?

V

From "Wittgenstein's Lectures in 1930–1933"

G. E. Moore

[IN THE FOLLOWING EXCERPT from Moore's report of Wittgenstein's lectures at Cambridge in 1930–1933, "this discussion" referred to in line 2 dealt with "the difference between the proposition which is expressed by the words 'I have got tooth-ache,' and those which are expressed by the words 'You have got tooth-ache' or 'He has got tooth-ache,'" as Moore indicates earlier in his report.—*Ed.*]

He [Wittgenstein] spent . . . a great deal of time on this discussion, and I am very much puzzled as to the meaning of much that he said, and also as to the connexion between different things which he said. It seems to me that his discussion was rather incoherent, and my account of it must be incoherent also, because I cannot see the connexion between different points which he seemed anxious to make. He said very early in the discussion that the whole subject is "extraordinarily difficult" because "the whole field is full of misleading notations";

and that its difficulty was shown by the fact that the question at
issue is the question between Realists, Idealists, and Solipsists.
And he also said, more than once, that many of the difficulties
are due to the fact that there is a great temptation to confuse
what are merely experiential propositions, which might, therefore, not have been true, with propositions which are necessarily
true or are, as he once said, "tautological or grammatical statements". He gave, as an instance of a proposition of the latter
sort, "I can't feel your toothache", saying that "If you feel it,
it isn't mine" is a "matter of grammar", and also that "I can't
feel your toothache" means the same as " 'I feel your toothache'
has no sense"; and he contrasted this with "I hear my voice
coming from somewhere near my eyes", which he said we think
to be necessary, but which in fact is not necessary "though it
always happens". In this connexion he gave the warning "Don't
be prejudiced by anything which *is* a fact, but which *might* be
otherwise". And he seemed to be quite definite on a point which
seems to me certainly true, *viz.* that I might see without physical
eyes, and even without having a body at all; that the connexion
between seeing and physical eyes is merely a fact learnt by
experience, not a necessity at all; though he also said that "the
visual field" has certain internal properties, such that you can
describe the motion of certain things in it as motions towards or
away from "your eye"; but that here "your eye" does not mean
your physical eye, nor yet anything whatever which is *in* the
visual field. He called "your eye", in this sense, "the eye of the
visual field", and said that the distinction between motion
towards it and away from it was "on the same level" as "the
distinction between 'curved' and 'straight' ".

However, he began the discussion by raising a question, which
he said was connected with Behaviourism, namely, the question
"When we say 'He has tooth-ache' is it correct to say that his
tooth-ache is only his behaviour, whereas when I talk about my
tooth-ache I am not talking about my behaviour?"; but very
soon he introduced a question expressed in different words,
which is perhaps not merely a different formulation of the same
question, *viz.* "Is another person's toothache 'tooth-ache' in

the same sense as mine?" In trying to find an answer to this question or these questions, he said first that it was clear and admitted that what verifies or is a criterion for "I have tooth-ache" is quite different from what verifies or is a criterion for "He has tooth-ache", and soon added that, since this is so, the *meanings* of "I have toothache" and "he has tooth-ache" must be different. In this connexion he said later, first, that the meaning of "verification" is different, when we speak of verifying "I have" from what it is when we speak of verifying "He has", and then, later still, that there is no such thing as a verification for "I have", since the question "How do you know that you have tooth-ache?" is nonsensical. He criticized two answers which might be given to this last question by people who think it is not nonsensical, by saying (1) that the answer "Because I feel it" won't do, because "I feel it" means the same as "I have it", and (2) that the answer "I know it by inspection" also won't do, because it implies that I can "look to see" whether I have it or not, whereas "looking to see whether I have it or not" has no meaning. The fact that it is nonsense to talk of verifying the fact that I have it, puts, he said, "I have it" on "a different level" in grammar from "he has it". And he also expressed his view that the two expressions are on a different grammatical level by saying that they are not both values of a single propositional function "x has tooth-ache"; and in favour of this view he gave two definite reasons for saying that they are not, namely, (1) that "I don't know whether I have tooth-ache" is always absurd or nonsense, whereas "I don't know whether he has tooth-ache" is not nonsense, and (2) that "It seems to me that I have tooth-ache" is nonsense, whereas "It seems to me that he has" is not.

He said, that when he said this, people supposed him to be saying that other people never really have what he has, but that, if he did say so, he would be talking nonsense; and he seemed quite definitely to reject the behaviourist view that "he has tooth-ache" means only that "he" is behaving in a particular manner; for he said that "tooth-ache" doesn't in fact only mean a particular kind of behaviour, and implied that when we

pity a man for having toothache, we are not pitying him for
putting his hand to his cheek; and, later on, he said that we
conclude that another person has toothache from his behaviour,
and that it is legitimate to conclude this on the analogy of the
resemblance of his behaviour to the way in which we behave
when we have toothache. It seemed, therefore, that just as to
his first question he meant to give definitely the answer "No",
so to his second question he meant to give definitely the answer
"Yes"; the word "toothache" is used in the same sense when
we say that he has it (or "you have it") as when we say that
I have it, though he never expressly said so; and though he
seemed to throw some doubt on whether he meant this by
saying "I admit that other people do have tooth-ache—this
having *the meaning which we have given it*".

It seemed, therefore, that he did not think that the difference
between "I have tooth-ache" and "He has tooth-ache" was
due to the fact that the word "tooth-ache" was used in a different sense in the two sentences. What then was it due to?
Much that he said seemed to suggest that his view was that the
difference was due to the fact that in "He has toothache" we
were necessarily talking of a physical body, whereas in "I have
tooth-ache" we were not. As to the first of these two propositions he did not seem quite definite; for though at first he
said that "my voice" means "the voice which comes from my
mouth", he seemed afterwards to suggest that in "He has
toothache" (or "You have") we were not necessarily referring
to a *body*, but might be referring only to a *voice*, identified as
"his" or "yours" without reference to a body. But as to the
second proposition, the one about "I have tooth-ache", the
point on which he seemed most anxious to insist was that what
we call "having tooth-ache" is what he called a "primary
experience" (he once used the phrase "direct experience" as
equivalent to this one); and he said that "what characterizes
'primary experience'" is that in its case " 'I' does not denote a
possessor". In order to make clear what he meant by this he
compared "I have tooth-ache" with "I see a red patch"; and
said of what he called "visual sensations" generally, and in

particular of what he called "the visual field", that "the idea
of a person doesn't enter into the description of it, just as a
[physical] eye doesn't enter into the description of what is
seen"; and he said that similarly "the idea of a person" doesn't
enter into the description of "having tooth-ache". How was he
here using the word "person"? He certainly meant to deny that
the idea of a physical body enters necessarily into the description; and in one passage he seemed to imply that he used "person" to mean the same as "physical body", since he said "A
description of a sensation does not contain a description of a
sense-organ, nor, *therefore*, of a person". He was, therefore, still
maintaining apparently that one distinction between "I have
toothache" and "He has toothache" was due to the fact that
the latter necessarily refers to a physical body (or, perhaps, to
a voice instead) whereas the former does not. But I think this
was not the only distinction which he had in mind, and that he
was not always using "person" to mean the same as physical
body (or, perhaps, a voice instead). For he said that "Just as
no [physical] eye is involved in seeing, so no Ego is involved in
thinking or in having toothache"; and he quoted, with apparent
approval, Lichtenberg's saying "Instead of 'I think' we ought
to say 'It thinks'" ("it" being used, as he said, as "Es" is
used in "Es blitzet"); and by saying this he meant, I think,
something similar to what he said of "the eye of the visual
field" when he said that it is not anything which is *in* the
visual field. Like so many other philosophers, in talking of "visual
sensations" he seemed not to distinguish between "what I see"
and "my seeing of it"; and he did not expressly discuss what
appears to be a possibility, namely, that though no person enters
into what I see, yet some "person" other than a physical body
or a voice, may "enter into" my seeing of it.

In this connexion, that in "I have toothache" "I" does not
"denote a possessor", he pointed out that, when I talk of "*my*
body", the fact that the body in question is "mine" or "belongs
to me", cannot be verified by reference to that body itself, thus
seeming to imply that when I say "This body belongs to me",
"me" is used in the second of the senses which he distinguished

for "I", *viz.* that in which, according to him, it does not "denote a possessor". But he did not seem to be quite sure of this, since he said in one place "*If* there is an ownership such that I possess a body, this isn't verified by reference to a body", *i.e.* that "This is *my* body" can't possibly mean "This body belongs to this body". He said that, where "I" is replaceable by "this body" "I" and "he" are "on the same [grammatical] level". He was quite definite that the word "I" or "any other word which denotes a subject" is used in "two utterly different ways", one in which it is "on the level with other people", and one in which it is not. This difference, he said, was a difference in "the grammar of our ordinary language". As an instance of one of these two uses, he gave "I've got a match-box" and "I've got a bad tooth", which he said were "on a level" with "Skinner has a match-box" and "Skinner has a bad tooth". He said that in these two cases "I have . . ." and "Skinner has . . ." really were values of the same propositional function, and that "I" and "Skinner" were both "possessors". But in the case of "I have tooth-ache" or "I see a red patch" he held that the use of "I" is utterly different.

In speaking of these two senses of "I" he said, as what he called "a final thing", "In one sense 'I' and 'conscious' are equivalent, but not in another", and he compared this difference to the difference between what can be said of the pictures on a film in a magic lantern and of the picture on the screen; saying that the pictures in the lantern are all "on the same level" but that the picture which is at any given time on the screen is not "on the same level" with any of them, and that if we were to use "conscious" to say of one of the pictures in the lantern that it was at that time being thrown on the screen, it would be meaningless to say of the picture on the screen that it was "conscious". The pictures on the film, he said, "have neighbours", whereas that on the screen has none. And he also compared the "grammatical" difference between the two different uses of "I" with the difference between the meaning of "has blurred edges" as applied to the visual field, and the meaning of the same expression as applied to any drawing you might make of the visual field: your drawing might be imagined to have sharp edges instead of blurred ones, but this is unimaginable in the case of the visual field. The visual field, he said, has no outline or boundary, and he equated this with "It has no sense to say that it has one".

In connexion with his statement that "I", in one of its uses, is equivalent to "conscious", he said something about Freud's use of the terms "conscious" and "unconscious". He said that Freud had really discovered phenomena and connexions not previously known, but that he talked as if he had found out that there were in the human mind "unconscious" hatreds, volitions, etc., and that this was very misleading, because we think of the difference between a "conscious" and an "unconscious" hatred as like that between a "seen" and an "unseen" chair. He said that, in fact, the grammar of "felt" and "unfelt" hatred is quite different from that of "seen" and "unseen" chair, just as the grammar of "artificial" flower is quite different from that of "blue" flower. He suggested that "unconscious toothache", if "unconscious" were used as Freud used it, might be necessarily bound up with a physical body, whereas "conscious toothache" is not so bound up.

As regards Solipsism and Idealism he said that he himself had been often tempted to say "All that is real is the experience of the present moment" or "All that is certain is the experience of the present moment"; and that any one who is at all tempted to hold Idealism or Solipsism knows the temptation to say "The only reality is the present experience" or "The only reality is *my* present experience". Of these two latter statements he said that both were equally absurd, but that, though both were fallacious, "the idea expressed by them is of enormous importance". Both about Solipsism and about Idealism he had insisted earlier that neither of them pretends that what it says is learnt by experience—that the arguments for both are of the form "you can't" or "you must", and that both these expressions "cut [the statement in question] out of our language". Elsewhere he said that both Solipsists and Idealists would say they "couldn't imagine it otherwise", and that, in reply to this, he would say, "If so, your statement has no sense" since "nothing can characterize reality, except as opposed to something else which is not the case". Elsewhere he had said that the Solipsist's statement "Only my experience is real" is absurd "as a statement of fact", but that the Solipsist sees that a person who says "No: my experience is real too" has not really refuted him, just as Dr. Johnson did not refute Berkeley by kicking a stone. Much later he said that Solipsism is right if it merely says that "I have tooth-ache" and "He has tooth-ache" are "on quite a different level", but that "if the Solipsist says that he has something which another hasn't, he is absurd and is making the very mistake of putting the two statements on the same level". In this connexion he said that he thought that both the Realist and the Idealist were "talking nonsense" in the particular sense in which "nonsense is produced by trying to express by the use of language what ought to be embodied in the grammar"; and he illustrated this sense by saying that "I can't feel his toothache" means " 'I feel his toothache' has no sense" and therefore does not "express a fact" as "I can't play chess" may do.

VI

Persons

P. F. Strawson

I

IN THE *TRACTATUS* (5.631–5.641), Wittgenstein writes of the I which occurs in philosophy, of the philosophical idea of the subject of experiences. He says first: "The thinking, presenting subject—there is no such thing." Then, a little later: "*In an important sense* there is no subject." This is followed by: "The subject does not belong to the world, but is a limit of the world." And a little later comes the following paragraph: "There is [therefore] really a sense in which in philosophy we can talk non-psychologically of the I. The I occurs in philosophy through the fact that the 'world is my world.' The philosophical I is not the man, not the human body, or the human soul of which psychology treats, but the metaphysical subject, the limit—not a part of the world." These remarks are impressive, but also puzzling and obscure. Reading them, one might think: Well, let's settle for the human body and the human soul of which psychology treats, and which is a part of the world, and let the metaphysical subject go. But again we might think: No, when I talk of myself, I do after all talk of that which has all of my experiences, I do talk of the subject of my experiences—and yet also of something that is part of the world in that it, but not the world, comes to an end when I die. The limit of *my* world is not—and is not so thought of by me—the limit of *the* world. It may be difficult to explain the idea of something which is both a subject of experiences and a part of the world. But it is an idea we have: it should be an idea we can explain.

Let us think of some of the ways in which we ordinarily talk of ourselves, of some of the things which we ordinarily ascribe to ourselves. They are of many kinds. We ascribe to ourselves *actions and intentions* (I am doing, did, shall do this); *sensations* (I am warm, in pain); *thoughts and feelings* (I think, wonder, want this, am angry, disappointed, contented); *perceptions and memories* (I see this, hear the other, remember that). We ascribe to ourselves, in two senses, position: *location* (I am on the sofa) and *attitude* (I am lying down). And of course we ascribe to ourselves not only temporary conditions, states, and situations, like most of these, but also enduring characteristics, including such physical characteristics as height, coloring, shape, and weight. That is to say, among the things we ascribe to ourselves are things of a kind that we also ascribe to material bodies to which we would not dream of ascribing others of the things that we ascribe to ourselves. Now there seems nothing needing explanation in the fact that the particular height, coloring, and physical position which we ascribe to ourselves, should be ascribed to *something or other;* for that which one calls one's body is, at least, a body, a material thing. It can be picked out from others, identified by ordinary physical criteria and described in ordinary physical terms. But it can seem, and has seemed, to need explanation that one's states of consciousness, one's thoughts and sensations, are ascribed *to the very same thing* as that to which these physical characteristics, this physical situation, is ascribed. Why are one's states of consciousness ascribed to the very same thing as certain corporeal characteristics, a certain physical situation, etc.? And once this question is raised, another question follows it, viz.: Why are one's states of consciousness ascribed to (said to be of, or to belong to) anything at all? It is not to be supposed that the answers to these questions will be independent of one another.

It might indeed be thought that an answer to both of·them could be found in the unique role which each person's body plays in his experience, particularly his perceptual experience. All philosophers who have concerned themselves with these questions have referred to the uniqueness of this role. (Descartes was well enough aware of its uniqueness: "I am *not* lodged in my body like a pilot in a vessel.") In what does this uniqueness consist? Well, of course, in a great many facts. We may summarize some of these facts by saying that for each person there is one body which occupies a certain *causal* position in relation to that person's perceptual experience, a causal position which is in various ways unique in relation to each of the various kinds of perceptual experience he has; and—as a further consequence —that this body is also unique for him as an *object* of the various kinds of perceptual experience which he has. This complex uniqueness of the single body appears, moreover, to be a contingent matter, or rather a cluster of contingent matters; we can, or it seems that we can, imagine many peculiar combinations of dependence and independence of aspects of our perceptual experience on the physical states or situation of more than one body.

Now I must say, straightaway, that this cluster of apparently contingent facts about the unique role which each person's body plays in his experience does not seem to me to provide, *by itself*, an answer to our questions. Of course these facts explain *something*. They provide a very good reason why a subject of experience should have a *very special regard* for just one body, why he should think of it as unique and perhaps more important than any other. They explain—if I may be permitted to put it so —why I feel *peculiarly attached* to what in fact I call my own body; they even might be said to explain why, granted that I am going to speak of one body as *mine*, I should speak of this body (the body that I do speak of as mine) as mine. But they do not explain why I should have the concept of *myself* at all, why I should ascribe my thoughts and experiences to *anything*. Moreover, even if we were satisfied with some other explanation of why one's states of consciousness (thoughts and feelings and perceptions) were ascribed to *something*, and satisfied that the facts in question sufficed to explain why the "possession" of a particular body should be ascribed to the *same* thing (i.e., to explain why a particular body should be spoken of as standing in some special relation, called "being possessed by" to that thing), yet the facts in question still do not explain why we should, as we do, ascribe certain corporeal characteristics not simply to the body standing in this special relation to the thing to which we ascribe thoughts, feelings, etc., but to the thing itself to which we ascribe those thoughts and feelings. (For we say "I am bald" as well as "I am cold," "I am lying on the hearthrug" as well as "I see a spider on the ceiling.") Briefly, the facts in question explain why a subject of experience should pick out one body from others, give it, perhaps, an honored name and ascribe to it whatever characteristics it has; but they do not explain why the experiences should be ascribed to any subject at all; and they do not explain why, if the experiences are to be ascribed to something, they *and* the corporeal characteristics which might be truly ascribed to the favored body, should be ascribed to the same thing. So the facts in question do not explain the use that we make of the word "I", or how any word has the use that word has. They do not explain the concept we have of a person.

II

A possible reaction at this point is to say that the concept we have is wrong or confused, or, if we make it a rule not to say that the concepts we have are confused, that the usage we have, whereby we ascribe, or seem to ascribe, such different kinds of predicate to one and the same thing, is confusing, that it conceals the true nature of the concepts involved, or something of this sort. This reaction can be found in two very important types of view about these matters. The first type of view is Cartesian, the view of Descartes and of others who think like him. Over the attribution of the second type of view I am more hesitant; but there is some evidence that it was held, at one period, by Wittgenstein and possibly also by Schlick. On both of these views, one of the questions we are considering, namely "Why do we ascribe our states of consciousness to the very same thing as certain corporeal characteristics, etc.?" is a question which does not arise; for on both views it is only a linguistic illusion that both kinds of predicate are properly ascribed to one and the same thing, that there is a common owner, or subject, of both types of predicate. And on the second of these views, the other question we are considering, namely "Why do we ascribe our states of consciousness to anything at all?" is also a question which does not arise; for on this view, it is only a linguistic illusion that one ascribes one's states of consciousness at all, that there is any proper subject of these apparent ascriptions, that states of consciousness belong to, or are states of, anything.

That Descartes held the first of these views is well enough known. When we speak of a person, we are really referring to one or both of two distinct substances (two substances of different types), each of which has its own appropriate type of states and properties; and none of the properties or states of either can be a property or state of the other. States of consciousness belong to one of these substances, and not to the other. I shall say no more about the Cartesian view at the moment—what I have to say about it will emerge later on—except to note again that while it escapes one of our questions, it does not escape, but indeed invites, the other: "Why are one's states of consciousness *ascribed* at all, to *any* subject?"

The second of these views I shall call the "no-ownership" or "no-subject" doctrine of the self. Whether or not anyone has explicitly held this view, it is worth reconstructing, or constructing, in outline.[1] For the errors into which it falls are instructive. The "no-ownership" theorist may be presumed to start his explanations with facts of the sort which illustrate the unique causal position of a certain material body in a person's experience. The theorist maintains that the uniqueness of this body is sufficient to give rise to the idea that one's experiences can be ascribed to some particular individual thing, can be said to be possessed by, or owned by, that thing. This idea, he thinks, though infelicitously and misleadingly expressed in terms of ownership, would have some validity, would make some sort of sense, so long as we thought of this individual thing, the possessor of the experiences, as the body itself. So long as we thought in this way, then to ascribe a particular state of consciousness to this body, this individual thing, would at least be to say something contingent, something that might be, or might have been, false. It might have been a misascription; for the experience in question might be, or might have been, causally dependent on the state of some other body; in the present admissible, though infelicitous, sense of "belong", it might have belonged to some other individual thing. But now, the theorist

[1] The evidence that Wittgenstein at one time held such a view is to be found in the third of Moore's articles in *Mind* on "Wittgenstein's Lectures in 1930–33" (*Mind*, 1955, especially pp. 13–14) [See Selection V in this anthology especially pp. 122–124—*Ed*]. He reportedly held t' the use of "I" was utterly different in the case of "I have a tooth-ache" or "I see a red patch" om its use in the case of "I've got a bad tooth" or "I've got a matchbox." He thought that there were two uses of "I" and that in one of them "I" was replaceable by "this body". So far the view might be Cartesian. But he also said that in the other use (the use exemplified by "I have a tooth-ache" as opposed to "I have a bad tooth"), the "I" *does not denote a possessor*, and that no ego is involved in thinking or in having tooth-ache; and referred with apparent approval to Lichtenberg's dictum that, instead of saying "I think," we (or Descartes!) ought to say "There is a thought" (i.e., "Es denkt").

The attribution of such a view to Schlick would have to rest on his article "Meaning and Verification," Pt. V (*Readings in Philosophical Analysis*, H. Feigl and W. Sellars, eds.). Like Wittgenstein, Schlick quotes Lichtenberg, and then goes on to say: "Thus we see that unless we choose to call our body the owner or bearer of the data [the data of immediate experience]— which seems to be a rather misleading expression—we have to say that the data have no owner or bearer." The full import of Schlick's article is, however, obscure to me, and it is quite likely that a false impression is given by the quotation of a single sentence. I shall say merely that I have drawn on Schlick's article in constructing the case of my hypothetical "no-subject" theorist; but shall not claim to be representing his views.

Lichtenberg's anti-Cartesian dictum is, as the subsequent argument will show, one that I endorse, if properly used. But it seems to have been repeated, without being understood, by many of Descartes' critics.

The evidence that Wittgenstein and Schlick ever held a "no-subject" view seems indecisive, since it is possible that the relevant remarks are intended as criticisms of a Cartesian view rather than as expositions of the true view.

suggests, one becomes confused: one slides from this admissible, though infelicitous, sense in which one's experiences may be said to belong to, or be possessed by, some particular thing, to a wholly inadmissible and empty sense of these expressions; and in this new inadmissible sense, the particular thing which is supposed to possess the experiences is not thought of as a body, but as something else, say an ego.

Suppose we call the first type of possession, which is really a certain kind of causal dependence, "having$_1$", and the second type of possession, "having$_2$"; and call the individual of the first type "B" and the supposed individual of the second type "E". Then the difference is that while it is genuinely a contingent matter that *all my experiences are had$_1$ by B*, it appears as a necessary truth that *all my experiences are had$_2$ by E*. But the belief in E and in having$_2$ is an illusion. Only those things whose ownership is logically transferable can be owned at all. So experiences are not owned by anything except in the dubious sense of being causally dependent on the state of a particular body. This is at least a genuine relationship to a thing, in that they might have stood in it to another thing. Since the whole function of E was to own experiences in a logically non-transferable sense of "own", and since experiences are not owned by anything in this sense, for there is no such sense of "own", E must be eliminated from the picture altogether. It only came in because of a confusion.

I think it must be clear that this account of the matter, though it contains *some* of the facts, is not coherent. It is not coherent, in that one who holds it is forced to make use of that sense of possession of which he denies the existence, in presenting his case for the denial. When he tries to state the contingent fact, which he thinks gives rise to the illusion of the "ego," he has to state it in some such form as "All *my* experiences are had$_1$ by (uniquely dependent on the state of) body B." For any attempt to eliminate the "my", or some other expression with a similar possessive force, would yield something that was not a contingent fact at all. The proposition that *all* experiences are causally dependent on the state of a single body B, for example, is just false. The theorist means to speak of all the experiences *had by a certain person* being contingently so dependent. And the theorist cannot consistently argue that "all the experiences of person P" *means the same thing* as "all experiences contingently dependent on a certain body B"; for then his proposition would not be contingent, as his theory requires, but analytic. He must mean to be speaking of some class of experiences of the members of which it is in fact contingently true that they are all dependent on body B. And the defining characteristic of this class is in fact that they are "*my* experiences" or "the experiences *of* some person," where the sense of "possession" is the one he calls into question.

This internal incoherence is a serious matter when it is a question of denying what prima facie is the case: that is, that one does genuinely ascribe one's states of consciousness to something, viz., oneself, and that this kind of ascription is precisely such as the theorist finds unsatisfactory, i.e., is such that it does not seem to make sense to suggest, for example, that the identical pain which was in fact one's own might have been another's. We do not have to seek far in order to understand the place of this logically non-transferable kind of ownership in our general scheme of thought. For if we think of the requirements of identifying reference, in speech, to *particular* states of consciousness, or private experiences, we see that such particulars cannot be thus identifyingly referred to except as the states or experiences *of* some identified *person*. States, or experiences, one might say, *owe* their identity as particulars to the identity of the person whose states or experiences they are. And from this it follows immediately that if they can be identified as particular states or experiences at all, they must be possessed or ascribable in just that way which the no-ownership theorist ridicules, i.e., in such a way that it is logically impossible that a particular state or experience in fact possessed by someone should have been possessed by anyone else. The requirements of identity rule out logical transferability of ownership. So the theorist could maintain his position only by denying that we could ever refer to particular states or experiences at all. And *this* position is ridiculous.

We may notice, even now, a possible connection between the no-ownership doctrine and the Cartesian position. The latter is, straight-forwardly enough, a dualism of two subjects (two types of subject). The former could, a little paradoxically, be called a dualism too: a dualism of one subject (the body) and one non-subject. We might surmise that the second dualism, para-doxically so called, arises out of the first dualism, nonpara-doxically so called; in other words, that if we try to think of that to which one's states of consciousness are ascribed as something utterly different from that to which certain corporeal characteristics are ascribed, then indeed it becomes difficult to see why states of consciousness should be ascribed, thought of as belonging to, anything at all. And when we think of this pos-sibility, we may also think of another: viz., that both the Cartesian and the no-ownership theorist are profoundly wrong in holding, as each must, that there are two uses of "I" in one of which it denotes something which it does not denote in the other.

III

The no-ownership theorist fails to take account of all the facts. He takes account of some of them. He implies, correctly, that the unique position or role of a single body in one's experience is not a sufficient explanation of the fact that one's experiences, or states of consciousness, are ascribed to something which *has* them, with that peculiar nontransferable kind of possession which is here in question. It may be a necessary part of the explanation, but it is not, by itself, a sufficient explanation. The theorist, as we have seen, goes on to suggest that it is perhaps a sufficient explanation of something else: viz., of our confusedly and mistakenly *thinking* that states of consciousness are to be ascribed to something in this special way. And this suggestion, as we have seen, is incoherent: for it involves the denial that someone's states of consciousness are anyone's. We avoid the incoherence of this denial, while agreeing that the special role

of a single body in someone's experience does not suffice to
explain why that experience should be ascribed to anybody. The
fact that there is this special role does not, by itself, give a
sufficient reason why what we think of as a subject of experience
should have any use for the conception of himself as such a
subject.

When I say that the no-ownership theorist's account fails
through not reckoning with all the facts, I have in mind a very
simple but, in this question, a very central, thought: viz., that
it is a necessary condition of one's ascribing states of consciousness, experiences, to oneself, in the way one does, that one should
also ascribe them (or be prepared to ascribe them) to others
who are not oneself.[2] This means not less than it says. It means,
for example, that the ascribing phrases should be used in just
the same sense when the subject is another, as when the subject
is oneself. Of course the thought that this is so gives no trouble
to the non-philosopher: the thought, for example, that "in
pain" means the same whether one says "I am in pain" or "He
is in pain." The dictionaries do not give two sets of meanings
for every expression which describes a state of consciousness: a
first-person meaning, and a second- and third-person meaning.
But to the philosopher this thought has given trouble; indeed it
has. How could the sense be the same when the method of verification was so different in the two cases—or, rather, when there

---

[2] I can imagine an objection to the unqualified form of this statement, an objection which might
be put as follows. Surely the idea of a uniquely applicable predicate (a predicate which *in fact*
belongs to only one individual) is not absurd. And, if it is not, then surely the most that can be
claimed is that a necessary condition of one's ascribing predicates of a certain class to one
individual (oneself) is that one should be prepared, or ready, on appropriate occasions, to ascribe
them to other individuals, and hence that one should have a conception of what those appropriate
occasions for ascribing them would be; but not, necessarily, that one should actually do so on any
occasion.

The shortest way with the objection is to admit it, or at least to refrain from disputing it; for
the lesser claim is all that the argument strictly requires, though it is slightly simpler to conduct
it on the basis of the larger claim. But it is well to point out further that we are not speaking of a
single predicate, or merely of some group or other of predicates, but of the whole of an enormous
class of predicates such that the applicability of those predicates or their negations determines a
major logical type of category of individuals. To insist, at this level, on the distinction between the
lesser and the larger claims is to carry the distinction over from a level at which it is clearly
correct to a level at which it may well appear idle or, possibly, senseless.

The main point here is a purely logical one: the idea of a predicate is correlative with that
of a range of distinguishable individuals of which the predicate can be significantly, though not
necessarily truly, affirmed.

was a method of verification in the one case (the case of others) and not, properly speaking, in the other case (the case of one-self)? Or, again, how can it be right to talk of *ascribing* in the case of oneself? For surely there can be a question of ascribing only if there is or could be a question of identifying that to which the ascription is made? And though there may be a question of identifying the one who is in pain when that one is another, how can there be such a question when that one is oneself? But this last query answers itself as soon as we remember that we speak primarily to others, for the information of others. In one sense, indeed, there is no question of my having to *tell who it is* who is in pain, when I am. In another sense I may have to *tell who it is*, i.e., to let others know who it is.

What I have just said explains, perhaps, how one may properly be said to ascribe states of consciousness to oneself, given that one ascribes them to others. But how is it that one can ascribe them to others? Well, one thing is certain: that *if* the things one ascribes states of consciousness to, in ascribing them to others, are thought of as a set of Cartesian egos to which *only* private experiences can, in correct logical grammar, be ascribed, *then* this question is unanswerable and this problem insoluble. If, in identifying the things to which states of consciousness are to be ascribed, private experiences are to be all one has to go on, then, just for the very same reason as that for which there is, from one's own point of view, no question of telling that a private experience is one's own, there is also no question of telling that a private experience is another's. All private experiences, all states of consciousness, will be mine, i.e., no one's. To put it briefly: one can ascribe states of consciousness to oneself only if one can ascribe them to others; one can ascribe them to others only if one can identify other subjects of experience; and one cannot identify others if one can identify them *only* as subjects of experience, possessors of states of consciousness.

It might be objected that this way with Cartesianism is too short. After all, there is no difficulty about distinguishing bodies from one another, no difficulty about identifying bodies. And does not this give us an indirect way of identifying subjects of experience, while preserving the Cartesian mode? Can we not identify such a subject as, for example, "the subject that stands to that body in the same special relation as I stand to this one"; or, in other words, "the subject of those experiences which stand in the same unique causal relation to body N as *my* experiences stand to body M"? But this suggestion is useless. It requires me to have noted that *my* experiences stand in a special relation to body M, when it is just the right to speak of *my* experiences at all that is in question. (It requires me to have noted that *my* experiences stand in a special relation to body M; but it requires me to have noted this as a condition of being able to identify other subjects of experience, i.e., as a condition of having the idea of myself as a subject of experience, i.e., as a condition of thinking of any experience as *mine*.) So long as we persist in talking, in the mode of this explanation, of experiences on the one hand, and bodies on the other, the most I may be allowed to have noted is that experiences, *all* experiences, stand in a special relation to body M, that body M is unique in just this way, that this is what makes body M unique among bodies. (This "most" is, perhaps, too much—because of the presence of the word "experiences".) The proffered explanation runs: "Another subject of experience is distinguished and identified as the subject of those experiences which stand in the same unique causal relationship to body N as *my* experiences stand to body M." And the objection is: "But what is the word 'my' doing in this explanation? (It could not get on without it.)"

What we have to acknowledge, in order to begin to free ourselves from these difficulties, is the *primitiveness* of the concept of a person. What I mean by the concept of a person is the concept of a type of entity such that *both* predicates ascribing states of consciousness *and* predicates ascribing corporeal characteristcs, a physical situation, etc. are equally applicable to a single individual of that single type. And what I mean by saying that this concept is primitive can be put in a number of ways. One way is to return to those two questions I asked earlier: viz., (1) why are states of consciousness ascribed to anything at all? and (2) why are they ascribed to the very same thing as certain corporeal characteristics, a certain physical situation, etc.? I remarked at the beginning that it was not to be supposed that the answers to these questions were independent of each other. And now I shall say that they are connected in this way: that a necessary condition of states of consciousness being ascribed at all is that they should be ascribed to the *very same things* as certain corporeal characteristics, a certain physical situation, etc. That is to say, states of consciousness could not be ascribed at all, *unless* they were ascribed to persons, in the sense I have claimed for this word. We are tempted to think of a person as a sort of compound of two kinds of subject—a subject of experiences (a pure consciousness, an ego), on the one hand, and a subject of corporeal attributes on the other.

Many questions arise when we think in this way. But, in particular, when we ask ourselves how we come to frame, to get a use for, the concept of this compound of two subjects, the picture—if we are honest and careful—is apt to change from the picture of two subjects to the picture of one subject and one non-subject. For it becomes impossible to see how we could come by the idea of different, distinguishable, identifiable subjects of experiences—different consciousnesses—*if this idea is thought of as logically primitive*, as a logical ingredient in the compound idea of a person, the latter being composed of two subjects. For there could never be any question of assigning an experience, as such, to any subject other than oneself; and therefore never any question of assigning it to oneself either, never any question of ascribing it to a subject at all. So the concept of the pure individual consciousness—the pure ego— is a concept that cannot exist; or, at least, cannot exist as a primary concept in terms of which the concept of a person can be explained or analyzed. It can only exist, if at all, as a secondary, nonprimitive concept, which itself is to be explained, analyzed, in terms of the concept of a person. It was the entity corresponding to this illusory primary concept of the pure consciousness, the ego-substance, for which Hume was seeking, or ironically pretending to seek, when he looked into himself, and complained that he could never discover himself without a perception and could never discover anything but the perception. More seriously—and this time there was no irony, but a confusion, a Nemesis of confusion for Hume—it was this entity of which Hume vainly sought for the principle of unity, confessing himself perplexed and defeated; sought vainly because there is no principle of unity where there is no principle of differentiation. It was this, too, to which Kant, more perspicacious here than Hume, accorded a purely formal ("analytic") unity: the unity of the "I think" that accompanies all my perceptions and therefore might just as well accompany none. And finally it is this, perhaps, of which Wittgenstein spoke when he said of the subject, first, that there is no such thing, and, second, that it is not a part of the world, but its limit.

So, then, the word "I" never refers to this, the pure subject. But this does not mean, as the no-ownership theorist must think and as Wittgenstein, at least at one period, seemed to think, that "I" in some cases does not refer at all. It refers, because I am a person among others. And the predicates which would, *per impossible*, belong to the pure subject if it could be referred to, belong properly to the person to which "I" does refer.

The concept of a person is logically prior to that of an individual consciousness. The concept of a person is not to be analyzed as that of an animated body or of an embodied anima. This is not to say that the concept of a pure individual consciousness might not have a logically secondary existence, if one thinks, or finds, it desirable. We speak of a dead person—a body —and in the same secondary way we might at least think of a disembodied person, retaining the logical benefit of individuality from having been a person.[3]

IV

It is important to realize the full extent of the acknowledgment one is making in acknowledging the logical primitiveness of the concept of a person. Let me rehearse briefly the stages of the

---

[3] A little further thought will show how limited this concession is. But I shall not discuss the question now.

argument. There would be no question of ascribing one's own states of consciousness, or experiences, to anything, unless one also ascribed states of consciousness, or experiences, to other individual entities of the same logical type as that thing to which one ascribes one's own states of consciousness. The condition of reckoning oneself as a subject of such predicates is that one should also reckon others as subjects of such predicates. The condition, in turn, of this being possible, is that one should be able to distinguish from one another (pick out, identify) different subjects of such predicates, i.e., different individuals of the type concerned. And the condition, in turn, of this being possible is that the individuals concerned, including oneself, should be of a certain unique type: of a type, namely, such that to each individual of that type there *must* be ascribed, or ascribable, *both* states of consciousness *and* corporeal characteristics. But this characterization of the type is still very opaque and does not at all clearly bring out what is involved. To bring this out, I must make a rough division, into two, of the kinds of predicates properly applied to individuals of this type. The first kind of predicate consists of those which are also properly applied to material bodies to which we would not dream of applying predicates ascribing states of consciousness. I will call this first kind M-predicates: and they include things like "weighs 10 stone", "is in the drawing room", and so on. The second kind consists of all the other predicates we apply to persons. These I shall call P-predicates. And P-predicates, of course, will be very various. They will include things like "is smiling", "is going for a walk", as well as things like "is in pain", "is thinking hard", "believes in God", and so on.

So far I have said that the concept of a person is to be understood as the concept of a type of entity such that *both* predicates ascribing states of consciousness *and* predicates ascribing corporeal characteristics, a physical situation, etc. are equally applicable to an individual entity of that type. And all I have said about the meaning of saying that this concept is primitive is that it is not to be analyzed in a certain way or ways. We are not, for example, to think of it as a secondary kind of entity in relation to two primary kinds, viz., a particular consciousness and a particular human body. I implied also that the Cartesian error is just a special case of a more general error, present in a different form in theories of the no-ownership type, of thinking of the designations, or apparent designations, of persons as *not* denoting precisely the same thing, or entity, for all kinds of predicate ascribed to the entity designated. That is, if we are to avoid the general form of this error we must *not* think of "I" or "Smith" as suffering from type-ambiguity. (If we want to locate type-ambiguity somewhere, we would do better to locate it in certain predicates like "is in the drawing room", "was hit by a stone", etc., and say they mean one thing when applied to material objects and another when applied to persons.)

This is all I have so far said or implied about the meaning of saying that the concept of a person is primitive. What has to be brought out further is what the implications of saying this are as regards the logical character of those predicates in which we ascribe states of consciousness. And for this purpose we may well consider P-predicates in general. For though not all P-predicates are what we should call "predicates ascribing states of consciousness" (for example, "going for a walk" is not), they may be said to have this in common, that they imply the possession of consciousness on the part of that to which they are ascribed.

What then are the consequences of this view as regards the character of P-predicates? I think they are these. Clearly there is no sense in talking of identifiable individuals of a special type, a type, namely, such that they possess both M-predicates and P-predicates, unless there is in principle some way of telling, with regard to any individual of that type, and any P-predicate, whether that individual possesses that P-predicate. And, in the case of at least some P-predicates, the ways of telling must constitute in some sense logically adequate kinds of criteria for the ascription of the P-predicate. For suppose in no case did these ways of telling constitute logically adequate kinds of criteria. Then we should have to think of the relation between the ways of telling and what the P-predicate ascribes (or a part of what it ascribes) always in the following way: we should have to think of the ways of telling as *signs* of the presence, in the individual concerned, of this different thing (the state of consciousness). But then we could only know that the way of telling was a sign of the presence of the different thing ascribed by the P-predicate, by the observation of correlations between the two. But this observation we could each make only in one case, namely, our own. And now we are back in the position of the defender of Cartesianism, who thought our way with it was too short. For what, now, does "our own case" mean? There is no sense in the idea of ascribing states of consciousness to oneself, or at all, unless the ascriber already knows how to ascribe at least some states of consciousness to others. So he cannot (or cannot generally) argue "from his own case" to conclusions about how to do this; for unless he already knows how to do this, he has no conception of *his own case*, or any *case* (i.e., any subject of experiences). Instead, he just has evidence that pain, etc. may be expected when a certain body is affected in certain ways and not when others are.

The conclusion here is, of course, not new. What I have said is that one ascribes P-predicates to others on the strength of observation of their behavior; and that the behavior criteria one goes on are not just signs of the presence of what is meant by the P-predicate, but are criteria of a logically adequate kind for the ascription of the P-predicate. On behalf of this conclusion, however, I am claiming that it follows from a consideration of the conditions necessary for any ascription of states of consciousness to anything. The point is not that we must accept this conclusion in order to avoid skepticism, but that we must accept it in order to explain the existence of the conceptual scheme in terms of which the skeptical problem is stated. But once the conclusion is accepted, the skeptical problem does not arise. (And so with the generality of skeptical problems: their statement involves the pretended acceptance of a conceptual scheme and at the same time the silent repudiation of one of the conditions of its existence. This is why they are, in the terms in which they are stated, insoluble.) But this is only half the picture about P-predicates.

Now let us turn to the other half. For of course it is true, at least of some important classes of P-predicates, that when one ascribes them to oneself, one does not do so on the strength of observation of those behavior criteria on the strength of which one ascribes them to others. This is not true of all P-predicates. It is not, in general, true of those which carry assessments of character and capability: these, when self-ascribed, are in general ascribed on the same kind of basis as that on which they are ascribed to others. And of those P-predicates of which it is true that one does not generally ascribe them to oneself on the basis of the criteria on the strength of which one ascribes them to others, there are many of which it is also true that their ascription is liable to correction by the self-ascriber on this basis. But there remain many cases in which one has an entirely adequate basis for ascribing a P-predicate to oneself, and yet in which this basis is quite distinct from those on which one ascribes the predicate to another. (Thus one says, reporting a present state of mind or feeling: "I feel tired, am depressed, am in pain.") How can this fact be reconciled with the doctrine that the criteria on the strength of which one ascribes P-predicates to others are criteria of a logically adequate kind for this ascription?

The apparent difficulty of bringing about this reconciliation may tempt us in many directions. It may tempt us, for example, to deny that these self-ascriptions are really ascriptions at all; to *assimilate* first-person ascriptions of states of consciousness to those other forms of behavior which constitute criteria on the basis of which one person ascribes P-predicates to another. This device seems to avoid the difficulty; it is not, in all cases, entirely inappropriate. But it obscures the facts, and is needless. It is merely a sophisticated form of failure to recognize the special character of P-predicates (or at least of a crucial class of P-predicates). For just as there is not (in general) one primary process of learning, or teaching oneself, an inner private meaning for predicates of this class, then another process of learning to apply such predicates to others on the strength of a correlation, noted in one's own case, with certain forms of behavior, so—and equally—there is not (in general) one primary process of learning to apply such predicates to others on the strength of behavior criteria, and then another process of acquiring the secondary technique of exhibiting a new form of behavior, viz., first-person P-utterances. Both these pictures are refusals to acknowledge the unique logical character of the predicates concerned.

Suppose we write 'Px' as the general form of propositional function of such a predicate. Then according to the first picture, the expression which primarily replaces "x" in this form is "I", the first-person singular pronoun; its uses with other replacements are secondary, derivative, and shaky. According to the second picture, on the other hand, the primary replacements of "x" in this form are "he", "that person", etc., and its use with "I" is secondary, peculiar, not a true ascriptive use. But it is essential to the character of these predicates that they have both first- and third-person ascriptive uses, that they are both self-ascribable otherwise than on the basis of observation of the behavior of the subject of them, and other-ascribable on the basis of behavior criteria. To learn their use is to learn both aspects of their use. In order to *have* this type of concept, one must be both a self-ascriber and an other-ascriber of such predicates, and must see every other as a self-ascriber. And in order to *understand* this type of concept, one must acknowledge that there is a kind of predicate which is unambiguously and adequately ascribable *both* on the basis of observation of the subject of the predicate *and* not on this basis (independently of observation of the subject): the second case is the case where the ascriber is also the subject. If there were no concepts answering to the characterization I have just given, we should indeed have no philosophical problem about the soul; but equally we should not have *our* concept of a person.

To put the point—with a certain unavoidable crudity—in terms of one particular concept of this class, say, that of depression, we speak of behaving in a depressed way (of depressed behavior) and also of feeling depressed (of a feeling of depression). One is inclined to argue that feelings can be felt, but not observed, and behavior can be observed, but not felt, and that therefore there must be room here to drive in a logical wedge. But the concept of depression spans the place where one wants to drive it in. We might say, in order for there to be such a concept as that of X's depression, the depression which X has, the concept must cover both what is felt, but not observed, by X and what may be observed, but not felt, by others than X (for all values of X). But it is perhaps better to say: X's depression *is* something, one and the same thing, which is felt but not observed by X and observed but not felt by others than X. (And, of course, what can be observed can also be faked or disguised.) To refuse to accept this is to refuse to accept the structure of the language in which we talk about depression. That is, in a sense, all right. One might give up talking; or devise, perhaps, a different structure in terms of which to soliloquize. What is not all right is simultaneously to pretend to accept that structure and to refuse to accept it; i.e., to couch one's rejection in the language of that structure.

It is in this light that we must see some of the familiar philosophical difficulties in the topic of the mind. For some of them spring from just such a failure to admit, or fully appreciate, the character which I have been claiming for at least some P-predicates. It is not seen that these predicates could not have either aspect of their use (the self-ascriptive and the non-self-ascriptive) without having the other aspect. Instead, one aspect of their use is taken as self-sufficient, which it could not be, and then the other aspect appears as problematical. And so we oscillate between philosophical skepticism and philosophical behaviorism. When we take the self-ascriptive aspect of the use of some P-predicates (say, "depressed") as primary, then a logical gap seems to open between the criteria on the strength of which we say that another is depressed, and the actual state of depression. What we do not realize is that if this logical gap is allowed to open, then it swallows not only his depression, but our depression as well. For if the logical gap exists, then depressed behavior, however much there is of it, is no more than a sign of depression. And it can become a sign of depression only because of an observed correlation between it and depression. But whose depression? Only mine, one is tempted to say. But if *only* mine, then *not* mine at all. The skeptical position customarily represents the crossing of the logical gap as at best a shaky inference. But the point is that not even the syntax of the premises of the inference exists if the gap exists.

If, on the other hand, we take the other-ascriptive uses of these predicates as self-sufficient, we may come to think that all there is in the meaning of these predicates, as predicates, is the criteria on the strength of which we ascribe them to others. Does this not follow from the denial of the logical gap? It does not follow. To think that it does is to forget the self-ascriptive use of these predicates, to forget that we have to do with a class of predicates to the meaning of which it is essential that they should be both self-ascribable and other-ascribable to the same individual, when self-ascriptions are not made on the observational basis on which other-ascriptions are made, but on another basis. It is not that these predicates have two kinds of meaning. Rather, it is essential to the single kind of meaning that they do have that both ways of ascribing them should be perfectly in order.

If one is playing a game of cards, the distinctive markings of a certain card constitute a logically adequate criterion for calling it, say, the Queen of Hearts; but, in calling it this, in the context of the game, one is also ascribing to it properties over and above the possession of those markings. The predicate gets its meaning from the whole structure of the game. So it is with the language which ascribes P-predicates. To say that the criteria on the strength of which we ascribe P-predicates to others are of a logically adequate kind for this ascription is not to say that all there is to the ascriptive meaning of these predicates is these criteria. To say this is to forget that they are P-predicates, to forget the rest of the language-structure to which they belong.

V

Now our perplexities may take a different form, the form of the question "But how can one ascribe to oneself, not on the basis of observation, *the very same thing* that others may have, on the basis of observation, a logically adequate reason for ascribing to one?" And this question may be absorbed in a wider one, which might be phrased: "How are P-predicates possible?" or "How is the concept of a person possible?" This is the question by which we replace those two earlier questions, viz.: "Why are states of consciousness ascribed at all, ascribed to anything?" and "Why are they ascribed to the very same thing as certain corporeal characteristics, etc.?" For the answer to these two initial questions is to be found nowhere else but in the admission of the primitiveness of the concept of a person, and hence of the unique character of P-predicates. So residual perplexities have to frame themselves in this new way. For when we have acknowledged the primitiveness of the concept of a person and, with it, the unique character of P-predicates, we may still want to ask what it is in the natural facts that makes it intelligible that we should have this concept, and to ask this in the hope of a non-trivial answer.[4] I do not pretend to be able to satisfy this demand at all fully. But I may mention two very different things which might count as beginnings or fragments of an answer.

And, first, I think a beginning can be made by moving a certain class of P-predicates to a central position in the picture. They are predicates, roughly, which involve doing something, which clearly imply intention or a state of mind or at least consciousness in general, and which indicate a characteristic pattern, or range of patterns, of bodily movement, while not indicating at all precisely any very definite sensation or experience. I mean such things as "going for a walk", "furling a rope", "playing ball", "writing a letter". Such predicates have the interesting characteristic of many P-predicates that one does not, in general, ascribe them to oneself on the strength of observa-

---

[4] I mean, in the hope of an answer which does not *merely* say: Well, there are people in the world.

tion, whereas one does ascribe them to others on the strength of observation. But, in the case of these predicates, one feels minimal reluctance to concede that what is ascribed in these two different ways is the same. And this is because of the marked dominance of a fairly definite pattern of bodily movement in what they ascribe, and the marked absence of any distinctive experience. They release us from the idea that the only things we can know about without observation, or inference, or both, are private experiences; we can know also, without telling by either of these means, about the present and future movements of a body. Yet bodily movements are certainly also things we can know about by observation and inference.

Among the things that we observe, as opposed to the things we know without observation, are the movements of bodies similar to that about which we have knowledge not based on observation. It is important that we understand such observed movements; they bear on and condition our own. And in fact we understand them, we interpret them, only by seeing them as elements in just such plans or schemes of action as those of which we know the present course and future development without observation of the relevant present movements. But this is to say that we see such movements (the observed movements of others) as *actions*, that we interpret them in terms of intention, that we see them as movements of individuals of a type to which also belongs that individual whose present and future movements we know about without observation; that we see others, as self-ascribers, not on the basis of observations, of what we ascribe to them on this basis.

Of course these remarks are not intended to suggest how the "problem of other minds" could be solved, or our beliefs about others given a general philosophical "justification." I have already argued that such a "solution" or "justification" is impossible, that the demand for it cannot be coherently stated. Nor are these remarks intended as a priori genetic psychology. They are simply intended to help to make it seem intelligible to us, at this stage in the history of the philosophy of this subject, that we have the conceptual scheme we have. What I am suggesting is that it is easier to understand how we can see each other (and ourselves) as persons, if we think first of the fact that we act, and act on each other, and act in accordance with a common human nature. "To see each other as persons" is a lot of things; but not a lot of separate and unconnected things. The class of P-predicates that I have moved into the center of the picture are not unconnectedly there, detached from others irrelevant to them. On the contrary, they are inextricably bound up with the others, interwoven with them. The topic of the mind does not divide into unconnected subjects.

I spoke just now of a common human nature. But there is also a sense in which a condition of the existence of the conceptual scheme we have is that human nature should not be common, should not be, that is, a community nature. Philosophers used to discuss the question of whether there was, or could be, such a thing as a "group mind." And for some the idea had a peculiar fascination, while to others it seemed utterly absurd and nonsensical and at the same time, curiously enough, pernicious. It is easy to see why these last found it pernicious: they found something horrible in the thought that people should cease to have toward individual persons the kind of attitudes that they did have, and instead have attitudes in some way analogous to those toward groups; and that they might cease to decide individual courses of action for themselves and instead merely participate in corporate activities. But their finding it pernicious showed that they understood the idea they claimed to be absurd only too well. The fact that we find it natural to individuate as persons the members of a certain class of what might also be individuated as organic bodies does not mean that such a conceptual scheme is inevitable for any class of beings not utterly unlike ourselves.

Might we not construct the idea of a special kind of social world in which the concept of an individual person has no employment, whereas an analogous concept for groups does have employment? Think, to begin with, of certain aspects of actual human existence. Think, for example, of two groups of human beings engaged in some competitive but corporate activity, such as battle, for which they have been exceedingly well trained. We may even suppose that orders are superfluous, though information is passed. It is easy to imagine that, while absorbed in such activity, the members of the groups make no references to individual persons at all, have no use for personal names or pronouns. They do, however, refer to the groups and apply to them predicates analogous to those predicates ascribing purposive activity which we normally apply to individual persons. They may, *in fact*, use in such circumstances the plural forms "we" and "they"; but these are not genuine plurals, they are plurals without a singular, such as we use in sentences like these: "We have taken the citadel," "We have lost the game." They may also refer to elements in the group, to members of the group, but exclusively in terms which get their sense from the parts played by these elements in the corporate activity. (Thus we sometimes refer to what are in fact persons as "stroke" or "tackle".)

When we think of such cases, we see that we ourselves, over a part of our social lives—not, I am thankful to say, a very large part—do operate conceptual schemes in which the idea of the individual person has no place, in which its place is taken, so to speak, by that of a group. But might we not think of communities or groups such that this part of the lives of their members was the dominant part—or was the whole? It sometimes happens, with groups of human beings, that, as *we* say, their members think, feel, and act "as one." The point I wish to make is that a condition for the existence, the use, of the concept of an individual person is that this should happen *only sometimes*.

It is absolutely useless to say, at this point: But all the same, even if this happened all the time, every member of the group would have an individual consciousness, would be an individual subject of experience. The point is, once more, that there is no sense in speaking of the individual consciousness just as such, of the individual subject of experience just as such: for there is no way of identifying such pure entities.[5] It is true, of course, that in suggesting this fantasy, I have taken our concept of an in-

---

[5] More accurately: their identification is necessarily secondary to the identification of persons.

dividual person as a starting point. It is this fact which makes
the useless reaction a natural one. But suppose, instead, I had
made the following suggestion: that each part of the human
body, each organ and each member, had an individual consciousness, was a separate center of experiences. This, in the same
way, but more obviously, would be a useless suggestion. Then
imagine all the intermediate cases, for instance these. There is
a class of moving natural objects, divided into groups, each
group exhibiting the same characteristic pattern of activity.
Within each group there are certain differentiations of appearance accompanying differentiations of function, and in particular there is one member of each group with a distinctive
appearance. Cannot one imagine different sets of observations
which might lead us, in the one case, to think of the particular
member as the spokesman of the group, as its mouthpiece; and
in the other case to think of him as its mouth, to think of the
group as a single *scattered* body? The point is that as soon as
we adopt the latter way of thinking then we want to drop the
former; we are no longer influenced by the human analogy in
its first form, but only in its second; and we no longer want to
say: "Perhaps the members have consciousness." To understand
the movement of our thought here, we need only remember the
startling ambiguity of the phrase "a body and its members".

VI

I shall not pursue this attempt at explanation any further. What
I have been mainly arguing for is that we should acknowledge
the logical primitiveness of the concept of a person and, with
this, the unique logical character of certain predicates. Once
this is acknowledged, certain traditional philosophical problems are seen not to be problems at all. In particular, the
problem that seems to have perplexed Hume [6] does not exist—
the problem of the principle of unity, of identity, of the particular consciousness, of the particular subject of "perceptions"
(experiences) considered as a primary particular. There is no
such problem and no such principle. If there were such a prin-

[6] Cf. the Appendix to the *Treatise of Human Nature.*

ciple, then each of us would have to apply it in order to decide whether any contemporary experience of his was his or someone else's; and there is no sense in this suggestion. (This is not to deny, of course, that one *person* may be unsure of his own identity in some way, may be unsure, for example, whether some particular action, or series of actions, had been performed by him. Then he uses the same methods (the same in principle) to resolve the doubt about himself as anyone else uses to resolve the same doubt about him. And these methods simply involve the application of the ordinary criteria for *personal* identity. There remains the question of what exactly these criteria are, what their relative weights are, etc.; but, once disentangled from spurious questions, this is one of the easier problems in philosophy.)

Where Hume erred, or seems to have erred, both Kant and Wittgenstein had the better insight. Perhaps neither always expressed it in the happiest way. For Kant's doctrine that the "analytic unity of consciousness" neither requires nor entails any principle of unity is not as clear as one could wish. And Wittgenstein's remarks (at one time) to the effect that the data of consciousness are not owned, that "I" as used by Jones, in speaking of his own feelings, etc., does not refer to what "Jones" as used by another refers to, seem needlessly to flout the conceptual scheme we actually employ. It is needlessly paradoxical to deny, or seem to deny, that when Smith says "Jones has a pain" and Jones says "I have a pain," they are talking about the same entity and saying the same thing about it, needlessly paradoxical to deny that Jones can *confirm* that he has a pain. Instead of denying that self-ascribed states of consciousness are really ascribed at all, it is more in harmony with our actual ways of talking to say: For each user of the language, there is just one person in ascribing to whom states of consciousness he does not need to use the criteria of the observed behavior of that person (though he does not necessarily not do so); and that person is himself. This remark at least respects the structure of the conceptual scheme we employ, without precluding further examination of it.

VII

Wittgenstein's Conception of a Criterion

Carl Wellman

ONE OF THE KEY words in the vocabulary of Ludwig Wittgenstein is "criterion." He gives this word a somewhat different meaning from that which is usual in ordinary philosophical discourse, although his special use is obviously derived from everyday usage. His conception of a criterion is the pivot upon which turn his theory of the nature of descriptive language, his claim that certain seeming assertions are meaningless, his view of the nature of philosophical questions, and his rejection of the view that empirical knowledge rests ultimately upon private sensations. Obviously, one cannot really understand the philosophy of Wittgenstein until one has grasped the special sense in which he uses the term "criterion." In addition, many of the philosophers who have been influenced by him have adopted and extended his use of the term. Thus it is doubly important that his conception of a criterion be clearly understood.

There have been at least two attempts to explain this conception, each helpful in its own way. Norman Malcolm indicates clearly the core of this conception.[1] Unfortunately, he is so faithful to the language of Wittgenstein that he leaves obscure exactly what is obscure in the original. Rogers Albritton does not hesitate to torture the original language in an effort to translate its meaning into more precise terms.[2] In this process of translation, however, he loses sight of the fundamental unity in Wittgenstein's view. Therefore, I should like to make a third attempt at explanation which will, I hope, clarify a little more than Malcolm's and torture a little less than Albritton's.

Wittgenstein's writings have a tendency to be as difficult to interpret as they are suggestive to read. Even a careful study of the passages in which the term "criterion" occurs leaves his conception rather obscure. Because of his style of philosophical writing, grasping his conception is very much like putting together a jigsaw puzzle; one must collect his scattered remarks and fit them together to reconstruct his view. Let me try to arrange the pieces of this puzzle in a manner which, to me at least, presents a fairly clear picture of what Wittgenstein means. For the convenience of the reader I have given each "piece" a number.

1. The term "criterion" is a relative one in the sense that a criterion is always a criterion *for* something. What is this something for which Wittgenstein is seeking a criterion? In various places he writes as though a criterion were a criterion for an expression, for the use of an expression, for something being the case, for a state of affairs, or for a class or characteristic.[3] It is quite in the idiom of Wittgenstein to speak of the criterion (1) for "He has angina," (2) for saying "He has angina," (3) for it being the case that he has angina, (4) for his having angina, or (5) for angina. These various forms of expression are hardly incompatible; in fact, they are clearly correlative ways of saying the same thing. Let us try to find a single formulation which will

---

[1] "Wittgenstein's *Philosophical Investigations*," *Philosophical Review*, LXIII (1954), 530–559. [See Selection II in this anthology.—*Ed.*]

[2] "On Wittgenstein's Use of the Term 'Criterion,'" *Journal of Philosophy*, LVI (1959), 845–857.

[3] Ludwig Wittgenstein, *The Blue and Brown Books* (Oxford, 1958), pp. 104, 138, 24, 185, 61.

make sense of all these ways of speaking of a criterion. A criterion may be said to be a criterion for a linguistic expression fitting its object. By an object I do not necessarily mean a physical object, but whatever the expression refers to, is applied to, or is about. By fitting I mean is true of or applied to, but in a very special way. An expression fits an object when it is linguistically, rather than factually, correct to apply it to that object. There is a difference between saying "It is an *X*" on the grounds that this is what we mean by the term "*X*" and on the grounds that there is empirical evidence for its being an *X*.

2. A criterion is always a criterion for a linguistic expression fitting its object. In all the passages with which I am familiar the expression that Wittgenstein has in mind is, or could be interpreted to be, a descriptive one. It is probably no accident that Wittgenstein developed his conception of a criterion in connection with descriptive language, for one leads naturally to the other.

3. To describe something is to specify what it is like and what it is unlike. In this sense descriptive terms are always used to classify or to divide things into kinds.[4] This seems to imply that to use descriptive language a person must be able to distinguish between the different kinds of things. Unless a person were able to recognize members of a given class, he could hardly use the class name very effectively. To be able to use or understand descriptions one must be able to tell which objects fit a given description and which descriptive expressions fit a given object. But how does one know whether or not a specified description fits a given object? This is the question which Wittgenstein's conception of a criterion is intended to answer.

4. Let us take a special case of this problem. Suppose that I am given a descriptive expression and asked to find an object which fits it. I am, perhaps, told to go to the store and buy a lemon. But how can I recognize a lemon when I find one? I go to the store, look over the various objects which I find there, and sooner or later pick up a lemon. But how could I tell which object to pick up? How did I know that this object in my hand

[4] *Ibid.*, pp. 159–160.

was a lemon? By observing certain characteristics of it.[5] I noticed
that it was greenish-yellow, waxy, ovoid, smallish, and so forth.
These observable characteristics by which one identifies an object
as an instance of some descriptive expression are what Wittgenstein calls "criteria."

5.   But surely, one is tempted to reply, these cannot be the real
criteria. There must be more to recognizing an X than just
noticing one or more characteristics of it. How does one know
that he has recognized these characteristics correctly? How can
one be sure that what seems to him to be lemon yellow is not
really apple green? One must have some criterion in his mind,
perhaps an image or concept, which he compares with what he
observes in the object. But, Wittgenstein asks, do you always
find this mental picture when you introspect? [6] Do you need
another mental picture to recognize the agreement of this first
mental picture with the observed characteristic in the object?
And how do you know that you have called to mind the right
mental picture? [7] No mental picture, whether image or concept,
could serve as our ultimate criterion of whether a descriptive
expression fits an object.

6.   Granted that we do not relate the word to the observable
characteristics in the object through some mediating mental
picture, how is the word related to the object? Not by some
mysterious single relation of word meaning object, but by all the
particular connections which exist within the actual activities of
using the word in our language.[8] For example, when one first
learned the use of the word "lemon," the characteristic color,
texture, shape, and size of lemons were pointed out. When one
later called an orange a "lemon," the fact that this object was not
greenish-yellow or ovoid was mentioned pointedly. And in the
everyday activities of ordering lemons from the store, asking for
lemon in one's tea, and declining a second helping of lemon
meringue pie the word "lemon" continues to be used in situations

[5] *Ibid.*, pp. 182–183.
[6] *Ibid.*, p. 165.
[7] *Ibid.*, p. 3.
[8] *Ibid.*, pp. 172–173.

involving greenish-yellow, waxy, ovoid, smallish objects. All of
these various connections make up the meaning relation between
word and object.

7.   It follows that a descriptive term has no meaning at all
until it is connected with certain observable characteristics of the
objects to which it is intended to apply.[9] The term is then used
to stand for or refer to these observable characteristics, and they
serve as criteria for its use. Therefore, anyone who does not know
the criteria for the use of a descriptive expression literally does
not understand its meaning. Correspondingly to give the criteria
for the use of an expression is to give an explanation of that
expression's meaning.[10] Thus the criteria for the use of a descriptive expression are central to its meaning and would be mentioned in any definition of that expression.

8.   As a result, one can justify his use of a descriptive expression by means of the criteria for its application.[11] On my return
from the store I hand my wife an object and say "Here is the
lemon you wanted." Let us imagine that my wife inspects the
object skeptically and asks "What reason do you have to call this
a lemon?" I can reply by pointing to its greenish-yellow color,
its smallish size, its waxy texture, and its ovoid shape. Since the
word "lemon" is used to refer to objects with these characteristics, their presence in something constitutes a justification for
applying the term to that object. This kind of justification
appeals to the meaning of an expression, to its definition, or to a
convention.

9.   When one gets down to convention, one strikes bedrock.
Suppose my wife asks "But how do you know that that color
which we both observe is really greenish-yellow?" No further
reply is possible.[12] However, many philosophers insist that there
must be a reply. If I cannot justify calling this color "greenish-
yellow," then pointing to this color cannot justify me in calling
the object a "lemon." One is tempted to say that his real reason
for calling the object a "lemon" is not the publicly observable

9 *Ibid.*, pp. 8–9.
10 *Ibid.*, p. 24.
11 *Ibid.*, pp. 24–25.
12 *Ibid.*, p. 24.

color in the object but the greenish-yellow sensation in his mind. But this is no help, for what is one's criterion for the greenish-yellowness of the sensation? The desire to go beyond publicly observable characteristics to private sensation is primarily a reluctance to admit that the chain of reasons comes to an end.[13] As soon as one realizes that this simply postpones the evil day, he sees that this move is pointless. Our ultimate criteria for the use of descriptive language are publicly observable features of the situations in which we use that language.

10.   One must distinguish between the kind of justification we have just been discussing and a quite different kind. Sometimes one justifies a description by giving criteria and sometimes by giving symptoms. Criteria are observable features which are directly connected to an expression by its meaning; symptoms are features which are indirectly connected to the expression by being associated with the criteria in our experience. To justify one's use of a description by giving criteria is to appeal to a convention; to justify one's use of a description by giving symptoms is to appeal to an empirical generalization. These are, of course, learned in very different ways. The convention is learned by training in the use of the word; the empirical generalization is learned by observation and experimentation.[14]

11.   Whereas the connotations of the terms "criterion" and "symptom" are distinct, their denotations are harder to distinguish. Normally we use descriptive expressions without deciding which phenomena are to be taken as criteria and which as symptoms.[15] Nor is there any point in trying to discover which characteristics are really criteria for some specified expression, for expressions have no meaning except that which we have given them.[16] Since there is no sharp line between essential and nonessential characteristics, it is a mistake to look for some essence common to all instances of a term. Instead, a term is usually applied on the basis of many overlapping characteristics

13 *Ibid.*, p. 73.
14 *Ibid.*, pp. 24–25.
15 *Ibid.*, p. 25.
16 *Ibid.*, p. 28.

which form a family likeness.[17] As a rule there is no such thing as *the* criterion for the use of a descriptive expression.

12.   This implies that in justifying the use of an expression by giving its criteria one will normally have to give more than one criterion. Whether or not a word correctly applies will usually depend upon several characteristics which may be present or absent in varying degree. Upon occasion these various criteria may even conflict with one another. Which criteria are relevant to the use of a term on any particular occasion will depend primarily upon the circumstances under which it is to be used. All of this means that the kind of justification which can be given for applying a descriptive expression is much more complicated than appeared at first glance.

13.   There is one piece of the puzzle which does not seem to fit into the picture at all. Suppose that, when asked to pick out something red from a collection of objects presented to him, a person selects a red pencil. How does he know which object to choose? What reason does he have to believe that the word "red" fits the pencil? Wittgenstein seems to say that there is no reason for such a choice.[18]

If Wittgenstein really means what he seems to mean, then his conception of a criterion is indeed a puzzling one. If there is no reason to justify applying the word "red" to a red pencil, then either "red" is not a descriptive expression, or some descriptive expressions have no criteria, or some criteria cannot be used as reasons. It seems hardly likely that Wittgenstein would wish to say that in their ordinary use color words do not describe. It is possible that he would wish to say that there are certain descriptive expressions for which there are no criteria. But to say this would be to admit that criteria are not essential to the descriptive use of language. If some descriptions can be used without criteria, why not all? Certainly one could no longer claim, as Wittgenstein does, that a purported description is really meaningless on the grounds that no criteria have been specified for it.[19] The remain-

---

[17] *Ibid.*, p. 17.
[18] *Ibid.*, pp. 148–149.
[19] *Ibid.*, pp. 8–10.

ing alternative is not much more attractive. Suppose that color words do have criteria but that these cannot be used as reasons to justify the use of these words. Why not? Color words have been connected with their criteria by the same process of learning and repeated use that connect any other words with their criteria. If appealing to these conventions ever constitutes a justification, it should do so here. My conclusion, which I draw with some trepidation, is that Wittgenstein does not really mean what he seems to be saying.

What, then, does he mean? A close rereading of certain passages suggests that we should distinguish between the object and its color.[20] When one predicates a color word of an object, he purports to *describe* the object but to *name* its color. Thus it is possible to justify the application of the word "red" to this pencil simply by pointing to its publicly observable color. What cannot be justified is calling this particular color "red." Here one is simply down to convention, and no mental picture or private sensation can guarantee that one has remembered the convention correctly. This means that one's criterion for the use of a color word is the publicly observable color of the object to which the word is applied but that there is no *further* criterion for whether or not one has correctly connected the color word and its criterion. What Wittgenstein wishes to stress is his belief that the ultimate criteria for our descriptive expressions are always publicly observable characteristics. It is because he is so insistent upon the ultimacy of these criteria that he sometimes seems to be denying their existence.

I have tried to collect and fit together the pieces of this puzzle found in the *Blue and Brown Books.* Can we now see the unity in these fragmentary remarks which makes this conception of a criterion a single picture rather than a patchwork of gay but unrelated colors? I think that we can. From first to last Wittgenstein is concerned with one underlying problem: how does one know whether a descriptive expression fits an object? This general problem takes on various forms under various circumstances. To a person who is given a descriptive expression the

[20] *Ibid.,* pp. 88, 128–129, 148–149.

question is "How can I recognize which objects fit this description?" To a person given an object the question becomes "How can I discover which descriptions are true of this object?" To a person who has applied a descriptive expression to an object the question remains "How can I justify my description?" At bottom, however, these are all forms of the one problem of justifying the claim that the expression fits the object. If I am correct, there is no need to distinguish, as Albritton does, between the conception of a criterion predominant in the *Blue and Brown Books* and another conception in the *Philosophical Investigations*.[21] The notion of justification is central to Wittgenstein's view from the start.

Although I cannot find two distinct conceptions of a criterion in the writings of Wittgenstein, I would like to make a distinction within his single conception. It would be helpful to know which of his remarks simply explicate the special sense he has given to the term "criterion" and which remarks go beyond this meaning. Therefore, I would like to distinguish between Wittgenstein's definition of the term "criterion" and his theory about criteria.

As far as I know, there is no explicit definition of the term "criterion" in any of Wittgenstein's writings; the closest he comes is the passage in which he distinguishes between criteria and symptoms.[22] Let us go beyond this passage to suggest a definition which seems to be implicit in his use of the term throughout his writings: a criterion is a purely linguistic ground for judging that it is or is not correct to apply a given expression to some object.

If this is what one means by a criterion, it is obviously possible to have many different theories about what in fact our criteria are and how they function. Wittgenstein discusses and rejects the views that our criteria are mental pictures or that they are private sensations. His own theory seems to contain at least eight theses. (1) Our ultimate criteria are always publicly observable characteristics of the object to which the expression is applied. (2) Criteria are first connected to the expression by the process

[21] Albritton, *op. cit.*, pp. 854–855.
[22] Wittgenstein, *op. cit.*, pp. 24–25.

of learning its meaning. (3) Expression and criteria continue to
be connected in the everyday activities of using the expression.
(4) It is these connections with its criteria which give the expression its meaning. (5) There is usually no single criterion which
determines the meaning of an expression. (6) The use of an
expression can be justified by pointing to the presence of its
criteria in the object to which it has been applied. (7) In justifying one's use of an expression by pointing to its criteria one is
appealing to a linguistic convention. (8) Beyond this appeal no
further justification is possible or necessary.

Assuming that this is Wittgenstein's conception of a criterion,
what are we to say of it? Many things, no doubt, but let me limit
myself to three critical remarks. First, there is one point on which
Wittgenstein seems to me to be correct. He contends that in most
cases we apply descriptive expressions on the basis of several
criteria which may be present or absent in varying degrees and
no set of which is both necessary and sufficient for the application
of the term. He has argued this point in terms of numerous
examples. In some cases he has attempted to bring out how varied
are the considerations which are relevant to the application of
the word; in other cases he has simply challenged his reader to
indicate anything shared by all the instances where the term can
be correctly applied. Although such a line of argument is not
conclusive, I have found it convincing.

The importance of Wittgenstein's conclusion is obvious, for it
undercuts a very long philosophical tradition. Since the time of
Socrates it has usually been assumed that all the instances of a
descriptive predicate have some one thing in common. This
assumption has been accepted both by those ontologically
oriented philosophers who conceive of philosophy as discovering
the real natures of the basic kinds of entities and by those
analytic philosophers who aim only at stating precisely the
necessary and sufficient conditions for the application of some
linguistic expression. To have challenged this assumption and to
have partially explored an alternative to it is surely a major
contribution to the progress of philosophy.

Second, there is one point on which Wittgenstein is lamentably vague. He does not explain clearly why it is that our use of descriptive predicates presupposes that we have criteria of application. Which aspect of descriptive language is it which requires that we have criteria? Three possible answers suggest themselves at once. (*a*) It might be the classificatory nature of descriptive language which requires criteria. To apply a descriptive expression is to put the object into one class and exclude it from all contrary classes. Thus to call this paper "white" is to compare it with clouds and snow and to contrast it with blood and grass. But how does one know how to classify any given object? If classification is more than sorting at random, one must have certain criteria on the basis of which he distinguishes one kind of thing from another. (*b*) It might be the assertive nature of descriptive language which requires criteria. To utter a description is to make an assertion, to claim that one's utterance is true. But the distinction between truth and falsity presupposes some basis for determining which assertions are correct and which incorrect. Thus asserting necessarily involves certain criteria for the correctness of what is asserted. (*c*) It might be the conventional nature of descriptive language which requires criteria. Any descriptive sentence belongs to some particular language, such as English or Chinese; and every language is governed by certain conventions. To use a descriptive expression correctly one must use it according to the conventions of the language, and to violate those conventions is to misuse the words they govern. This distinction between proper and improper use implies that there are certain criteria for the correct usage of any expression in the language. In my exposition I have emphasized the first of these three possible answers. Unfortunately, Wittgenstein does not distinguish sharply between them or indicate which is involved in his conception of a criterion. Until this confusion is resolved this conception remains unclear and, to that extent, inadequate.

This unclarity becomes crucial as soon as one turns to nondescriptive language. Certain philosophers have adopted (often indirectly, incompletely, and unconsciously) the conception of a criteron Wittgenstein developed in connection with descriptive language and have used it in their analyses of ethical language. For example, R. M. Hare contends that ethical terms are applied on the basis of criteria even though their meaning is not descriptive.[23] Apparently he links the need for criteria to the assertive rather than the classificatory nature of language. But the question remains as to how an expression applied on the basis of criteria can be nondescriptive. Presumably ethical words either have a different kind of criteria from descriptive ones or their criteria control their application in a different way. Hare does not spell out either alternative for us, but it is clear that this vagueness in Wittgenstein's conception must be removed before it can be usefully employed in the analysis of ethical language.

This lack of clarity becomes even more confusing when one turns to what might be called the expressive use of language. Wittgenstein's discussion of this kind of language seems to imply that we do not use expressive sentences on the basis of criteria.[24] Yet it seems clear that even here there are criteria for whether the language has been used correctly.[25] To say "Whoopee" when one wishes to express pain is just as incorrect English as to say "red" when one wishes to describe the midday sky. Possibly Wittgenstein would wish to say that, although there are criteria for whether an expressive sentence has been used correctly, no criteria are involved in using such sentences.[26] In any event, the need for further clarification is obvious.

Third, there is one fundamental point on which Wittgenstein is mistaken. One of his main theses is that our ultimate criteria are *publicly* observable features of the situations in which we use the language. He does not argue for this thesis directly. In fact, it would be inconsistent with his conception of philosophy to consider it a thesis at all; he does not regard it as a theory to be asserted and defended. Instead he is trying to free us from the muddles which he believes arise from the opposite picture of

[23] *The Language of Morals* (Oxford, 1952), ch. vi.
[24] Wittgenstein, *op. cit.*, p. 68.
[25] P. F. Strawson, *"Philosophical Investigations," Mind*, LXIII (1954), 99. [See Selection I in this anthology.—*Ed.*]
[26] Wittgenstein, *op. cit.*, p. 13.

language. Thus his argument consists in trying to show that the view that our criteria are private involves certain fatal confusions.

He considers two forms which this conception of private criteria might take, the view that our ultimate criteria are mental pictures and the view that they are sensations. I have no quarrel with his refutation of the first alternative. It seems to me that he has shown conclusively that, whether or not such mental pictures exist, they are neither the whole nor the final story in our application of descriptive predicates. However, I am not convinced by his attacks on the view that our ultimate criteria are private experiences.

He contends, you will remember, that the desire to go beyond publicly observable characteristics to private sensations is primarily a reluctance to admit that the chain of reasons comes to an end. This move (positing private sensations as our criteria for the application of descriptive predicates to publicly observable characteristics) turns out to be pointless. It is Wittgenstein's view, I am sure, that this move is doubly pointless; nothing is gained and everything is lost. Nothing is gained because the chain of reasons still comes to an end; everything is lost because private sensations cannot serve as reasons at all. Let us consider these claims separately.

It is true that the chain of reasons still comes to an end. The appeal from publicly observable characteristics to private sensations simply adds one more link to the chain. One can now justify his application of the word to the characteristic on the basis of his sensation, but how can he justify his application of the word to his sensation? He cannot. If the purpose of this appeal to sensations is really to avoid the admission that ultimately one must come to a reason which cannot itself be justified, then this move is indeed useless.

However, this is not the real motivation of the move at all. Those who make this move do so because they believe, as does Wittgenstein, that only an observable criterion could be of any use in the application of descriptive predicates and, what Wittgenstein denies, that the only things we can observe directly are private experiences. This assertion that the only things actually given in experience are private sensations is not a gratuitous assumption, but a conclusion indicated by certain facts. (1) People differ in their powers of discrimination. A glaring example is that the color-blind person cannot distinguish between hues which appear quite different to the person with normal vision. It is also well known that as we grow older we find it harder to tell one flavor from another. It might seem that such lack of discrimination exists only in abnormal observers, but psychological experimentation has shown that differences in sensory discrimination are the rule rather than the exception. The obvious explanation is that different people have different experiences when confronted with the same object. (2) This conclusion is re-enforced by what we have learned about the process of perception itself. What one sees when he looks at a printed page, for example, varies with the amount and color of the illumination, the amount of fog or smoke in the air, how long one has been reading, the structure and condition of the eye, general fatigue, emotional blocks, and many other factors as well as what is actually on that page. Thus what one perceives is causally dependent upon the perceiver as well as the object of perception. (3) Another fact which suggests that what is given in experience is not identical with the public object is the existence of perceptual error. Such illusions range all the way from the elaborate mirage sometimes seen in the desert to the everyday experience of feeling that a room is chilly when the thermometer assures one that it is warm as toast. It is difficult to explain such errors on the assumption that we experience the real object as it actually is; however, explanation is easy if one distinguishes between what is actually given in experience and the interpretation put upon that given. (4) There are some experiences, such as dreams and hallucinations, where the object of awareness does not seem to belong to the public world at all. Yet the fact that these private objects are sometimes taken to be real indicates that dreams and hallucinations are not obviously different from ordinary perceptual experiences. Perhaps the content of every experience is a private object and public objects are inferred rather than given. These four sets of facts all suggest that our knowledge of public objects is based upon our private sensations. Thus the view that our basic criteria are private sensations is not simply an attempt to avoid the ultimacy of our ultimate criteria, but an attempt to preserve their observability.

It is equally incorrect to say that everything is lost by this move. Wittgenstein believes that sensations are rendered incapable of serving as criteria because of their privacy. Above all, a criterion is something to which one can appeal to justify his use of a descriptive expression, but sensations cannot be of any use in this process of justification. Obviously I cannot justify to you my use of an expression by appealing to any sensation, for I do not have your sensations and I cannot show you mine. Still, it might be thought that I could use my own sensations to justify my use of the expression to myself. But my sensation is a reason for applying the word "red," for example, only if it is in fact a red rather than a green or yellow sensation. How do I know that I have correctly identified my sensation as red? Since I have no way to check the correctness of my identification, I have no reason to think that the mere presence of the sensation of my experience justifies my use of the word "red."

These two difficulties, the fact that I cannot show my sensation to you and the fact that I cannot check my identification of it, are connected in the mind of Wittgenstein. It is *because* I cannot show my sensation to you that I cannot check my identification. If I could show it to you, I could use your identification to corroborate my own. This reasoning seems to me to put the cart before the horse. One cannot claim that the credibility of the identification depends entirely upon the possibility of corroboration, for of what value is checking one identification against another unless each has some independent credibility? Actually, corroboration is a test of correctness only because the identifications which support one another each have some antecedent claim to correctness. Thus it is the corroboration which depends upon the identification and not vice versa.

Still, one might wonder what reason one has prior to corroboration to trust his identification. Well, why *am* I so sure that I have correctly identified my sensation as red? It is because I am confident that I remember how the word "red" is used. Notice that this is exactly the same reason I might have if I were identifying a publicly observable characteristic as red. Thus the question as to whether identification, public or private, has any claim to validity comes down to the question of the validity of memory. This is a vexing question which I do not propose to discuss here. It is clear, however, that Wittgenstein is faced with an awkward dilemma. Either there is some justification prior to corroboration for trusting one's memory or there is not. If there is, even a private identification has some claim to validity; if there is not, even a public identification has no claim to validity. Therefore, either Wittgenstein's objection to private sensations serving as criteria is mistaken, or his own theory that publicly observable characteristics serve as criteria is inadequate.

VIII

Operationalism and Ordinary Language:
A Critique of Wittgenstein

C. S. Chihara and J. A. Fodor

THIS PAPER EXPLORES some lines of argument in Wittgenstein's post-*Tractatus* writings in order to indicate the relations between Wittgenstein's philosophical psychology on the one hand and his philosophy of language, his epistemology, and his doctrines about the nature of philosophical analysis on the other. We shall hold that the later writings of Wittgenstein express a coherent doctrine in which an operationalistic analysis of confirmation and language supports a philosophical psychology of a type we shall call "logical behaviorism."

We shall also maintain that there are good grounds for re-

This work was supported in part by the U.S. Army, Navy, and Air Force under Contract DA 36–039–AMC–03200(E); in part by the National Science Foundation (Grant GP–2495), the National Institutes of Health (Grant MH–04737–04), the National Aeronautics and Space Administration (Ns G–496), the U.S. Air Force (ESD Contract AF 19 (628)-2487), the National Institute of Mental Health (Grant MPM 17, 760); and, in addition, by a University of California Faculty Fellowship.

In making references to Part I of Ludwig Wittgenstein's *Philosophical Investigations* (New York, 1953), cited here as PI, we shall give section numbers, e.g. (PI, § 13), to Part II, we shall give page numbers, e.g. (PI, p. 220). In referring to his *The Blue and Brown Books* (New York, 1958), cited here as BB, we give page numbers. References to his *Remarks on the Foundations of Mathematics* (New York, 1956), cited here as RFM, will include both part and section numbers, e.g. (RFM, II, § 26).

jecting the philosophical theory implicit in Wittgenstein's other works. In particular we shall first argue that Wittgenstein's position leads to some implausible conclusions concerning the nature of language and psychology; second, we shall maintain that the arguments Wittgenstein provides are inconclusive; and third, we shall try to sketch an alternative position which avoids many of the difficulties implicit in Wittgenstein's philosophy. In exposing and rejecting the operationalism which forms the framework of Wittgenstein's later writings, we do not, however, suppose that we have detracted in any way from the importance of the particular analyses of particular philosophical problems which form their primary content.

I

Among the philosophical problems Wittgenstein attempted to dissolve is the "problem of other minds." One aspect of this hoary problem is the question: What justification, if any, can be given for the claim that one can tell, on the basis of someone's behavior, that he is in a certain mental state? To this question, the sceptic answers: No good justification at all. Among the major motivations of the later Wittgenstein's treatment of philosophical psychology is that of showing that this answer rests on a misconception and is *logically* incoherent.

Characteristically, philosophic sceptics have argued in the following way. It is assumed as a premiss that there are no logical or conceptual relations between propositions about mental states and propositions about behavior in virtue of which propositions asserting that a person behaves in a certain way provide support, grounds, or justification for ascribing the mental states to that person. From this, the sceptic deduces that he has no compelling reason for supposing that any person other than himself is ever truly said to feel pains, draw inferences, have motives, etc. For, while his first-hand knowledge of the occurrence of such mental events is of necessity limited to his own case, it is entailed by the premiss just cited that application of mental predicates to others must depend upon logically fallible inferences. Furthermore, attempts to base such inferences on analogies and correlations fall short of convincing justifications.

Various replies have been made to this argument which do not directly depend upon contesting the truth of the premiss. For example, it is sometimes claimed that, at least in some cases, no *inference* from behavior to mental states is at issue in psychological ascriptions. Thus, we sometimes *see* that someone is in pain, and in these cases, we cannot be properly said to *infer* that he is in pain. However, the sceptic might maintain against this argument that it begs the question. For the essential issue is whether anyone is *justified* in claiming to see that another is in pain. Now a physicist, looking at cloud-chamber tracks, may be justified in claiming to see that a charged particle has passed through the chamber. That is because in this case there is justification for the claim that certain sorts of tracks show the presence and motion of particles. The physicist can explain not only how he is able to detect particles, but also why the methods he uses are methods of detecting *particles.* Correspondingly, the sceptic can argue that what is required in the case of another's pain is some justification for the claim that, by observing a person's behavior, one can *see* that he is in *pain.*

Wittgenstein's way of dealing with the sceptic is to attack his premiss by trying to show that there do exist conceptual relations between statements about behavior and statements about mental events, processes, and states. Hence, Wittgenstein argues that in many cases our knowledge of the mental states of some person rests upon something other than an observed empirical correlation or an analogical argument, viz. a conceptual or linguistic connection.

To hold that the sceptical premiss is false is *ipso facto* to commit oneself to some version of *logical behaviorism* where by "logical behaviorism" we mean the doctrine that there are logical or conceptual relations of the sort denied by the sceptical premiss.[1] Which form of logical behaviorism one holds

[1] Philosophers of Wittgensteinian persuasion have sometimes heatedly denied that the term "behaviorism" is correctly applied to the view that logical connections of the above sort exist. We do not feel that very much hangs on using the term "behaviorism" as we do, but we are prepared to give some justification for our terminology. "Behaviorism" is, in the first instance, a term

depends on the nature of the logical connection one claims obtains. The strongest form maintains that statements about mental states are translatable into statements about behavior. Wittgenstein, we shall argue, adopts a weaker version.

II

It is well known that Wittgenstein thought that philosophical problems generally arise out of misrepresentations and misinterpretations of ordinary language (PI, § 109, § 122, § 194). "Philosophy," he tells us, "is a fight against the fascination which forms of expression exert upon us" (BB, p. 27). Thus, Wittgenstein repeatedly warns us against being misled by superficial similarities between certain forms of expression (BB, p. 16) and tells us that, to avoid philosophical confusions, we must distinguish the "surface grammar" of sentences from their "depth grammar" (PI, § 11, § 664). For example, though the grammar of the sentence "*A* has a gold tooth" seems to differ in no essential respect from that of "*A* has a sore tooth," the apparent similarity masks important conceptual differences (BB, pp. 49, 53; PI, § 288–293). Overlooking these differences leads philosophers to suppose that there is a problem about our knowledge of other minds. It is the task of the Wittgensteinian philosopher to dissolve the problem by obtaining a clear view of the workings of pain language in this and other cases.

The Wittgensteinian method of philosophical therapy involves taking a certain view of language and of meaning. Throughout the *Investigations*, Wittgenstein emphasizes that "the speaking of language is part of an activity" (PI, § 23) and that if we are

---

applied to a school of psychologists whose interest was in placing constraints upon the conceptual equipment that might be employed in putative psychological explanations, but who were *not* particularly interested in the analysis of the mental vocabulary of ordinary language. The application of this label to a philosopher bent upon this latter task must therefore be, to some extent, analogical. Granted that there has been some tendency for the term "behaviorism" to be preempted, even in psychology, for the position held by such *radical* behaviorists as Watson and Skinner, who require that all psychological generalizations be defined over observables, insofar as C. L. Hull can be classified as a behaviorist, there does seem to be grounds for our classification. Hull's view, as we understand it, is that mental predicates are in no sense "eliminable" in favor of behavioral predicates, but that it is a condition upon their coherent employment that they be severally related to behavioral predicates and that some of these relations be logical rather than empirical—a view that is strikingly similar to the one we attribute to Wittgenstein. Cf. C. F. Hull, *Principles of Behavior* (New York, 1943).

to see the radically different roles superficially similar expressions play, we must keep in mind the countless kinds of language-using activities or "language-games" in which we participate (BB, pp. 67–68).

It is clear that Wittgenstein thought that analyzing the meaning of a word involves exhibiting the role or use of the word in the various language-games in which it occurs. He even suggests that we "think of words as instruments characterized by their use . . ." (BB, p. 67).

This notion of analysis leads rather naturally to an operationalistic view of the meaning of certain sorts of predicates. For, in those cases where it makes sense to say of a predicate that one has determined that it applies, one of the central language-games that the fluent speaker has learned to play is that of making and reporting such determinations. Consider, for example, one of the language-games that imparts meaning to such words as "length," i.e., that of reporting the dimensions of physical objects. To describe this game, one would have to include an account of the procedures involved in measuring lengths; indeed, mastering (at least some of) those procedures would be an essential part of learning this game. "The meaning of the word 'length' is learnt among other things, by learning what it is to determine length" (PI, p. 225). As Wittgenstein comments about an analogous case, "Here the teaching of language is not explanation, but training" (PI, § 5). For Wittgenstein, "To understand a sentence means to understand a language." "To understand a language means to be master of a technique" (PI, § 199).

In short, part of being competent in the language-game played with "length" consists in the ability to arrive at the truth of such statements as "x is three feet long" by performing relevant operations with, e.g., rulers, range-finders, etc. A philosophic analysis of "length," insofar as it seeks to articulate the language-game played with that word, must thus refer to the operations which determine the applicability of length predicates. Finally, insofar as the meaning of the word is itself determined by the rules governing the language-games in which it occurs, a reference to these operations will be essential in characterizing the meaning of such predicates as "three feet long." It is in this manner that we are led to the view that the relevant operations for determining the applicability of a predicate are conceptually connected with the predicate.[2]

By parity of reasoning, we can see that to analyze such words as "pain," "motive," "dream," etc., will *inter alia* involve articulating the operations or observations in terms of which we determine that someone is in pain, or that he has such and such a motive, or that he has dreamed, etc. (PI, p. 224). But clearly, such determinations are ultimately made on the basis of the behavior of the individual to whom the predicates are applied (taking behavior in the broad sense in which it includes verbal reports). Hence, for Wittgenstein, reference to the characteristic features of pain behavior on the basis of which we determine that someone is in pain is essential to the philosophical analysis of the word "pain" just as reference to the operations by which we determine the applicability of such predicates as "three feet long" is essential to the philosophical analysis of the word "length." In both cases, the relations are conceptual and the rule of language which articulates them is in that sense a rule of logic.

III

But what, specifically, is this logical connection which, according to Wittgenstein, is supposed to obtain between pain behavior and pain? Obviously, the connection is not that of simple entailment. It is evident that Wittgenstein did not think that some proposition to the effect that a person is screaming, wincing, groaning, or moaning could entail the proposition that the person is in pain. We know that Wittgenstein used the term "criterion" to mark this special connection, but we are in need of an explanation of this term.

We have already remarked that one of the central ideas in

[2] Cf. "Let us consider what we call an 'exact' explanation in contrast with this one. Perhaps something like drawing a chalk line round an area? Here it strikes us at once that the line has breadth. So a color-edge would be more exact. But has this exactness still got a function here: isn't the engine idling? And remember too that we have not yet defined what is to count as overstepping this exact boundary; *how, with what instruments, it is to be established*" (PI, § 88, italics ours). Cf., also RFM, I, § 5.

Wittgenstein's philosophy is that of a "language-game." Apparently Wittgenstein was passing a field on which a football game was being played when the idea occurred to him that "in language we play *games* with *words*." [3] Since this analogy dominated so much of the later Wittgenstein's philosophical thinking, perhaps it would be well to begin the intricate task of explicating Wittgenstein's notion of criterion by considering some specific game.

Take basketball as an example. Since the object of the game is to score more points than one's opponents, there must be some way of telling if and when a team scores. Now there are various ways of telling that, say, a field goal has been scored. One might simply keep one's eyes on the scoreboard and wait for two points to be registered. Sometimes one realizes that a field goal has been scored on the basis of the reactions of the crowd. But these are, at best, indirect ways of telling, for if we use them we are relying on someone else: the score-keeper or other spectators. Obviously, not every way of telling is, in that sense, indirect; and anyone who is at all familiar with the game knows that, generally, one *sees* that a field goal has been scored in seeing the ball shot or tipped through the hoop. And if a philosopher asks, "Why does the fact that the ball went through the basket show that a field goal has been scored?" a natural reply would be, "That is what the rules of the game say; that is the way the game is played." The ball going through the basket satisfies a *criterion* for scoring a field goal.

Notice that though the relation between a criterion and that of which it is a criterion is a logical or conceptual one, the fact that the ball goes through the hoop does not entail that a field goal has been scored. First, the ball must be "in play" for it to be possible to score a field goal by tossing the ball through the basket. Second, even if the ball drops through the hoop when "in play," it need not follow that a field goal has been scored, for the rules of basketball do not cover all imaginable situations. Suppose, for example, that a player takes a long two-handed shot and that the ball suddenly reverses its direction, and after soar-

---

[3] Norman Malcolm, *Ludwig Wittgenstein: a Memoir* (Oxford, 1958), p. 65.

ing and dipping through the air like a swallow in flight, grace-
fully drops through the player's own basket only to change into
a bat, which immediately entangles itself in the net. What do
the rules say about that?

An analogous situation would arise, in the case of a "language-
game," if what seemed to be a chair suddenly disappeared, re-
appeared, and, in general, behaved in a fantastic manner. Wittgenstein's comment on this type of situation is:

> Have you rules ready for such cases—rules saying whether one
> may use the word "chair" to include this kind of thing? But do
> we miss them when we use the word "chair"; and are we to say
> that we do not really attach any meaning to this word, because we
> are not equipped with rules for every possible application of it?
> (PI, § 80)

For Wittgenstein, a sign "is in order—if, under normal circumstances it fulfils its purpose." (PI, § 87).

> It is only in normal cases that the use of a word is clearly pre-
> scribed; we know, are in no doubt, what to say in this or that
> case. The more abnormal the case, the more doubtful it becomes
> what we are to say. (PI, § 142)

Let us now try to make out Wittgenstein's distinction between
criterion and *symptom*, again utilizing the example of basketball. Suppose that, while a game is in progress, a spectator
leaves his seat. Though he is unable to see the playing court, he
might realize that the home team had scored a field goal on the
basis of a symptom—say, the distinctive roar of the crowd—
which he had observed to be correlated with home-team field
goals. This correlation, according to Wittgenstein, would have
to be established *via* criteria, say, by noting the sound of the
cheering when the home team shot the ball through the basket.
Thus, a symptom is "a phenomenon of which experience has
taught us that it coincided, in some way or other, with the phenomenon which is our defining criterion" (BB, p. 25). Though

both symptoms and criteria are cited in answer to the question, "How do you know that so-and-so is the case?" (BB, p. 24), symptoms, unlike criteria, are discovered through experience or observation: that something is a symptom is not given by the rules of the "language-game" (not deducible from the rules alone). However, to say of a statement that it expresses a symptom is to say something about the relation between the statement and the rules, viz., that it is not derivable from them. Hence, Wittgenstein once claimed that "whereas 'When it rains the pavement gets wet' is not a grammatical statement at all, if we say 'The fact that the pavement is wet is a *symptom* that it has been raining' this statement is 'a matter of grammar'." [4] Furthermore, giving the criterion for (e.g.) another's having a toothache "is to give a grammatical explanation about the word 'toothache' and, in this sense, an explanation concerning the meaning of the word 'toothache' " (BB, p. 24). However, given that there is this important difference between criteria and symptoms, the fact remains that Wittgenstein considered both symptoms and criteria as "evidences" (BB, p. 51).

Other salient features of criteria can be illuminated by exploiting our illustrative example. Consider Wittgenstein's claim that "in different circumstances we apply different criteria for a person's reading" (PI, § 164). It is clear that in different circumstances we apply different criteria for a person's scoring a field goal. For example, the question whether a player scored a field goal may arise even though the ball went nowhere near the basket: in a "goal-tending" situation, the question will have to be decided on the basis of whether the ball had started its descent before the defensive player had deflected it. According to the rules it would be a decisive reason for not awarding a field goal that the ball had not reached its apogee when it was blocked.

One can now see that to claim that X is a criterion of Y is not to claim that the presence, occurrence, existence, etc., of X is a necessary condition of the applicability of 'Y', and it is not

---

[4] G. E. Moore, "Wittgenstein's Lectures in 1930–33," *Philosophical Papers* (London, 1959), pp. 266–267.

to claim that the presence, occurrence, existence, etc., of X is a sufficient condition of Y, although if X is a criterion of Y, it may be the case that X is a necessary or a sufficient condition of Y.

Again, consider the tendency of Wittgenstein, noted by Albritton,[5] to write as if X (a criterion of Y) just *is* Y or is what is called 'Y' in certain circumstances. We can understand a philosopher's wanting to say that shooting the ball through the basket in the appropriate situation just *is* scoring a field goal or is what we called "scoring a field goal."

Consider now the following passage from the *Investigations* (§ 376) which suggests a kind of test for "non-criterionhood":

> When I say the ABC to myself, what is the criterion of my doing the same as someone else who silently repeats it to himself? It might be found that the same thing took place in my larynx and in his. (And similarly when we both think of the same thing, wish the same, and so on.) But then did we learn the use of the words: "to say such-and-such to oneself" by someone's pointing to a process in the larynx or the brain?

Obviously not. Hence, Wittgenstein suggests, something taking place in the larynx cannot be the criterion. The rationale behind this "test" seems to be this: For the teaching of a particular predicate 'Y' to be successful, the pupil must learn the rules for the use of 'Y' and hence must learn the criteria for 'Y' if there are such criteria. Thus, if the teaching could be entirely successful without one learning that X is something on the basis of which one tells that 'Y' applies, X cannot be a criterion of Y. For example, since a person could be taught what "field goal" means without learning that one can generally tell that the home team has scored a field goal by noting the roar of the home crowd, the roar of the home crowd cannot be a criterion of field goals.

Finally, let us examine the principle, which Wittgenstein appears to maintain, that any change of criteria of X involves

---

[5] Rogers Albritton, "On Wittgenstein's Use of the Term 'Criterion'," *Journal of Philosophy*, vol. 56 (1959), pp. 851–854.

changing the concept of X. In the *Investigations*, Wittgenstein
makes the puzzling claim:

> There is *one* thing of which one can say neither that it is one
> metre long, nor that it is not one metre long, and that is the stand-
> ard metre in Paris.—But this is, of course, not to ascribe any
> extraordinary property to it, but only to mark its peculiar role in
> the language-game of measuring with a metre-rule.—Let us im-
> agine samples of colour being preserved in Paris like the standard
> metre. We define: "Sepia" means the colour of the standard sepia
> which is there kept hermetically sealed. Then it will make no sense
> to say of this sample either that it is of this colour or that it is
> not. (PI, § 50)

Wittgenstein evidently is maintaining not only that the senses of
the predicates "x is one meter long" and "x is sepia" are given
by the operations which determine the applicability of the respective predicates (the operations of comparing objects in certain ways with the respective standards),[6] but also that these
operations cannot be performed on the standards themselves and
hence neither standard can be said to be an instance of either
the *predicate* for which it is a standard or of its negation. (Cf.,
"A thing cannot be at the same time the measure and the thing
measured" [RFM, I, § 40, notes].)

Wittgenstein would undoubtedly allow that we might introduce a new language-game in which "meter" is defined in terms
of the wave length of the spectral line of the element krypton
of atomic weight 86.[7] In this language-game, where such highly
accurate and complex measuring devices as the interferometer
are required, the standard meter does not have any privileged
position: it, too, can be measured and "represented." In this

---

[6] Note Wittgenstein's suggestion that we can "give the phrase 'unconscious pain' sense by fixing experiential criteria for the case in which a man has pain and doesn't know it" (BB, p. 55). Cf., also: "If however we do use the expression 'the thought takes place in the head,' we have given this expression its meaning by describing the experience which would justify the *hypothesis* that the thought takes place in our heads, by describing the experience which we wish to call observing thought in our brain" (BB, p. 8).

[7] Adopted by the eleventh General International Conference on Weights and Measures in the fall of 1960.

language-game, the standard meter is or is not a meter. But here, Wittgenstein would evidently distinguish two senses of the term "meter." Obviously what is a meter in one language-game need not be a meter in the other. Thus, Wittgenstein's view seems to be that by introducing a new criterion for something's being a meter long, we have introduced a new language-game, a new sense of the term "meter," and a new concept of meter. Such a position is indicated by Wittgenstein's comment:

> We can speak of measurements of time in which there is a different, and as we should say a greater, exactness than in the measurement of time by a pocket-watch; in which the words "to set the clock to the exact time" have a different, though related meaning. . . . (PI, § 88)

Returning to our basketball analogy, suppose that the National Collegiate Athletic Association ruled that, henceforth, a player can score a field goal by pushing the ball *upward* through the basket. Obviously, this would involve changing the rules of basketball. And to some extent, by introducing this new criterion, the rules governing the use or "grammar" of the term "field goal" would be altered. To put it somewhat dramatically (in the Wittgensteinian style), a new *essence* of field goal would be created. (Cf. "The mathematician creates *essence*" [RFM, I, § 32].) For Wittgenstein, not only is it the case that the criteria we use "give our words their common meanings" (BB, p. 57) and that to explain the criteria we use is to explain the meanings of words (BB, p. 24), but also it is the case that to introduce a new criterion of Y is to define a new concept of Y.[8]

In summary, we can roughly and schematically characterize Wittgenstein's notion of criterion in the following way: X is a criterion of Y in situations of type S if the very meaning or definition of 'Y' (or, as Wittgenstein might have put it, if the "grammatical" rules for the use of 'Y') [9] justify the claim that

---

[8] RFM, II, § 24; III, § 29; and I, Appendix I, § 15–16. See also C. S. Chihara "Mathematical Discovery and Concept Formation," *The Philosophical Review*, vol. 72 (1963), pp. 17–34.

[9] Cf., "The person of whom we say 'he has pain' is, *by the rules of the game*, the person who cries, contorts his face, etc." (BB, p. 68, italics ours).

one can recognize, see, detect, or determine the applicability of 'Y' on the basis of X in *normal* situations of type S. Hence, if the above relation obtains between X and Y, and if someone admits that X but denies Y, the burden of proof is upon him to show that something is abnormal in the situation. In a normal situation, the problem of gathering evidence which justifies concluding Y from X simply does not arise.

IV

The following passage occurs in the *Blue Book* (p. 24):

> When we learnt the use of the phrase "so-and-so has toothache" we were pointed out certain kinds of behavior of those who were said to have toothache. As an instance of these kinds of behavior let us take holding your cheek. Suppose that by observation I found that in certain cases whenever these first criteria told me a person had toothache, a red patch appeared on the person's cheek. Supposing I now said to someone "I see A has toothache, he's got a red patch on his cheek." He may ask me "How do you know A has toothache when you see a red patch?" I would then point out that certain phenomena had always coincided with the appearance of the red patch.
>
> Now one may go on and ask: "How do you know that he has got toothache when he holds his cheek?" The answer to this might be, "I say, *he* has toothache when he holds his cheek because I hold my cheek when I have toothache." But what if we went on asking: "And why do you suppose that toothache corresponds to his holding his cheek just because your toothache corresponds to your holding your cheek?" You will be at a loss to answer this question, and find that here we strike rock bottom, that is we have come down to conventions.

It would seem that, on Wittgenstein's view, empirical justification of the claim to see, recognize, or know that such and such is the case *on the basis of some observable feature or state of affairs,* would have to rest upon inductions from observed correlations, so that, if a person claims that Y is the case on the grounds that X is the case, in answer to the question "Why does the fact that X show that Y?" he would have to cite either conventions or observed correlations linking X and Y. Thus, Wittgenstein appears to be arguing that the possibility of ever inferring a person's toothache from his behavior requires the existence of a criterion of toothache that can sometimes be observed to obtain. A generalized form of this argument leads to the conclusion that "an 'inner process' stands in need of outward criteria" (PI, § 580).

As an illustration of Wittgenstein's reasoning, consider the following example: It appears to be the case that the measurement of the alcohol content of the blood affords a reasonably reliable index of intoxication. On the basis of this empirical information, we may sometimes justify the claim that X is intoxicated by showing that the alcohol content of his blood is higher than some specified percentage. But now consider the justification of the claim that blood-alcohol is in fact an index of intoxication. On Wittgenstein's view, the justification of *this* claim must rest ultimately upon correlating cases of intoxication with determinations of high blood-alcohol content. But, the observations required for this correlation could be made only if there exist independent techniques for identifying each of the correlated items. In any particular case, these independent techniques may themselves be based upon further empirical correlations; we might justify the claim that the blood-alcohol content is high by appealing to some previously established correlation between the presence of blood-alcohol and some test result. But ultimately according to Wittgenstein, we must come upon identifying techniques based not upon further empirical correlations, but rather upon definitions or conventions which determine criteria for applying the relevant predicates. This is why Wittgenstein can say that a symptom is "a phenomenon of which experience has taught us that it coincided, in some way or other with the phenomenon which is our defining criterion" (BB, p. 25).

A similar argument has recently been given by Sidney Shoemaker who writes:

If we know psychological facts about other persons at all, we know them on the basis of their behavior (including, of course, their verbal behavior). Sometimes we make psychological statements about other persons on the basis of bodily or behavioral facts that are only contingently related to the psychological facts for which we accept them as evidence. But we do this only because we have discovered, or think we have discovered, empirical correlations between physical (bodily and behavioral) facts of a certain kind and psychological facts of a certain kind. And if *all* relations between physical and psychological facts were contingent, it would be impossible for us to discover such correlations. . . . Unless some relationships between physical and psychological states are not contingent, and can be known prior to the discovery of empirical correlations, we cannot have even indirect inductive evidence for the truth of psychological statements about other persons, and cannot know such statements to be true or even probably true.[10]

Malcolm argues in a similar manner in *Dreaming*.[11]

Of course, Wittgenstein did not claim that all predicates presuppose criteria of applicability. For example, Wittgenstein probably did not think that we, in general, see, tell, determine, or know that something is red on the basis of either a criterion or a symptom. The relevant difference between ascriptions of "red" and third-person ascriptions of "pain" is that we generally see, recognize, determine, or know that another is in pain on the basis of something which is not the pain itself (as for example, behavior and circumstances) whereas, if it made any sense at all to say we generally see, recognize, etc., that an object is red on the basis of something, what could this something be other than just the object's redness? But Wittgenstein's use of the term "criterion" seems to preclude redness being a criterion of redness. If someone asks "How do you know or tell that an object is red?" it would not, in general, do to answer "By its redness." (Cf. Wittgenstein's comment "How do I know that this color is

[10] Sidney Shoemaker, *Self-knowledge and Self-identity* (Ithaca, 1963), pp. 167–168.
[11] Norman Malcolm, *Dreaming* (London, 1959), pp. 60–61. [Pp. 215–226 in this anthology.—*Ed.*]

red?—It would be an answer to say: 'I have learnt English' "
[PI, § 381].) Evidently, some color predicates and, more generally, what are sometimes called "sense datum" predicates
(those that can be known to apply—as some philosophers put it
—*immediately*), do not fall within the domain of arguments of
the above type. But the predicates with which we assign "inner
states" to another person are not of this sort. One recognizes that
another is in a certain mental state, Y, on the basis of something,
say, X. Now it is assumed that X must be either a criterion or
symptom of Y. If X is a symptom, X must be known to be correlated with Y, and we may then inquire into the way in which
this correlation was established. Again, X must have been observed to be correlated with a criterion of Y or with a symptom,
X_1, of Y. On the second alternative, we may inquire into the
basis for holding that X_1 is a symptom of Y. . . . Such a chain
may go on for any distance you like, but it cannot go on indefinitely. That is, at some point, we must come to a criterion of
Y. But once this conclusion has been accepted, there appears to
be no reasonable non-sceptical alternative to Wittgenstein's
logical behaviorism, for if "inner" states require "outward"
criteria, behavioral criteria are the only plausible candidates.

V

As a refutation of scepticism, the above argument certainly will
not do; for, at best, it supports Wittgenstein's position only on
the assumption that the sceptic is not right. That is, it demon-
strates that there must be criteria for psychological predicates
by assuming that such predicates are sometimes applied justi-
fiably. A sceptic who accepts the argument of Section IV could
maintain his position only by allowing that no one could have
any idea of what would show or even indicate that another is in
pain, having a dream, thinking, etc. In this section we shall
show how Wittgenstein argues that that move would lead the
sceptic to the absurd conclusion that it must be impossible to
teach the meaning of these psychological predicates.

"What would it be like if human beings showed no outward signs of pain (did not groan, grimace, etc.)? Then it would be impossible to teach a child the use of the word 'toothache'" (PI, § 257). For just imagine trying to teach a child the meaning of the term "toothache," say, on the supposition that there is absolutely no way of telling whether the child—or anyone else for that matter—is actually in pain. How would one go about it, if one had no reason for believing that gross damage to the body causes pain or that crying out, wincing, and the like indicate pain? ("How could I even have come by the idea of another's experience if there is no possibility of any evidence for it?" [BB, p. 46; cf. also BB, p. 48].)

Again, what would show us that the child had grasped the teaching? If anything would, the argument of Section IV requires that there be a criterion of having succeeded in teaching the child. (As Wittgenstein says of an analogous case, "If I speak of communicating a feeling to someone else, mustn't I in order to understand what I say know what I shall call the criterion of having succeeded in communicating?" [BB, p. 185].) But the only plausible criterion of this would be that the child applies the psychological predicates correctly (cf. PI, § 146); and since the sceptical position implies that there is no way of knowing if the child correctly applies such predicates, it would seem to follow that nothing could show or indicate that the child had learned what these terms mean.

We now have a basis for explicating the sense of "logical" which is involved in the claim that scepticism is a logically incoherent doctrine. What Wittgenstein holds is not that "*P* and not-*P*" are strictly deducible from the sceptic's position, but rather that the sceptic's view presupposes a deviation from the rules for the use of key terms. In particular, Wittgenstein holds that if the sceptic were right, the preconditions for teaching the meaning of the mental predicates of our ordinary language could not be satisfied.[12]

---

[12] Cf., " 'Before I judge that two images which I have are the same, I must recognize them as the same.' . . . Only if I can express my recognition in some other way, and if it is possible for someone else to teach me that 'same' is the correct word here" (PI, § 378).

We now see too the point to the insistence that the sceptic's position must incorporate an extraordinary and misleading use of mental predicates. The sceptic's view is logically incompatible with the operation of the ordinary language rules for the application of these terms, and these rules determine their meanings. (Cf. "What *we* do is to bring words back from their metaphysical to their everyday usage" [PI, § 116].) As Wittgenstein diagnoses the sceptic's view, the sceptic does not have in mind any criteria of third person ascriptions when he denies that he can know if anyone else has pains (cf. PI, § 272). The sceptic tempts us to picture the situation as involving "a barrier which doesn't allow one person to come closer to another's experience than to the point of observing his behavior"; but, according to Wittgenstein, "on looking closer we find that we can't apply the picture" (BB, p. 56); no clear meaning can be attached to the sceptic's claim: no sense can even be given the hypothesis that other people feel "pains," as the sceptic uses the term "pain." ("For how can I even make the hypothesis if it transcends all possible experience?" [BB, p. 48].) And if the sceptic says, "But if I suppose that someone has a pain, then I am simply supposing that he has just the same as I have so often had." Wittgenstein can reply:

That gets us no further. It is as if I were to say: "You surely know what 'It is 5 o'clock here' means; so you also know what 'It's 5 o'clock on the sun' means. It means simply that it is just the same time there as it is here when it is 5 o'clock."—The explanation by means of *identity* does not work here. For I know well enough that one can call 5 o'clock here and 5 o'clock there "the same time," but what I do not know is in what cases one is to speak of its being the same time here and there. (PI, § 350)

Thus, we can see how Wittgenstein supports his logical behaviorism: the argument in Section IV purports to show that the only plausible alternative to Wittgenstein's philosophical psychology is radical scepticism; and the argument in the present section rules out this alternative. For Wittgenstein, then, "the person of whom we say 'he has pains' is, by the rules of the game, the person who cries, contorts his face, etc.," (BB, p. 68).

Undoubtedly, there is much that philosophers find comforting and attractive in Wittgenstein's philosophical psychology, but there are also difficulties in the doctrine which mar its attractiveness. To some of these difficulties, we shall now turn.

VI

In this section, we shall consider some consequences of applying the views just discussed to the analysis of dreaming, and we shall attempt to show that the conclusions to which these views lead are counter-intuitive.

According to Wittgenstein, we are to understand the concept of dreaming in terms of the language-game(s) in which "dream" plays a role and, in particular, in terms of the language-game of dream telling. For, to master the use of the word "dream" is precisely to learn what it is to find out that someone has dreamed, to tell what someone has dreamed, to report one's own dreams, and so on. Passages in the *Investigations* (e.g., PI, pp. 184, 222–223) indicate that, for Wittgenstein, a criterion of someone's having dreamed is the dream report. On this analysis, sceptical doubts about dreams arise when we fail to appreciate the logical bond between statements about dreams and statements about dream reports. The sceptic treats the dream report as, at best, an empirical correlate of the occurrence of a dream: a symptom that is, at any event, no more reliable than the memory of the subject who reports the dream. But, according to Wittgenstein, once we have understood the criterial relation between dream reporting and dreaming, we see that "the question whether the dreamer's memory deceives him when he reports the dream after waking cannot arise . . ." (PI, p. 222). (Compare: "Once we understand the rules for playing chess, the question whether a player has won when he has achieved check-mate cannot arise.")

The rules articulating the criteria for applying the word "dream" determine a logical relation between dreaming and reporting dreams. Moreover, the set of such rules fixes the language-game in which "dream" has its role and hence determines the meaning of the word.

It is important to notice that there are a number of *prima facie* objections to this analysis which, though perhaps not conclusive, supply grounds for questioning the doctrines which lead to it. Though we could perhaps learn to live with these objections were no other analyses available, when seen from the vantage point of an alternative theory they indicate deep troubles with Wittgenstein's views.

(1) Given that there exist no criteria for first person applications of many psychological predicates ("pain," "wish," or the like) it is unclear how the first person aspects of the game played with these predicates are to be described. Wittgenstein does not appear to present a coherent account of the behavior of predicates whose applicability is not determined by criteria. On the other hand, the attempt to characterize "I dreamt" as criterion-governed leads immediately to absurdities. Thus, in Malcolm's *Dreaming* it is suggested that:

> If a man wakes up with the impression of having seen and done various things, and if it is known that he did not see and do those things, then it is known that he dreamt them. . . . When he says "I dreamt so and so" he implies, first, that it seemed to him on waking up as if the so and so had occurred and second, that the so and so did not occur. (p. 66) [p. 225 in this anthology.—*Ed.*]

That this is an incredibly counter-intuitive analysis of our concept of dreaming hardly needs mentioning. We ask the reader to consider the following example: A person, from time to time, gets the strange feeling that, shortly before, he had seen and heard his father commanding him to come home. One morning he wakes with this feeling, knowing full well that his father is dead. Now we are asked by Malcolm to believe that the person *must have dreamt* that he saw and heard his father: supposedly, it would be logically absurd for the person to claim to have this feeling and deny that he had dreamt it!

(2) Wittgenstein's view appears to entail that no sense can be made of such statements as "Jones totally forgot the dream he had last night," since we seem to have no criteria for determining the truth of such a statement. (We have in mind the case in which Jones is totally unable to remember having dreamed and no behavioral manifestations of dreaming were exhibited.) It is sometimes denied that observations of what people ordinarily say are relevant to a description of ordinary language. But, insofar as statements about what we would say are susceptible to empirical disconfirmation, the claim that we would feel hesitation about saying that someone completely forgot his dream appears to be just false.[13]

(3) The Wittgensteinian method of counting concepts is certainly not an intuitive one. Consider Malcolm's analysis of dreaming again. Malcolm realizes that sometimes, on the basis of a person's behavior during sleep, we say that he had a dream, even though he is unable to recall a dream upon awaking. But, in such cases, Malcolm claims, "our words . . . have no clear sense" (*Dreaming*, p. 62) [p. 222 in this anthology.—Ed.]. On the other hand, Malcolm admits that there is a *sense* of the term "nightmare" where behavior during sleep is the criterion. However, a different concept of dreaming is supposedly involved in this case. An analogous situation is treated in the *Blue Book* (p. 63), where Wittgenstein writes:

If a man tries to obey the order "Point to your eye," he may do many different things, and there are many different criteria which he will accept for having pointed to his eye. If these criteria, as they usually do, coincide, I may use them alternately and in different combinations to show me that I have touched my eye. If they don't coincide, I shall have to distinguish between different senses of the phrase "I touch my eye" or "I move my finger towards my eye."

---

[13] Thus consider the following: "Up until the night I opened the door, I remembered my dreams. Soon after, I ceased to recall them. I still dreamed, but my waking consciousness concealed from itself what sleep revealed. If the recurrent nightmare of the iron fence awoke me, I recognized it. But if any other nightmare broke my sleep, I forgot what it was about by morning. And of all the other dreams I had during the night I remembered nothing" (Windham, D., "Myopia," *The New Yorker*, July 13, 1963).

Following this suggestion of Wittgenstein, Malcolm distinguishes not only different senses of the term "dream," but also different concepts of sleep—one based upon report, one based upon nonverbal behavior. But surely, this is an unnatural way of counting concepts. Compare Malcolm's two concepts of sleep with a case where it really does seem natural to say that a special concept of sleep has been employed, viz., where we say of a hibernating bear that it sleeps through the winter.

(4) As Malcolm points out, the language-game *now* played with "dream" seems to exhibit no criteria which would enable one to determine the precise duration of dreams. Hence, it would seem to follow (as Malcolm has noticed) that scientists who have attempted to answer such questions as, "How long do dreams last?" are involved in conceptual confusions rather than empirical determinations. For such questions cannot be answered without adopting criteria for ascribing the relevant properties to dreams. But since, on Wittgenstein's view, to adopt such new criteria for the use of a word is, to that extent, to change its meaning, it follows that the concept of "dream" that such researchers employ is not the ordinary concept and hence that the measurements they effect are not, strictly speaking, measurements of *dreams*.[14] The notion that adopting any test for dreaming which arrives at features of dreams not determinable from the dream report thereby alters the concept of a dream seems to run counter to our intuitions about the goals of psychological research. It is not immediately obvious that the psychologist who says he has found a method of measuring the duration of dreams *ipso facto* commits the fallacy of ambiguity.[15]

(5) Consider the fact that such measures as EEG, eye-move-

---

[14] In *Dreaming*, Malcolm gives a number of arguments, not to be found in Wittgenstein's published writings, for the position that psychologists attempting to discover methods of measuring the duration of dreams must be using the term "dream" in a misleading and extraordinary way. For a reply to these arguments, see C. S. Chihara "What Dreams are Made On" forthcoming in *Theoria*. See also H. Putnam's criticism of Malcolm, "Dreaming and 'Depth Grammar'," *Analytical Philosophy*, ed. by R. J. Butler (Oxford, 1962), pp. 211–235.

[15] The implausibility of this view is even more striking when Wittgenstein applies it in his philosophy of mathematics to arrive at the conclusion that every new theorem about a concept alters the concept or introduces a new concept. When the notion of conceptual change is allowed to degenerate this far, it is not easy to see that anything rides on the claim that a conceptual change has taken place. Cf. C. S. Chihara, "Mathematical Discovery and Concept Formation," *The Philosophical Review*, vol. 72 (1963), pp. 17–34.

ments and "dream-behavior" (murmuring, tossing, etc., during sleep) correlate reasonably reliably with one another and dream reports. The relation between, say, EEG and dream reports is clearly not criterial; no one holds that EEG is a criterion of dream reports. It would seem then that, on Wittgenstein's view, EEG provides us with, at best, a symptom of positive dream reports; and symptoms are supposedly discovered by observing co-occurrences. The difficulty, however, is that this makes it unclear how the expectation that such a correlation must obtain could have been a rational expectation even *before* the correlation was experimentally confirmed. One cannot have an inductive generalization over no observations; nor, in this case, was any higher level "covering law" used to infer the probability of a correlation between EEG and dream reports. Given Wittgenstein's analysis of the concept of dreaming, not only do the researches of psychologists into the nature of dreams appear mysterious, but even the expectations, based upon these researches, seem somewhat irrational.

The difficulties we have mentioned are not peculiar to the Wittgensteinian analysis of dreams. Most of them have counterparts in the analyses of sensation, perception, intention, etc. Whether or not these difficulties can be obviated, in some way, noticing them provides a motive for re-examining the deeper doctrines upon which Wittgensteinian analyses of psychological terms are based.

VII

The Wittgensteinian argument of Section IV rests on the premiss that if we are justified in claiming that one can tell, recognize, see, or determine that '*Y*' applies on the basis of the presence of *X*, then either *X* is a criterion of *Y* or observations have shown that *X* is correlated with *Y*. Wittgenstein does not present any justification for this premiss in his published writings. Evidently, some philosophers find it self-evident and hence in need of no justification. We, on the other hand, far from finding this premiss self-evident, believe it to be false. Consider: one standard instrument used in the detection of high-speed, charged

particles is the Wilson cloud-chamber. According to present
scientific theories, the formation of tiny, thin bands of fog on
the glass surface of the instrument indicates the passage of
charged particles through the chamber. It is obvious that the
formation of these streaks is not a Wittgensteinian criterion of
the presence and motion of these particles in the apparatus.
That one can detect these charged particles and determine their
paths by means of such devices is surely not, by any stretch of
the imagination, a *conceptual* truth. C. T. R. Wilson did not
learn what "path of a charged particle" means by having the
cloud-chamber explained to him: he *discovered* the method, and
the discovery was contingent upon recognizing the empirical
fact that ions could act as centers of condensation in a super-
saturated vapor. Hence, applying Wittgenstein's own test for
non-criterionhood (see above), the formation of a cloud-chamber
track cannot be a criterion of the presence and motion of charged
particles.

It is equally clear that the basis for taking these streaks as
indicators of the paths of the particles is not observed *correlations* between streaks and some criterion of motion of charged
particles. (What criterion for determining the path of an elec-
tron could Wilson have used to establish such correlations?)
Rather, scientists were able to give compelling explanations of
the formation of the streaks on the hypothesis that high-velocity,
charged particles were passing through the chamber; on this
hypothesis, further predictions were made, tested, and confirmed; no other equally plausible explanation is available; and
so forth.

Such cases suggest that Wittgenstein failed to consider all
the possible types of answers to the question, "What is the justification for the claim that one can tell, recognize, or determine
that Y applies on the basis of the presence of X?" For, where
Y is the predicate "is the path of a high-velocity particle," X
need not have the form of either a criterion or a correlate.

Wittgensteinians may be tempted to argue that cloud-chamber
tracks really are criteria, or symptoms observed to be correlated
with criteria, of the paths of charged particles. To obviate this

type of counter, we wish to stress that the example just given is by no means idiosyncratic. The reader who is not satisfied with it will easily construct others from the history of science. What is at issue is the possibility of a type of justification which consists in neither the appeal to criteria nor the appeal to observed correlations. If the Wittgensteinian argument we have been considering is to be compelling, some grounds must be given for the exhaustiveness of these types of justification. This, it would seem, Wittgenstein has failed to do.

It is worth noticing that a plausible solution to the problem raised in VI. 5 can be given if we consider experiments with dreams and EEG to be analogous to the cloud-chamber case. That is, we can see how it could be the case that the correlation of EEG with dream reports was anticipated prior to observation. The dream report was taken by the experiments to be an indicator of a psychological event occurring prior to it. Given considerations about the relation of cortical to psychological events, and given also the theory of EEG, it was predicted that the EEG should provide an index of the occurrence of dreams. From the hypothesis that dream reports and EEG readings are both indices of the same psychological events, it could be deduced that they ought to be reliably correlated with one another, and this deduction in fact proved to be correct.

This situation is not at all unusual in the case of explanations based upon theoretical inferences to events underlying observable syndromes. As Meehl and Cronbach have pointed out, in such cases the validity of the "criterion" is often nearly as much at issue as the validity of the indices to be correlated with it.[16] The successful prediction of the correlation on the basis of the postulation of a common etiology is taken both as evidence for the existence of the cause and as indicating the validity of each of the correlates as an index of its presence.

In this kind of case, the justification of existential statements

---

[16] P. M. Meehl and H. J. Cronbach, "Construct Validity in Psychological Tests," *Minnesota Studies in the Philosophy of Science*, vol. I, ed., by H. Feigl and M. Scriven (Minneapolis, 1956), pp. 174–204. We have followed Meehl and Cronbach's usage of the terms "reliability" and "validity" so that *reliability* is a measure of the correlation between criteria while *validity* is a measure of the correlation between a criterion and the construct whose presence it is supposed to indicate.

is thus identical neither with an appeal to criteria nor with an appeal to symptoms. Such justifications depend rather on appeals to the simplicity, plausibility, and predictive adequacy of an explanatory system as a whole, so that it is incorrect to say that relations between statements which are mediated by such explanations are either logical in Wittgenstein's sense or contingent in the sense in which this term suggests simple correlation.

It cannot be stressed too often that there exist patterns of justificatory argument which are not happily identified either with appeals to symptoms or with appeals to criteria, and which do not in any obvious way rest upon such appeals. In these arguments, existential claims about states, events, and processes, which are *not* directly observable are susceptible of justification despite the fact that no *logical* relation obtains between the predicates ascribing such states and predicates whose applicability *can* be directly observed. There is a temptation to hold that in such cases there *must* be a criterion, that there must be some set of possible observations which would settle *for sure* whether the theoretical predicate applies. But we succumb to this temptation at the price of postulating stipulative definitions and conceptual alterations which fail to correspond to anything we can discover in the course of empirical arguments. The counter-intuitive features of philosophic analyses based on the assumption that there must be criteria are thus not the consequences of a profound methodological insight, but rather a projection of an inadequate philosophical theory of justification.

VIII

It might be replied that the above examples do not constitute counter-instances to Wittgenstein's criterion-correlation premiss since Wittgenstein may have intended his principle to be applicable only in the case of ordinary language terms which, so it might seem, do not function within the framework of a theory. It is perhaps possible to have indicators that are neither criteria nor symptoms of such highly theoretical entities as electrons and positrons, but the terms used by ordinary people in everyday life are obviously (?) in a different category. (Notice that Wittgenstein considers "making scientific hypotheses and theories" a different "game" from such "language-games" as "describing an event" and "describing an immediate experience" [BB, pp. 67–68; Cf. PI, § 23].) Hence, Wittgenstein might argue, it is only in the case of ordinary language terms that the demand for criteria is necessary.

Once one perceives the presuppositions of Wittgenstein's demand for criteria, however, it becomes evident that alternatives to Wittgenstein's analyses of ordinary language mental terms should at least be explored. Perhaps, what we all learn in learning what such terms as "pain" and "dream" mean are not criterial connections which map these terms severally onto characteristic patterns of behavior. We may instead form complex conceptual connections which interrelate a wide variety of mental states. It is to such a conceptual system that we appeal when we attempt to explain someone's behavior by reference to his motives, intentions, beliefs, desires, or sensations. In other words, in learning the language, we develop a number of intricately interrelated "mental concepts" which we use in dealing with, coming to terms with, understanding, explaining, interpreting, etc., the behavior of other human beings (as well as our own). In the course of acquiring these mental concepts we develop a variety of beliefs involving them. Such beliefs result in a wide range of expectations about how people are likely to behave. Since only a portion of these beliefs are confirmed in the normal course, these beliefs and the conceptual systems which they articulate are both subject to correction and alteration as the consequence of our constant interaction with other people.

On this view, our success in accounting for the behavior on the basis of which mental predicates are applied might properly be thought of as supplying *evidence* for the existence of the mental processes we postulate. It does so by attesting to the adequacy of the conceptual system in terms of which the processes are understood. The behavior would be, in that sense, analogous to the cloud-chamber track on the basis of which we detect the presence and motion of charged particles. Correspondingly, the conceptual system is analogous to the physical *theory* in which the properties of these particles are formulated.

If something like this should be correct, it would be possible, at least in theory, to reconstruct and describe the conceptual system involved and then to obtain some confirmation that the putative system is in fact employed by English speakers. For example, confirmation might come *via* the usual methods of "reading off" the conceptual relation in the putative system and *matching them* against the linguistic intuitions of native speakers. Thus, given that a particular conceptual system is being employed, certain statements should strike native speakers as nonsensical, others should seem necessarily true, others should seem ambiguous, others empirically false, and so on, all of which would be testable.

To maintain that there are no criterial connections between pains and behavior does not commit us to holding that the fact that people often feel *pains* when they cry out is *just* a contingent fact (in the sense in which it is just a contingent fact that most of the books in my library are unread). The belief that other people feel pains is not gratuitous even on the view that there are no criteria of pains. On the contrary, it provides the only plausible explanation of the facts I know about the way that they behave in and *vis à vis* the sorts of situations I find painful. These facts are, of course, enormously complex. The "pain syndrome" includes not only correlations between varieties of overt behaviors but also more subtle relations between pain and motivations, utilities, desires, and so on. Moreover, I confidently expect that there must exist reliable members of this syndrome other than the ones with which I am currrently familiar. I am in need of an explanation of the reliability and fruitfulness of this syndrome, an explanation which reference to the occurence of pains supplies. Here, as elsewhere, an "outer" syndrome stands in need of an inner process.

Thus, it is at least conceivable that a non-Wittgensteinian account ought to be given of the way children learn the mental predicates. (It is, at any event, sufficient to notice that such an account *could* be given, that there exist alternatives to Wittgenstein's doctrine.) For example, if the concept of dreaming is *inter alia* that of an inner event which takes place during a definite stretch of "real" time, which causes such involuntary behavior as moaning and murmuring in one's sleep, tossing about, etc., and which is remembered when one correctly reports a dream, then there are a number of ways in which a child might be supposed to "get" this concept other than by learning criteria for the application of the word "dream." Perhaps it is true of many children that they learn what a dream is by being told that what they have just experienced was a dream. Perhaps it was also true of many children that, having grasped the notions of *imagining* and *sleep*, they learn what a dream is when they are told that dreaming is something like imagining in your sleep.

But does this imply that children learn what a dream is "from their own case?" If this is a logical rather than psychological question, the answer is "Not necessarily": a child who never dreamed, but who was very clever, might arrive at an understanding of what dreams are just on the basis of the sort of theoretical inference we have described above. For our notion of a dream is that of a mental event having various properties that are required in order to explain the characteristic features of the dream-behavior syndrome. For example, dreams occur during sleep, have duration, sometimes cause people who are sleeping to murmur or to toss, can be described in visual, auditory, or tactile terms, are sometimes remembered and sometimes not, are sometimes reported and sometimes not, sometimes prove frightening, sometimes are interrupted before they are finished, etc. But if these are the sorts of facts that characterize our concept of dream, then there seems to be nothing which would, in principle, prevent a child who never dreamed from arriving at this notion.

A similar story might be told about how such sensation terms as "pain" are learned and about the learning of such quasi-dispositionals as "having a motive." In each case, since the features that we in fact attribute to these states, processes, or dispositions are just those features we know they must have if they are to fulfill their role in explanations of behavior, etiology, personality, etc., it would seem that there is nothing about them the child could not in principle learn by employing the pattern of inference we have described above, and hence nothing that he could in principle learn *only* by an analogy to his own case.

Now it might be argued that the alternative to Wittgenstein's position we have been sketching is highly implausible. For, if children do have to acquire the complicated conceptual system our theory requires to understand and use mental predicates, surely they would have to be taught this system. And the teaching would surely have to be terribly involved and complex. But as a matter of fact, children do not require any such teaching at all, and hence we should conclude that our alternative to Wittgenstein's criterion view is untenable.

The force of this argument, however, can to some extent be dispelled if we consider the child's acquisition of, e.g., the grammar of a natural language. It is clear that, by some process we are only now beginning to understand, a child, on the basis of a relatively short "exposure" to utterances in his language, develops capacities for producing and understanding "novel" sentences (sentences which he has never previously heard or seen). The exercise of these capacities, so far as we can tell, "involve" the use of an intricate system of linguistic rules of very considerable generality and complexity.[17] That the child is not taught (in any ordinary sense) any such system of rules is undeniable. These capacities seem to develop naturally in the child in response to little more than contact with a relatively small number of sentences uttered in ordinary contexts in everyday life.[18] Granting for the moment that the apparent complexity of such systems of rules is not somehow an artifact of an unsatisfactory theory of language, the fact that the child develops these linguistic capacities shows that a corresponding "nat-

[17] This point is susceptible of direct empirical ratification, for it can be demonstrated that in perceptual analysis, speech is analyzed into segments which correspond precisely to the segmentation assigned by a grammar.
[18] Cf. N. Chomsky's "A Review of Skinner's *Verbal Behavior*," reprinted in J. Fodor and J. Katz, *The Structure of Language* (Englewood Cliffs, 1964).

ural" development of a system of mental concepts may not, as a matter of brute fact, require the sort of explicit teaching a person needs to master, say, calculus or quantum physics.

IX

It is easily seen that this unabashedly nonbehavioristic view avoids each of the difficulties we raised regarding Wittgenstein's analyses of mental predicates. Thus, the asymmetry between first and third person uses of "dream" discussed in Section VI need not arise since there need be no criteria for "X dreamed," *whatever* value X takes: we do not have the special problem of characterizing the meaning of "I dreamed" since "dream" in this context means just what it means in third person contexts, viz., "a series of thoughts, images, or emotions occurring during sleep." Again, it is now clear why people find such remarks as "Jones totally forgot what and that he dreamed last night" perfectly sensible. It is even clear how such assertions might be confirmed. Suppose, for example, that there exists a neurological state a such that there is a very high correlation between the presence of a and such dream behavior as tossing in one's sleep, crying out in one's sleep, reporting dreams, and so on. Suppose, too that there exists some neurological state β such that whenever β occurs, experiences that the subject has had just prior to β are forgotten. Suppose, finally, that sometimes we observe sequences, a, β, and that such sequences are not followed by dream reports though the occurrences of a are accompanied by other characteristic dream behaviors. It seems clear that the reasonable thing to say in such a case is that the subject has dreamed and forgotten his dream. And since we have postulated no criterion for dreaming, but only a syndrome of dream behaviors each related to some inner psychological event, we need have no fear that, in saying what it is reasonable to say, we have changed the meaning of "dream." We leave it to the reader to verify that the other objections we raised against the Wittgensteinian analysis of "dream" also fail to apply to the present doctrine.

Thus, once we have abandoned the arguments for a criterial

connection between statements about behavior and statements
about psychological states, the question remains open whether
applications of ordinary language psychological terms on the
basis of observations of behavior ought not themselves be treated
as theoretical inferences to underlying mental occurrences. The
question whether such statements as "He moaned because he
was in pain" function to explain behavior by relating it to an
assumed mental event cannot be settled simply by reference
to ordinary linguistic usage. Answering this question requires
broadly empirical investigations into the nature of thought and
concept formation in normal human beings. What is at issue is
the question of the role of theory construction and theoretical
inference in thought and argument outside pure science. Psychological investigations indicate that much everyday con-
ceptualization depends on the exploitation of theories and
explanatory models in terms of which experience is integrated
and understood.[19] Such pre-scientific theories, far from being
mere functionless "pictures," play an essential role in determining the sorts of perceptual and inductive expectations we
form and the kind of arguments and explanations we accept.
It thus seems *possible* that the correct view of the functioning
of ordinary language mental predicates would assimilate applying them to the sorts of processes of theoretical inference opera-
tive in scientific psychological explanation. If this is correct,
the primary difference between ordinary and scientific uses of
psychological predicates would be just that the processes of
inference which are made explicit in the latter case remain
implicit in the former.

We can now see what should be said in reply to Wittgenstein's
argument that the possibility of teaching a language rests upon
the existence of criteria. Perhaps teaching a word would be
impossible if it could not sometimes be determined that the
student has mastered the use of the word. But this does not

[19] Among the many psychological studies relevant to this point, the following are of special importance: F. Bartlett, *Remembering, A Study in Experimental and Social Psychology* (Cambridge,
1932); J. Piaget, *The Child's Conception of the World* (London, 1928); J. Brunner, "On Perceptual Readiness," reprinted in *Readings in Perception*, ed. M. Wertheimer and D. Beardsley
(Princeton, 1958), pp. 686–729.

entail that there need be *criteria* for "X learned the word *w*." All that is required is that we must sometimes have good reasons for saying that the word has been mastered; and this condition is satisfied when, for example, the simplest and most plausible explanation available of the verbal behavior of the student is that he has learned the use of the word.